Individuals and/or organizations who helped make the publication of this book possible:

Patrons

Mr. Lester Poretsky
Mr. Valdis Goncarovs
Research International

H0301191

Sponsors

The Honorable V. J. Adduci
The Honorable Kenneth E. Be Lieu
The Boek Family
The Honorable Elford A. Cederberg
Combined International Philippine American Association of Metropolitan Washington, DC
Mr. David C. Guillermo
Mr. David S. Gedney
Maj. Gen. Ira A. Hunt, Jr.
Mr. Albert S. Mazloom
Mr. Walter L. Mess, Esq.
Mr. Paul A. Witt

Contributors

Dr. Carsbie C. Adams
Potomac Point Health Center
The American Legion, Post 225 (Virginia)
Mr. Robert B. Blancato
Ms. Steffanie H. Burgevin
Vice President
Wheat First Securities
Mr. and Mrs. Amos T. Camp
Mr. Frank S. Chalmers
Lt. Commander P. B. Clagett
The Honorable John W. and Mrs. Corwin
Mr. Frank P. Davidson, Esq.
Captain William T. Dutton
Educational Digest Service, Inc.
The Honorable Dr. Orval Hansen
Mr. Nonoy Mendoza
Fil-Am Image
The Honorable John H. Reed
The Honorable Hugh Scott
The Honorable Elmer B. Staats
Mr. and Mrs. John W. Yaag

How to Establish a Democracy or Improve the One You Now Have is a sequel to ***The Evolution of a Democracy: This is Our Country, The United States of America.*** Authored by Walter E. Boek, PhD, these books are written in a highly readable style. The first one, with a Foreword by Warren E. Burger, Esq., Chief Justice of the Supreme Court of the United States (ret.), is a comprehensive history of the world's oldest democracy. The second book focuses on the values and principles that apply to democratic processes throughout the world. Both books are available from the College of Democracy, the publisher.

The College of Democracy

Designed with guidance of members of its Board of Advisors, consisting of distinguished individuals, many of whom have been United States Senators and Representatives, the College of Democracy is part of National Graduate University which is a private, independent and non-profit institution of higher education. Objective of the College is to strengthen democracies through interdisciplinary, relevant education and research.

BOARD OF ADVISORS of the COLLEGE OF DEMOCRACY

Mr. George W.Abbott
The Honorable V.J.Adduci*
The Honorable John B. Anderson*
The Honorable Kenneth E. Be Lieu*
Dr. Walter E. Boek*
The Honorable Dr. Peter G. Bourne
The Honorable David R. Bowen
The Honorable John H. Buchanan, Jr.
The Honorable Elford A. Cederberg*
The Honorable Anna C. Chennault
Mr. Frank P. Davidson, Esq.
The Honorable Benjamin O. Davis (LtGen USAF ret)
The Honorable John Erlenborn
Mr. Samuel Foggie
The Honorable Bill Frenzel
The Honorable Gilbert Gude
Mr. David C. Guillermo
The Honorable Dr. Orval Hansen
Mr. William S. Harps
Mr. William E.W. Howe
Maj. Gen. Ira A. Hunt, Jr. (USA ret)*
The Honorable Dr. Walter H. Judd
The Honorable Hastings Keith
The Honorable Martha Keys
Dr. George W. Koch
The Honorable John V. Lindsay
The Honorable Clark MacGregor
The Honorable Eugene McCarthy
Mr. Nonoy Mendoza
Mr. Walter L. Mess, Esq.*
The Honorable Alejandro Orfila
The Honorable Howard W. Pollock
The Honorable James M. Quigley
The Honorable John H. Reed*
The Honorable Vincent E. Reed
The Honorable John J. Rhodes
Mr. John T. Roberts
The Honorable John G. Schmitz
The Honorable Hugh Scott
The Honorable Carlton Sickles
Mr. Edwin L. Slusarczyk
The Honorable Henry P. Smith, III
The Honorable Dr. Elmer B. Staats
The Honorable Mick Staton
The Honorable Dr. John R. Steelman
Dr. Hatten S. Yoder, Jr.*
Admiral E.R. Zumwalt, Jr. (USN ret)

*Executive Committee

Board of Governors of National Graduate University

Chairman of the Board
Mr. David S. Gedney
Vice Chairman
Dr. Robert L. Barre
Treasurer
Mr. Lester Poretsky
Secretary
Mr. John W. Yaag
President
Dr. Walter E. Boek

Members
The Honorable Anna C. Chennault
The Honorable Benjamin O. Davis (LtGen USAF ret)
Dr. William Loveless
Mr. Albert S. Mazloom
Emeritus Member
Dr. Joseph Rogers Young

Foreword

by

Jimmy Carter

Thirty-ninth President
United States of America

In many parts of the world there is now an unprecedented opportunity for improvements in the quality of life. It is clear that the highest and best process of government is through direct citizen elections with an associated free market economic system. Already, the transformation of scores of governments into democracies has opened the doors to freedom and prosperity for millions.

If the dreams of citizens in the new democracies are to be realized, however, their conception of democracy needs to be realistic. This book helps to achieve this goal because it focuses on how to establish new democracies and to improve or maintain those already in operation. The modern meaning of democracy is used: a form of government in which the ultimate power rests with its citizens or their elected representatives. It is a government in which citizenship status is nonrestrictive and in which people can make their choices on a fair, timely, and confidential basis.

As is emphasized in this book, the positive results from democratic governments do not take place automatically. Far from being a magic formula guaranteeing freedom from tyranny and want, democratic governance requires a willingness of citizens to work unrelentingly to build and maintain cooperative relationships among themselves as well as with their neighbors across national borders. There have not been wars between democracies.

When people begin to plan and operate their governments, democratic processes sometimes appear complicated and the obstacles formidable. Individuals not accustomed to making governmental or economic decisions may become insecure because day-to-day activities will be much less predictable than they were in a controlled society. As a consequence, enlightened leaders, sincerely attempting to help their countries find freedom and equality of opportunity, are seeking guidance from those of us who have enjoyed the results of democratic governments designed by our own wise founders.

During conversations with many people at various leadership levels, I have observed their intense interest in democratic processes. They want to learn about the problems their governments may face along with alternatives that must be considered to avoid or reduce dangers to new democracies.

I am pleased to say that the urgent need for information that can be critical to the success of democracies was recognized by members of the United States Congress and other distinguished American citizens comprising the Board of Advisors of the College of Democracy when they requested that this book be written. Their objective to produce a book that would be easy to read, readily understandable, free from unnecessary jargon, and full of valid information has been achieved. Unequaled in its comprehensiveness and frank discussion of issues that must be faced in both old and young democracies, it is an important and powerful tool for everyone striving to establish and maintain the best form of government that exists.

This book carries a positive message. Democracies have proven to be superior forms of government. Such governments are achievable when people are willing to participate actively in the responsibilities of government. They are inevitable when everyone recognizes that the human rights of each person are sacred. But, the forces that endanger democratic principles must be identified, recognized as destructive, and controlled if we are to have new democracies and keep strong those democratic republics that already exist. Those seeking an understanding and appreciation of the critical issues that must be resolved in democracies will find reading this book a rewarding experience because it is full of suggestions they will find helpful.

April, 1993

****

President Jimmy Carter

James Earl Carter, Jr. was President of the United States from January 20, 1977 to January 20, 1981. During his Presidency, very significant achievements were made both internationally and domestically. Concerning world affairs, the long sought peace between Egypt and Israel was accomplished with the signing of the Camp David Accords. Similarly, treaties with Panama concerning the Canal and the Salt II treaty with the Soviet Union were completed and approved. While championing human rights, he was able to establish diplomatic relations between the United States and the People's Republic of China. Within the United States President Carter succeeded in reducing government regulations in energy, transportation, communications, and finance along with developing a comprehensive energy program, a major educational program and environmental protection legislation. His efforts resulted in new departments of Energy and Education and the Alaska Lands Act.

Following his Presidency, he was appointed University Distinguished Professor at Emory University. In cooperation with

Emory, he founded The Carter Center that includes The Jimmy Carter Library and Museum and addresses national and international issues of public policy, conflict resolution, democracy promotion, human rights protection and disease prevention. Under Center auspices, the Council of Freely Elected Heads of Governments was established, and President Carter has personally helped monitor elections in many Central and South American and African countries, thus encouraging honest elections and the peaceful transfer of power to newly elected officials. In 1991, he launched the Atlanta Project, a community-wide effort to work on social problems associated with poverty. He is a regular volunteer for and former Board member of Habitat for Humanity that builds homes for the needy.

President Carter attended Georgia Southwestern College and Georgia Institute of Technology before graduation with a degree in science from the United States Naval Academy. As Lieutenant Carter, he served on submarines in both the Atlantic and Pacific fleets before becoming a special advisor on the design of nuclear submarines.

Upon the death of his father, he resigned from the Navy and operated the family's farm and farm supply business. He soon was also helping to lead community, regional and state programs, especially in education and economic planning. In recognition of his ability, he was elected State Senator and later Governor of Georgia. He also was Chairman of the Southern Regional Education Board and Appalachian Regional Commission as well as Campaign Chairman of the Democratic National Committee.

President Carter's publications range in interest from human rights, health, agriculture, poverty alleviation, and homes for the needy. His books include *Why Not The Best?*, *Keeping Faith: Memoirs of a President*, *Negotiation: The Alternative to Hostility*, and *Turning Point: A Candidate, a State, and a Nation Come of Age*.

A Statement by Ronald Reagan

Fortieth President
United States of America

Because they consider President Ronald Reagan to be one of the most influential world leaders in advancing democracy, members of the College of Democracy Board of Advisors invited him to write a statement for this book. His Oxford Union Society speech was received in response to this invitation as its content related directly to the purpose of this book. President Reagan's call for more involvement of democratic nations in suppressing atrocities in various parts of the world is supported in the book by a prediction that the future will see this type of multi-national action to curtail inhuman totalitarianism wherever it occurs. Similarly, helping to achieve President Reagan's expectations for improvement in individual freedom and human dignity is the precise objective of this book.

". . . I have always believed, at home and abroad, that the only cure for what ails democracy is — more democracy. . . .

Among the many questions which cry out for our attention, none is more important than this: what will arise from the ashes of the old world order? Will it be a phoenix of freedom or a phoenix of fear? At the end of 1992 there appears no obvious answer. Indeed, if you look around the globe, the new world looks increasingly like one of disorder. . . .

[W]herever there are forces that would destroy the human spirit and diminish human potential, they must be recognized and they must be countered. . . .

[O]ur work is not yet done. A great cause remains. Whenever we look in this momentous season of change, old oppressions are crumbling even as new possibilities struggle for acceptance. Everywhere free men and free markets are on the march — from the Moscow City Council to the formerly one-party states of Africa. Yet the work of freedom is never done and the task of the peacemaker is never complete. . . . Twice in this century, the community of nations has grappled with the structure of peace. As a young man, I saw the tragedy of Woodrow Wilson as my country failed to seize the moment and Europe, shattered by war, unwittingly sowed the seeds of a still greater conflict to come.... At the very least I'm encouraged to continue questioning conventional wisdom. For there are worse things to be called than a dreamer.

So let me tell you of another dream I have, as achievable as my much maligned forecast about the collapse of the Soviet Union. It's a dream I have long had, and I have seen a glimmer of its fulfillment in recent days. Just as the world's democracies banded together to advance the cause of freedom in the face of totalitarianism, might we not now unite to impose civilized standards of behavior on those who flout every measure of human decency? Are we not nearing a point in world history where civilized nations can in unison stand up to the most immoral and deadly excesses against humanity, such as those now defacing Somalia and Bosnia? Already we have seen the potential of such action in the unprecedented coalition against Saddam Hussein, in the pivotal role played by multi-national U. N. peacekeeping forces in troublespots around the globe, and in the historic actions being taken by the U. N. this week. I heartily endorse these measures and I applaud their efforts.

If we are to fulfill the hope that the fall of communism has presented us, the world's democracies must enforce stricter humanitarian standards of international conduct. Is this not a moral cause and a great undertaking as profound as the struggle against totalitarianism?. . .

[E]veryone in this room wishes for the day when tyrants are no more. We all wish for a world in which military adventures are confined to the imagined ramparts of childhood. We wish for a time when every nation is free to develop its own resources and realize its own possibilities, unmindful of threats from abroad. But it is a sad, undeniable fact of modern life that wishes are no substitute for national will. And wishful thinking only encourages the tyrants for whom human rights are as easily trampled as protesters in a city square. . . .

In the past the divided world of the Cold War paralyzed global organizations. It was virtually impossible to achieve global cooperation on most subjects. But with the end of the Cold War, the U.N. was also liberated. With the fall of the Soviet Union, obstruction has been replaced by more cooperation. And with it, the noble vision of the U.N.'s founders is now closer to realization. . . .

[M]y generation defeated totalitarianism, and more recently we have begun to destroy the weapons of mass destruction. As a result your world is poised for better tomorrows. What will you do on *your* journey? As I see it, you have the opportunity to get and enforce international standards of civilized behavior. Does that sound unrealistic?. . .

I hope with all my heart that your days will be great, not on the battlefield, but in the science labs, the operating rooms, performing arts halls and wherever empires of the mind can be assembled. I hope that you will each make your presence felt in the world. And that you will collectively make your contribution to the age-old battle for individual freedom and human dignity. Do not forget those who suffer under tyranny and violence. Do not abandon them to the evils of totalitarian rule or democratic neglect. For the freedom we celebrate is not the freedom to starve, or the freedom to languish in a long, starless night of the soul. This, at least, is something that should be beyond debate. . . ."

****

President Ronald Reagan

Ronald Wilson Reagan was President of the United States from January 20, 1981 to Jan 20, 1989. During his tenure the economy was revitalized through a strategy of lower tax rates, controlling the growth of federal spending, regulatory reform and a stable monetary policy, resulting in the longest period of peacetime economic growth in the nations's history. President Reagan also rebuilt the country's military defenses and established the Strategic Defense Initiative which contributed greatly to the collapse of Communism and the end of the Cold War. At the same time, his historic meetings with Mikhail Gorbachev led to new understanding and important agreements between the United States and the former Soviet Union, thereby lessening world tensions and improving prospects for peace. Most significantly, President Reagan restored the spirit of the American people and provided an example of leadership, courage and optimism, which won acclaim throughout the world.

Following his second term, President Reagan wrote two books, *Speaking My Mind,* a collection of his major speeches, and *An*

American Life, his autobiography. The Ronald Reagan Library was established in California as a source for presidential scholars. He remains active on behalf of many charitable and civic organizations, and speaks to government, civic, business and student groups throughout the United States and abroad.

Before his presidency, President Reagan was a successful sports broadcaster and then had a film career encompassing 53 feature-length motion pictures. For three years during World War II he served in the Army Air Corps. He was president of the Screen Actors Guild for six terms and president of the Motion Picture Industry Council for two terms. He was elected Governor of California for two terms from 1966 - 1970. During this period he also was Chairman of the Republican Governors Association.

Many honors have been bestowed on President Reagan by nations and organizations. Her Majesty Queen Elizabeth II installed him as Honorary Knight of the Grand Cross Order of the Bath, and His Imperial Majesty, the Emperor of Japan awarded him the Grand Cordon of the Supreme Order of the Chrysanthemum. He also received a medal from President Gorbachev for his efforts on behalf of the Armenian people following an earthquake and the Grand Cross of the Order of Merit from the President of the Federal Republic of Germany.

****

A Statement from President Boris Yeltsin

These excerpts from President Boris Yeltsin's July 10, 1991 Inaugural Address directly relate to the objective of this book.

Russia Will Revive

State Power is Responsible to the People

For the first time in the history of Russia, the president has taken an oath to his compatriots. . . . For ages power and the people were at different poles in this country. . . . For ages the interests of the state were placed above the interests of people and their needs and aspirations. Unfortunately, we realized later than other civilized nations that a state is strong through the prosperity of its citizens.

. . .[T]he transition to a presidential system of government in the Russian Federation has a special significance for all of us. The time when the people were silent is gone for good. A year after the adoption of the declaration of state sovereignty, the citizens of Russia for the first time made their choice. They have chosen not only a personality and not only a president but first and foremost the path this country would follow. It is the path of democracy, reform, and revival of human dignity. For the first time ever a new, voluntary interdependence is emerging between power and the people.

. . . We have all opted for a peaceful, lawful, and democratic means of changing things. . . . A happy life . . . is created by initiative and free enterprise. Our state will revive through a spiritual revival of the people, genuine freedom of conscience, and a complete renunciation of any ideological dictatorship. . . Imperial ambitions are deeply alien to the political line chosen by the people.

The historical experience accumulated by the world community reaffirms that humane principles—freedom, property, legitimacy, and openness to the world—underlie progress. The support given by the people to the candidates of the democratic movement is the best confirmation of these universally accepted values in our life.

****

Boris N. Yeltsin

President, Russian Federation

Boris Nikolayevich Yeltsin was elected the first President of the Russian Federation on June 12, 1991, in a direct and open election. Since November 6, 1991, he has been Chairman of the Government, and from May 1992, Supreme Commander of the Armed Forces of the Russian Federation. Prior to this in March 1990, President Yeltsin had been a People's Deputy of the Russian Federation and in May of that year elected Chairman of the Supreme Soviet of the Russian Federation.

A 1968 graduate of the Ural Polytechnic in civil engineering, he started his engineering career and mastered 12 construction professions while working in positions including Chief of Construction and Chief of the Sverdlovsk Housekeeping Plant of Yuzhgorstroi. In 1955, President Yeltsin began to participate in Communist Party affairs in a variety of offices until October 21, 1987, when after a speech during which he criticized his country's leaders, he was removed from his post as First Secretary of the Moscow party committee and stripped of alternate membership in the Politburo of the Communist Party of the Soviet Union Central Committee. He continued, however, to hold various offices and in 1989 was elected People's Deputy of the Union of Soviet Socialist Republics in the first national territorial constituency of Moscow with 88 percent of the vote. This led to his election to the Supreme Soviet where he headed the Committee for Construction and Architecture.

President Yeltsin has written two books, *My Confession* and *Until the Very End.*

A Statement from President Vaclav Havel

President Havel has given us this statement for inclusion in this book. It is a remarkable personal testimony that examines the extraordinary condition the peoples of the world find themselves in following the collapse of communism. The message of this book is emphasized by his clear call for people to acquire better understandings of themselves as well as respect for the human rights of others as they develop democratic governments.

A broad range of geopolitical interests, rivalries and ambitions, dormant until recently, are coming back to life. Alliances unquestioned until recently are now being called in doubt, because the pressures that once made them necessary are disappearing. Particular interests buried by history are suddenly emerging and clashing with each other. There are even signs, here and there, of the temptation to exploit the end of the divided world to create new divisions. . . .

The fall of communism can be regarded as a sign that modern thought — based on the premise that the world is objectively knowable, and that the knowledge so obtained can be absolutely generalized — has come to a final crisis. . . . I think the end of communism is a serious warning to all mankind. It is a signal that the era of arrogant, absolutive reason is drawing to a close and that it is high time to draw conclusions from that fact.

Communism was not defeated by military force, but by life, by the human spirit, by conscience, by the resistance of Being and man to manipulation. It was defeated by a revolt of colour, authenticity, history in all its variety, and human individuality against imprisonment within a uniform ideology. . . .

The large paradox at the moment is that . . . we are trying to deal with what we have unleased by employing the same means we used to unleash it in the first place. We are looking for new scientific receipes, new ideologies, new control systems, new instruments to eliminate the dreadful consequences of [the] previous [ones]. . . . What is needed is something different, something larger. Man's attitude to the world must be radically changed. . . .

It is my profound conviction that we have to release from the sphere of private whim such forces as a natural, unique and unrepeatable experience of the world, an elementary sense of justice, the ability to see things as others do, a sense of transcendental responsibility, archetypal wisdom, good taste, courage, compassion, and faith in the importance of particular measures that do not aspire to be a universal key to salvation. Such forces must be rehabilitated. Things must once more be given a chance to present themselves as they are, to be perceived in their individuality. We must see the pluralism of the world, and not bind it by seeking common denominators or reducing everything to a single common equation. We must try harder to understand than to explain. The way forward is not in the mere construction of universal systemic solutions, to be applied to reality from the outside; it is also in seeking to get to the heart of reality through personal experience. Such an approach promotes an atmosphere of tolerant solidarity and unity in diversity based on mutual respect, genuine pluralism and parallelism. In a word, human uniqueness, human action and the human spirit must be rehabilitated. . . .

It is my impression that sooner or later politics will be faced with the task of finding a new, post-modern face. A politician must become a person again, someone who trusts not only a scientific representation and analysis of the world, but also the world itself. He must believe not only in sociological statistics, but in real people. He must trust not only an objective interpretation of reality, but also his own soul, not only an adopted ideology, but also his own thoughts; not only the summary reports he receives each morning, but also his own feeling. Soul, individual spirituality, first-hand personal insight into things, the courage to be himself and go the way his conscience points, humility in the face of the mysterious order of Being, confidence in its natural direction and, above all, trust in his own subjectivity as his principal link with the subjectivity of the world — these, in my view, are the qualities that politicians of the future should cultivate.

****

Vaclav Havel

In January 1993, Vaclav Havel was elected the first President of the new Czech Republic after securing an agreement that the President would be elected by both chambers of Parliament, could not be recalled by Parliament, had the right to dissolve Parliament and had the right to return laws to Parliament. Prior to this, in December 1989, he had been elected President of Czechoslovakia for a term to end after parliamentary elections. The freely elected Parliament re-elected him to the Presidency of the Czech and Slovak Federal Republic in July 1990 for a term of two years. While President, he gained international recognition and was a leading initiator of democratic changes within his own country.

President Havel resigned the Presidency of the Czech and Slovak Federal Republic on July 20, 1992, because he felt he could no longer fulfill commitments necessitated by the oath of allegiance in a manner that would harmonize with his convictions, dispositions and consciousness.

Long an advocate of democracy and a supporter of Czech culture, he wrote a number of plays beginning in 1963 that caused him to become known internationally as a representative of Czechoslovakian intellectual opposition to communist totalitarian oppression. The invasion of Czechoslovakia by Soviet troops in 1968 did not stem his protest against extensive oppression. As a co-founder of Charter 77 and a member of Unjustly Prosecuted, his activity caused him to be imprisoned five times. Among his writings, which brought him numerous prestigious international awards, was an essay, *The Power of The Powerless,* in which he described the means and mechanism used by the communist regime in its effort to create a powerless, resigned society consisting of timid and morally corrupt individuals. He was one of the founders of the Civic Forum in November 1989, thus becoming a key figure of the "Velvet Revolution."

A Statement for the Book from Lech Walesa, President, Republic of Poland

When we started our new revolution, we thought that all we would need to do is to give people freedom, and the rest would fall into place on its own. Today we are aware of how naive and romantic we were at that time. How carried away we were by our triumph, by the victory, which without one shot or a drop of blood, had demolished the Berlin Wall, destroyed the old order and changed the map of Europe.

Times of struggle are not conducive to reflection. Maybe that is why we looked towards the future through rose colored glasses. Maybe that is why we used so little imagination. We thought that if we elected our best people to our representative institutions - government and parliament - then we would be able to calmly go home. The politicians would solve all our problems, introduce democracy and pluralism.

Now we know better that we were mistaken in our way of thinking. Nowhere in the world can one find politicians or authorities able to change reality overnight, able to quickly and painlessly introduce difficult reforms and new democratic order; authorities, who would in a short period create a paradise out of a not very well developed, medium sized country.

After four years of freedom, we have parted with this kind of illusion. The establishment of democracy in Poland will be a long and complex process. The most talented and noble minded politicians will not be able to accelerate it, especially if they are left on their own, and the entire society fails to join in the process of structural transformation. Authorities whose hands are not watched, degenerate rapidly. They separate themselves from society and cease to represent its interests. Instead, they become solely concerned with their own affairs. On the other hand, the citizens who do not take part in solving the country's problems, merely turn into indifferent observers, critics of the actions of the authorities. A void is formed between those governing and the governed. Democratically elected institutions cease to fulfill their role. They turn into empty shells, and democracy is not very effective.

Something similar has happened to us. We have a democratically elected government, parliament, and President. Local self-governments exist. Despite all this, our democracy still remains fragile and superficial. Society is not sufficiently involved in the process of governing and decision making, relying on the politicians to do it for them. The latter should at the most open possibilities, create frameworks for effective action. The citizens, on the other hand, must fill these frames with substance. That is what happens in a healthy democratic country Poland would like to become.

That is why today we must remind ourselves of a few simple truths. First of all, freedom is always a challenge. It demands effort and courage, discipline, responsibility and imagination, capability of making decisions and choices from among various arguments and possibilities. Freedom must simply be learned. Everyone will have to learn - those governing and governed, authorities as well as citizens.

We are taking our first steps on this path. Today, we feel on our own backs what it means to be truly free - what it means to make independent decisions and take responsibility for them.

It is true that freedom has not turned out to be the same for everyone. Some have been a little lost, others disappointed. You may even hear some say that the old order was better - it provided a greater sense of security. Whose fault is it that we were not able to release the people's energy and enterprise? Why are so many of us standing aside, applauding the changes, but not participating in their implementation? As soon as possible we must deal with this problem. Otherwise, we will not be able to start, to move forward. After all, we cannot build our democracy for as long as it took in the West. We do not have that much time. Instead of two hundred years, we have only two decades to create the machinery which would guarantee the proper evolution of democratic structures.

When I was starting our revolution, I was saying: let's give freedom to society, and we will stop walking in one place. Without introduction of pluralism, we will not be able to solve fundamental matters. I still believe in this - I am not taking it back. However, after four years of building democracy, I wonder, what's next? Seeing the stagnation and sluggishness of our transformations, should we be tempted by a more effective political order - a presidential system, which, to tell you the truth, limits democracy, but it also allows for quicker reformation of the country? Or should we just wait patiently until democracy emerges and a free market economy takes shape out of this long and tedious process?

Today, other post-Communist countries are facing a similar dilemma. Some think that during this difficult period of structural transformation the first concept is preferable. It is often mentioned by Boris Yeltsin. I tend to think that he is right, even though we did not begin at the same starting point. In Poland we started reforming our country by building democracy - in Russia, by building the economy. Both ways have not brought the expected results. We have found ourselves at an impasse. How do we overcome it? This is the question which we are just now looking to answer. I do not think that answering it will be easy, but we have to face this challenge.

****

Lech Walesa

On December 9, 1990, Lech Walesa was elected President of the Republic of Poland. Earlier at the Second Congress of Solidarity, he was elected chairman of the Union by a vote of 77.5 percent. The founding of his Civic Committee in 1988 affiliated main leaders of the Polish Opposition to communist rule. After this, Solidarity was reinstated under law changing the state system. Following the June, 1989, partly free elections to the Sejm which defeated the communists, President Walesa asked the Democratic Party and the United Peasant Party to form a coalition in order to establish a government.

In 1970 at age 27, President Walesa had helped to lead a confrontation between the regime and the Gdansk Shipyard workers for which he was arrested. Later fired for criticizing communist trade unions, he, with other independent activists, began organizing free labor unions. In 1980 he led the Shipyard strike wave which changed into a bloodless national uprising aimed at the gradual liquidation of communist rule in Poland. His election as Solidarity Chairman at the First National Solidarity Congress in Gdansk in September, 1981, was followed three months later by his arrest under imposition of martial law. Imprisoned in isolation for 12 months, he was released and soon afterward headed the outlawed Solidarity.

His leadership of two protests in the Shipyard in 1988 started the fast process of transformation in Poland and Europe. At this turning point, members of the delegalized trade union started to organize en masse over the country. President Lech Walesa then met with state leaders of the United States, England, France, Russia, Spain, the Vatican, Japan, Czechoslovakia, and Argentina. President Walesa has received many international honors, including The Nobel Peace Prize, the Medal of Freedom, the Award of the Free World and the Europe award of Human Rights.

About the Author

Walter E. Boek, PhD

Walter E. Boek, PhD, President of the College of Democracy and National Graduate University, wrote this book as a sequel to his *The Evolution of a Democracy: This is Our Country, the United States of America,* following discussion with officials in Eastern Europe, North Africa and China and with members of the College's Board of Advisors. Reflected in this book are concerns expressed in these talks that leaders within existing and emerging democracies need practical information enabling them to understand the processes and the systems of values basic to establishing and strengthening democracies.

Recognized as a scientist, Dr. Boek has authored books and articles on such diverse topics as decision-making and power structures, political processes, public health and medical care, communication, village resettlement, minority issues, economic factors, industrial productivity, and organizational behavior. In addition, Dr. Boek's research in Canada and the United States led to his participation in international science conferences, and his meetings with colleagues and officials in 32 nations afforded him first-hand observation of different governments and traditions.

Dr. Boek received his baccalaureate in science, engineering, and journalism from Cornell University and his master's and doctoral degrees in anthropology and economics from Michigan State University. He then conducted research for the Health Information Foundation, New York State, Institute for Advancement of Medical Communication, Bureau of Social Science Research, University of Maryland, the Province of Manitoba and the Federal Government of Canada in the Western Arctic. He has had faculty appointments at several universities and lectured at many others.

In recognition of his achievements, he has been given various awards and elected a Fellow by the American Association for the Advancement of Science, Society for Applied Anthropology, American Public Health Association, New York Academy of Sciences, and Washington Academy of Sciences, for which he served as president. He also is an elected member of Sigma Xi and the Washington Academy of Medicine.

****

DEDICATION

This book is dedicated to you who strive to establish or improve democratic governments, for you toil for all of humanity.

PREFACE

This book is about democratic processes. It discusses the factors that make democracies possible and keep them functioning. These involve both the beliefs and actions of people. Because the very essence of democracy is liberty and the pursuit of happiness, the boundaries limiting individual behavior that enhance or damage democratic processes vary from one nation to another. That is, some of the characteristics discussed can be tolerated in one democracy but not in another. Thus, the concerns and possible solutions suggested in the book would not be as important in the first type of democracy as in the second. Because the central core of principles remain the same, however, the issues presented in this book should have meaning for most people.

How can democracies be established or existing ones improved? This question cannot be answered with a set one- two- three procedure. Rather, it can be answered by considering the characteristics of thought and action that make democratic governments prosper as distinguished from those that cause them to degenerate.

To some readers a concept described, already may be obvious depending on their past experiences and the current status of their nation's government. For others it may be a very salient and critical concept about which they can take preventative or corrective action. For still others, the concept may be known but accepted as something that has to be tolerated with little thought being given to how it may be made less deleterious to or more supportive of the goals of democratic self government.

The theme of the book is that transformation to a democracy from outmoded forms of government is not an achievement accomplished by magic formulas. Nor is it a natural government for people previously held in bondage by restrictive leaders or by the people's own value systems. Democratic principles and processes are accepted by children as they are maturing in the older democracies. In the newer democracies these concepts must be learned and practiced by the adults. During the learning process individuals must become accustomed to making decisions for themselves, their families, their enterprises, their neighborhoods, communities and their government. It is the acceptance of the important role all individuals play that makes democracies effective governments.

Information in this book is predicated on the premise that full democratic status for the emerging democracies is desirable. Further, that here is no need for citizens to be told that they have to wait for years while time consuming, step by step movement toward a representative government takes place. The evolution to a democracy can and should be direct.

It is recognized that the radical changes in the economic system from a centrally controlled one to an individualistic free market capitalistic economy may result in a period at the beginning during which essential food and consumer goods are in short supply. The endurance of such shortages, however, has an optimistic element because of the freedom that democratic governments provide. Short term improvements take place quickly as individuals begin to apply their ingenuity to solving immediate problems. This happens as soon as people realize the personal rewards they can receive while meeting essential food and material needs. Under freedom, political and economic systems become viable by reinforcing each other.

In this book readers are first invited to contemplate the

characteristics of an "ideal" government. The next consideration is the essential relationship between democracy and free enterprise. Following these presentations, attention is focused on some of the issues that must be resolved if democracies are to be maintained and new ones established. These issues include the military, religion, population growth, the human urge to control, government regulations, and bureaucracies. The essential function of the learning process in democracies is then emphasized in a discussion of formal education. The culmination of the discourse is a description of practical steps that may be taken toward achieving ideal democratic processes in the older as well as younger democracies.

An attempt was made to refrain from theoretical approaches to issues and grandiose schemes for achieving aims. Rather, it is posited that the determinant factors in the success of democracies rest with the acts of citizens and leaders in their day to day affairs. That is why it is suggested that study groups be formed for all types of people in each country. By systematically exploring with each other the various aspects of the social, economic and political spheres of their lives in a democracy, citizens should come to realize the important role their own beliefs and actions have in ensuring that their democracies continue to develop and flourish throughout the centuries to come.

If this book stimulates readers to consider the variables that affect the success of representative governments and then to act on the knowledge they acquire during that process, it will meet objectives of members of the College of Democracy's Board of Advisors and others who encouraged its writing and made possible its publication.

****

CONTENTS

Title Page i
About the Cover Picture of the Statue of Liberty ii
Individuals and/or organizations who helped make publication of this book possible iii
Board of Advisors of the College of Democracy iv
Board of Governors of National Graduate University iv
Foreword by President Jimmy Carter v
Biography of Jimmy Carter ix
A Statement by President Ronald Reagan xi
Biography of Ronald Reagan xiv
A Statement from President Boris Yeltsin xvi
Biography of Boris Yeltsin xvii
A Statement from President Vaclav Havel xviii
Biography of Vaclav Havel xx
A Statement from President Walesa xxi
Biography of Lech Walesa xxiii
About the Author xxiv
Dedication xxv
Preface xxvi
Contents xxix
List of Figures and Pictures xxxiv

Part A

Characteristics of Democratic Governments and Critical Issues in Establishing Them

Chapter I. The Ideal Government 3
A. What is Government? 3
B. Characteristics of An Ideal Government 5
C. Why Democratic Governments Today Vary from the Ideal ... 17
D. Summary 25

Chapter II. The Essential Bond Between Democracy and Free Enterprise 27
A. Introduction 27
B. Capitalism as an Economic System 28
C. Economic Growth and Capitalism 33
D. The Importance of Free Trade in Democracies 35
E. Summary 42

Chapter III. Maintaining the Subservient Role of the Military **43**
A. The Necessity for Civilian Governments to Completely Control the Military in Democracies 43
B. The Usual Reason Military Dictators Give for Taking Control of Civilian Governments 46
C. The Parliamentary System of Government and Military Takeovers 47
D. Is a National Military Force Necessary? 49
E. Forces Influencing Expansion of the Military 51
F. Possible Effects of the Practice of Visiting Dignitaries Reviewing the Troops 53
G. Military Structure, Organization and Objectives in Relation to Democracy Development 54
H. Techniques of Military Leaders to Enhance Their Power and Wealth When They Control a Nation 57
I. Summary 57

Chapter IV. Religion, Family, Population and Democracy **61**
A. Introduction 61
B. Evolution of Humans that Made it Possible for Them to seek Answers to Questions about Their Origins, Current Existence and Future 62
C. Religious Functions and How They Sometimes are Subverted 64
D. Religious Leaders Who Sometimes Control Societies in a Totalitarian Fashion 66
E. Religious Tyranny that may Result When Religion and Government are United 67
F. A Balance of Influence Between Government and Religion in a Democracy is Essential 68
G. The Evolution of Ancient Grecian and Modern Democracy 69
H. Protestantism and the Development of Capitalism 70
I. The Importance of Religion in the Formation of the United States Democracy 73
J. Characteristics of Religions that Inhibit Democratic Processes 75
K. The Role of Women and Democratic Governments 77
L. Family Size and Citizen Participation in Democracies 79

M. The Natural Occurrence of Family Size Limitation in Successful Democracies ... 81
N. The Family as the Foundation of All Human Societies ... 82
O. The Possible Negative Effect of Government Programs that are Supposed to Provide Economic Support to Families ... 85
P. Summary ... 86

Chapter V. Overcoming the Human Urge to Control ... 89

A. Introduction ... 89
B. Competition Among Animals for Social Advantages ... 90
C. The Evolutionary Process that Produced Humans and the Methods Used to Control Others ... 91
D. Competition in the Enculturation of Children and Youth ... 95
E. Conspicuous Consumption: A Method of Gaining Control ... 98
F. Variations Between Messages Children Receive From Adults and Adult Behavior They Observe ... 100
G. Bureaucratic Control ... 102
H. Participative Decision-Making ... 103
I. The Peaceful and Quick Transfer of the Powers and Responsibility of Offices by the Incumbents to Newly Elected Officials ... 106
J. The Corruption of some Democratically Elected Leaders ... 108
K. Treatment of Citizens Who Resist Totalitarian Government Leaders ... 109
L. Bribery as a Method of Obtaining Influence in Government ... 112
M. The Risk of Leadership ... 116
N. Summary ... 117

Chapter VI. Government Regulations and the Decline of Democratic Principles ... 119

A. Introduction ... 119
B. The Bond Between Citizens and Elected Officials in a Democracy ... 120
C. Origins of a Regulation ... 121
D. The Initiation and Expansion of a Regulatory Bureaucracy ... 125
E. Restrictions on Freedom Imposed by Regulations ... 128

F. Governmentocracy ... 130
G. The Difficulty Citizens Have in Attempting to Control Governmentocracy ... 133
H. The Necessity For Essential Regulations ... 136
I. Summary ... 139
Chapter VII. Bureaucratic Dangers to Democracy ... 141
A. The Necessity to Have Government Employees ... 141
B. The Bureaucratic Organization ... 141
C. Why Bureaucracies Grow ... 144
D. The Socialistic Tendency of Government Employees ... 147
E. Private Ownership and the Failure of the Socialistic Government of the Soviet Union ... 150
F. Bureaucracies in Private Enterprises ... 152
G. The Danger to Democracies of Bureaucracies ... 152
H. Bribing of Government Employees ... 156
I. Government Procurement Issues ... 160
J. Summary ... 162
Chapter VIII. The Essential Learning Process in Democracies ... 165
A. Introduction ... 165
B. The Learning Process and Governments ... 165
C. The Enculturation Process ... 166
D. The Significance of Human Interaction ... 169
E. How Children Learn Democratic Principles ... 171
F. The Decision-Making Process ... 175
G. The Importance of Normal Enculturation ... 177
H. The Importance of Two-parent Families ... 180
I. Democratic Values and Formal Education ... 183
J. The Necessity for Immigrants to Learn Democratic Principles ... 184
K. The Importance of Local Control of Public Schools ... 189
L. Sharing of Freedoms in a Democracy ... 192
M. Summary ... 193

Part B
Practical Suggestions to Achieve an Ideal Democracy

Chapter IX. A Review of the Objectives of This Book ... 197
Chapter X. Sources of Advice ... 201

Chapter XI. Issues in the Establishment and Maintenance of Democratic Governments **207**
A. Initial Elections and Constitutions 207
B. Ameliorating Critical Differences Among the Citizens of a Nation 216
C. Conflict Resolution 221
D. The Election Process 237
E. Political Parties 242
F. Corruption Controls 248
G. Democracy From the Grass Roots to the National Level 253
H. Establishing a Free Press and Ensuring Free Speech 270
I. Citizen Voluntary Activities 271
J. Judicial System 278
K. Maintaining Law and Order 283
L. The Tax System 285
M. Controlling Bureaucracies 288
N. Controlling Government Regulations 296
O. Controlling the Military 301
Chapter XII. Economic Factors in Democracies **307**
A. Property Ownership **307**
B. Free Market/Free Enterprise Capitalism 314
C. Training for Successful Businesses 327
D. Supervised Credit for Small Businesses 331
E. The Limitations of Cooperatives 336
F. International Trade 340
G. Improving and Maintaining the Country's Economic Infrastructure 346
Chapter XIII. Social and Educational Aspects of Democracies **353**
A. Religion and Freedom 353
B. Population Planning 355
C. Social Stratification 364
D. Social Welfare 367
E. Education 376
F. Science and Technology 382
G. Democracy/Free Enterprise Study Groups 387
Chapter XIV. Successful Democracies **393**

Index **401**

****

FIGURES

1. The Interdependence of Democracy and Capitalism 42
2. Effect of Government Regulations on an Individual's Freedom 131
3. A Bureaucratic Type of Organizational Structure 143
4. The Enculturation Process 168
5. Interactional Equilibrium Diagrams 229
6. Government Jurisdictions from the Local Towns and Villages to the National 269
7. Social Status and the Life Cycle 371
8. Proposed Social Status and the Life Cycle 371

PICTURES

President Jimmy Carter ix
President Ronald Reagan xiv
President Boris Yeltsin xvii
President Vaclav Havel xx
President Lech Walesa xxiii
Walter E. Boek, PhD xxiv
The Immigration Reception Building on Ellis Island in New York Harbor of the United States of America 186
A Town Board Meeting 261
Trucks Lined up at the Border of a Newer Democracy Waiting for Customs Officers to Process their Papers 294
Carefully Taken Care of Gardens With Small Weekend Houses in a Former Socialist Country 310
A New Automobile Dealership in a New Democracy 318
President Harry S. Truman of the United States and Dr. John R. Steelman Conferring in the President's Automobile 322
Family Farming in a Former Communist Controlled Country with the Use of Horses and Small Tractors for Power and Family Labor 338
Rusted Steel Girders Beside a Bridge that Cannot be Used Until it is Rebuilt 349
A Public Health Physician at a Medical and Family Planning Clinic 360
Scientists at Work 384
A Study Group 388

****

Part A

Characteristics of Democratic Governments and Critical Issues in Establishing Them

Our constitution... favors the many instead of the few; this is why it is called a democracy.

—*Pericles*

An elective despotism was not the government we fought for, but one which should not only be founded on free principles but in which the powers of government should be so divided and balanced amongst several bodies of majesties as that no one could transcend their legal limits without being effectually checked and restrained by the others.

—*Thomas Jefferson*

Democracy is based upon the conviction that there are extraordinary possibilities in ordinary people.

—*Harry Emerson Fosdick*

I believe in as little government as possible, in complete freedom of thought and speech; and in all of the things which support the dignity of the individual man as against an all-powerful state.

—*Bartley C. Crum*

Chapter I.
The Ideal Government

A. What is Government?

Fortunately, the major physiological adjustments to their environment by humans occurring during the millions of years since their origination have produced a superior organism. Humans, in comparison with other forms of life, are organisms who think and talk about where they came from, how they evolved, why they still exist and what the future might be for them as individuals and for the groups to which they belong. With such mental ability, it is reasonable and, in fact, rational for humans to contemplate and work toward the development of ideal relationships with each other.

How the relationships between and among people are arranged and maintained is government. The means by which a few people govern themselves in small groups are complicated, just as they are when there are hundreds of millions of people. When there are few people and when people are homogeneous and lack physical mobility, kinship rules define behavior toward others. This complicated kinship knowledge is acquired beginning when the baby is born. When the society is composed of large numbers of people from varied backgrounds who are highly mobile, who your parents are as a determinant of your status and role is largely replaced by informal and formal rules established by the community. These rules are learned beginning as soon as the child moves a few feet away from its parents while they are shopping or visiting with other people. Whether integrated or operating separately, the two sets of behavioral rules just mentioned—the kinship and community — are the governments under which humans live.

How a person reacts to others is learned and thus also the type of government under which people function. Because new ways of organizing governments as well as improvements in old governments can be learned, the description of the ideal government in this book is not limited to existing governments. Instead, attention is focused on how human potentiality can best be fulfilled by a government.

Human experience with governments range from the utopian dream of individuals living together unfettered by any rules, to conglomerations of human masses held together by vicious life and death power over them by dictators. Among the numerous carefully planned experimental and haphazardly formed governments, is a superior type under which human potentialities are realized much better than any other. It is the democratic republic form controlled by citizens. Although the provision of full human potentialities for all citizens are not yet realized, variations of democracy have been in operation in a number of countries long enough — including the United States' over 210 consecutive years of operation — to provide identifiable characteristics of successful democracies.

B. Characteristics of An Ideal Government

When the characteristics of an ideal government are discussed, they are not about a "utopian" government. Utopian schemes by which humans supposedly can live together in harmony have been defined and tried out many times in a number of locations around the world. They last until normal human differences arise to destroy their founders' unrealistic dreams. Recent attempts that failed have been made by groups such as "hippies" (people, primarily youth, who rejected the values of most people in their societies). Hippies organized communes in which each member was to share in the work as well as the benefits of the commune. A commune is made up of individuals and families who live together and carry on agricultural and other occupational activities from which they obtain products and funds that make it possible for members of the group to live.

This book is focused, therefore, on the type of government that enhances human dignity, fulfills human potential, and fosters meaningful productivity while operating among people with systems of values and patterns of

behavior that vary from one another. The ideal democratic government posited has the flexibility to function with citizens who believe in its fundamental premises, but otherwise have widely divergent views and ways of life. Although people in such a government may openly oppose each other's views and actions, they stand firmly together voluntarily when their type of government is challenged from without. It is a government in which every individual shares in the consideration of the problems that relate to his or her welfare and is willing to surrender some freedoms in respect for the wishes of other people. It is one in which determining the responsibilities, duties and limits of the government is the responsibility of the citizens.

In democracies, as in most governments, the major responsibilities are carried out by these three branches: the **legislative**, the **judicial** and the **executive**. In the legislative branch, the laws are made, while in the judicial, decisions are made as to whether or not the laws are in accordance with the government's constitution. The executive branch has the responsibility of organizing and administering the programs authorized by the laws.

These are some of the characteristics of an ideal democratic government:

1. It is guided and limited by a written and published set of rules, a Constitution, that ensures the freedom of the

people and defines the limitations of government officials, both elected and appointed. The Constitution provides the blueprint for the government. It indicates how the legislative, judicial and administrative functions are organized.

Governmental restraints on individual liberty and property rights are written into the Constitution as is the establishment of the judicial system that is independent from control by legislators or other government officials.

2. The "common law," consisting of the customary way of solving problems and settling disputes and upon which the courts base some of their interpretations of the Constitution, in no way conflicts with the Constitution's stipulations of the freedoms of individuals and the restrictions on government control of citizens, nor is it in any way deemed a divine law or a natural law and thus superior to the Constitution.

3. The government is responsive to citizens. They control it. The people are sovereign.

4. Representatives of the people who make the laws (the legislators) are selected, elected and rejected by the people.

5. The length of time a person can remain in an elected legislative or executive office without having to

submit to reelection is predetermined and limited to six years or less. When judges are elected, as is true in some democracies at specified court levels, their terms are longer as set by the Constitution or by the legislative process and they cannot be removed from office except for malfeasance.

6. An independent judicial system whose judges continually decide whether or not acts of legislators, government employees, and lower courts are in accord with the Constitution. Such judges are empowered to strike down legislative statutes and executive branch regulations they deem unreasonable in relation to the intentions of the Constitution and thereby prevent people through such acts from violating stipulations of the Constitution.

7. The executive or administrative part of the government that carries out responsibilities dictated by legislation, is directed by an individual or individuals elected by the citizens thus providing citizens with a method of controlling this branch of government. The administration of the government is carried out in a businesslike manner with compentent officials.

8. The government employees who do the work of government, dictated by legislation, are under the direction of the elected chief executive officer with duties sanctioned by the legislators. They operate within the stipulations of the Constitution in accor-

dance with interpretations by judges in the independent judicial system.

9. Legislators, members of the judicial system, and government employees are subject to the same laws governing their behavior toward other citizens as the citizens themselves. Citizens have the right to bring suit in a court of law against legislators and government employees for grievances.

10. The people who control the government through the decisions they make by voting, the citizens, vote in private and in secret even though they are free to express their opinion publicly on issues as well as about candidates for offices.

11. Full citizenship, which includes the privilege to vote and to seek elected offices, is not restricted by religion, ethnicity, economic status and gender. Nor is it by any other characteristic or type of behavior other than youthful age, a reasonable length of residence, and absence of certain past criminal activities against fellow citizens.

12. When one official or government employee is replaced by another one through an election process or whose appointment is terminated, that individual gives up the responsibilities of the office on the ap-

pointed date without objecting or withholding any records, equipment, or rights to the office.

13. Citizens and their enterprises are not taxed so excessively that it endangers free enterprise and individual initiative and creativeness, and every tax is decided by elected representatives of the people or by vote of the people.

14. Restrictions are not placed on the travel of citizens inside or outside of the country other than those for security purposes as determined by legislators through the legislative process.

15. Citizens are not restricted as to where they may reside or own land other than in areas determined through the legislative process.

16. The people enjoy full freedom of religion and freedom from the control of religion. That is, first, they can follow any religion they choose to as long as their religious rituals do not physically harm the adherents or nonmembers and, second, they do not have to practice any religion or belong to, or attend religious services in any church, temple, mosque or other type of religious facility.

17. All religions are free from government control as well as from government support and the government is not controlled by religious organizations.

18. All armed forces of the country are under the complete control of the civilian government.

19. When the country has a national military force, its function is to protect the nation from outside intervention. Only under extreme circumstances, such as when large segments of the population violate the rights of others, is it used to restore order among people living within the nation.

20. Citizens who serve in the military at every level accept civilian control, have full citizenship privileges, including voting, and are just as loyal to their government and respectfull of its Constitution as those not in the armed forces.

21. Police forces to combat crime within a nation are organized and controlled on as local a basis as possible. Local governmental jurisdictions have their own police who enforce laws of the nation in their geographical areas as well as local rules that are in accord with the national constitution. National coordination, but not control, of local police activities necessarily may exist to combat criminals operating on an areawide or nationwide basis such as in the illegal drug traffic. Such essential police services, as special crime research laboratories and a computer search system regarding data on criminals and crime are functions of the national coordinating office.

22. There is one official language in the entire country. All public documents are in this language and it is the primary language taught in schools.

23. The government has a compulsory educational achievement requirement for children under a specified age that may be met either in government operated and funded schools under control of local citizens or in qualified private schools.

24. Every citizen has the right to own property, including land, buildings, equipment and businesses. This is certified by laws which provide clear title to property for individuals along with the right to acquire and dispose of it.

25. Citizens' and other residents' property, whether it be where they live, work or relax must be held sacred and cannot be entered or searched without authorization by a relevant court or by prior legislation.

26. Through their personal endeavors, individuals may accumulate wealth, including that from interest gained from funds they have deposited in banks or invested in enterprises of others.

27. The nation has well-defined laws by which citizens may enter into contracts with each other, individually or through corporations they may form.

28. Every citizen has the right to form and to join organizations of his or her choosing, including political parties, and may not be excluded from membership on the basis of characteristics extraneous to its objectives.

29. The political process through which election for legislative, executive and judicial offices take place is not limited to a single party but instead provides for two or more parties to function. Depending on the interests of citizens, in no way does the government and its leaders inhibit multiple parties from functioning nor does it enhance any party through its actions or regulations that constitute unreasonable restrictions on who may run for office or be on ballots.

30. Citizens have the right to meet together to discuss issues of concern to them and to make known their opinions to the government as individuals or as a group. The freedom to talk, to write and to publish and distribute their ideas and opinions to members of organizations to which they belong, as well as to other citizens, are basic policies of the government that are steadfastly followed. This includes grievances with their legislators, executive administrators and the courts.

31. The informational media such as newspapers, magazines, radio and television are privately owned by citizens of the country and are free from government control.

32. The faculty of educational institutions, schools, colleges and universities have the freedom to relay knowledge to students as they see it and are not required to teach doctrine approved by the government or knowledge and attitudes currently labeled "politically correct."

33. Individuals cannot be held for crimes of which they are accused without being informed promptly of the charges against them and who is making them; they must be considered not guilty, and treated as such, until they have been found guilty by due process of law; they have the right to a trial by a jury of their peers; have the right to their freedom until found guilty or innocent, unless found by a court to be a serious danger to themselves or others or that it is highly unlikely that they will return for their trial; they have the right to qualified legal counsel, even when it has to be provided at the expense of the government ; they cannot be coerced into confessing crimes and must be treated humanely when held in prison.

34. All residents of the country have the right to protest government action against them in a court of law and to appeal decisions of lower courts to a higher court.

35. Citizens have the right to own arms that are reasonable in size and function.

36. The democratic philosophy pervades the whole

society. That is, government, business, religion, education and social organizations all follow democratic procedures in which policy is formulated through participation from their members. In essence, each is a small democracy.

37. Programs provided by the government for the benefit of the people such as welfare, medical care, retirement, and job security are limited so that they do not result in people giving up their independence from the government or productive endeavors.

38. Although people in the society may differ from one another in economic and social status, that is, some acquire more of the goods and services or have occupations or professions differing from one another, there are no social castes. Castes prevent individuals born in one from moving upward or downward in accordance with the relevant knowledge, skills and assets they acquire. Caste is the inherited status at birth of each individual stipulated in the traditions of the society.

39. There are no secret legislative, judicial or executive sessions other than those involving the security of the nation in terms of external threat from other countries. It is an open government whose officials trust the people so that the people can trust them.

These 39 characteristics represent most of those that

are important in determining the degree to which a government is democratic. By utilizing these to rate governments, some nations claiming to be democratic or that have democratic sounding names will be found not to be democratic. For example, the name "Peoples Democratic Government" may suggest a democratic government whereas in reality, it may be a totalitarian and intolerant dictatorship. Other nations may be partially democratic because they have some of the characteristics.

Similarly, ***the occurrence of elections by themselves do not make a country democratic.*** A "populist" election may be a populist tyranny wherein the leader is sovereign. Nor does the existence of a constitution in a country connote a democracy even though it contains glittering statements of freedom for citizens. Instead, the constitution may be the means by which tyranny in fact, rather than in law, is concealed from external observers. Under some constitutions an elected leader or leaders consider themselves sovereign and serve as the executive, legislative, and judicial branches of government without representation of citizens.

These characteristics of democracies may be used to obtain a score indicating how democratic a country is by judging how well the government meets the 39 criteria. A scale of from zero to five could be devised to rate each characteristic. A score of "five" would be the highest rating and indicate that the specific characteristic was completely met by the country whereas the score of "one" would suggest that much improvement was needed. Although some characteristics are more important than others, if an evaluation is done every few years and a comparison made of the total scores arrived at by adding the rating given to all the individual characteristics, this rating method might be useful as an indication of changes that are occurring in the country.

C. Why Democratic Governments Today Vary From the Ideal

There may be no greater disappointment than that felt by people who have carefully planned and established a society in which everyone is supposed to share equally in the responsibilities and rewards of its operation and live in peace and harmony with the others, when they finally realize that their "utopian" society has failed. Such societies fail, not because the planners' objectives are ignoble, but because the members of the society are humans with learned beliefs and ways of living varying from one another. Therefore, in a utopian society some will work hard to improve their living conditions while resenting those who do not work as hard yet receive the same benefits in the society.

Leaderless societies do not exist. Observation of those societies that are claimed to be equalitarian, quickly reveals the leadership structure that keeps them functioning.

Similarly, ***societies without social differences among their members do not exist.*** All societies consist of people who enjoy more or less of the goods and services than others. To understand the reasons for these facts about leadership and social variations requires knowledge of what humans are like and how they got that way.

Regardless of where and how they live in the world, people have the same effective brain capability. People in highly industrialized communities, however, grossly underestimate the brain capacity of those living in "primitive" societies as well as what they must know to survive. Similarly, those people living in rural and/or subsistence societies underestimate the potential mental ability of urban people to learn how to live as they do. The urban people label the others as "country hicks" or "peasants" whereas the rural ones call the others "city slickers." This stereotyping inhibits each group from recognizing the actual capabilities of the other as well as variations among individual members.

The equality of learning abilities among widely diverse peoples can easily be demonstrated from recent history. Individuals living in societies wholly dependent on food from small gardens, fishing and hunting, where men dressed in loin cloth and depended on their spears for hunting and protection against others and women in grass skirts tended gardens, quickly changed their way of living and their government following World War II. As a result of the intrusion into their society of other people and technology of modern war and its aftermath of self governing trends, these men and women, who once knew only the former way of life, adopted western clothes and type of government. Some of their leaders soon became distinguished United Nations representatives of their new governments with offices in skyscraper buildings in San Francisco and New York City. Back home, their relatives and neighbors changed their way of living and formed elected governing councils. Anyone knowing how these people drastically changed their way of life, added to their knowledge and skills, and altered their beliefs in a short period of time, should be convinced of the equality of brain capacities among all peoples.

Although equal to others in mental capacity, each individual has a unique personality. Their personalities differ even from their siblings with whom they were reared as members of the same family during their infancy, childhood and young adulthood. ***Personality is the physiological reactions of a person to events, people and objects. Personalities are formed as the infant interacts with individuals already in the society.*** It is the information flowing from parents and older children, at first, and later from teachers, fellow workers and others, to the new member of the family that molds his or her personality.

Because personalities are formed in this manner, restrictive societies, whether dictatorial, religious or communistic, go to great lengths to indoctrinate young children without their parents being present. Totalitarian governments have indoctrinating organizations for children and youth in addition to regular schools, so that much of the children's time is under supervision. This technique was applied in Germany under Hitler with Hitler youth organizations there and in the former Soviet Union with the "Young Pioneers" and "Komsomol" organizations. A government's objective in operating such groups is to train youths to think in the desired ways and to slant their knowledge of other philosophies, forms of government, or religions in a manner favoring their own government.

Children in the organizations in the Soviet Union also were used by the authorities to obtain information on their parents, other relatives and neighbors. With children from the same family in more than one organization because of age variations, their accounts were compared for consistencies. Parents making comments or involved in acts against the government and its policies were reprimanded by the authorities.

If children can be kept away from the influence of their parents, or taught to reject the thinking of their parents, children's personalities can be formed so that they will believe what they have been told by government authorities and be loyal to the intended cause, no matter how brutal or ethnocentric it may be.

It is much more difficult for adults to have their beliefs changed than it is for children. That is why a substantial number of people in the former Soviet Union still were religious and participated in religious services that their government attempted to prohibit despite 70 years of communistic rule. The stability of adult beliefs is the reason that brainwashing techniques were practiced by Chinese communists in North Korea and the communists in North Vietnam to change the thinking of captive soldiers of the democracies held as prisoners of war. Totalitarian governments establish what they call "relearning" centers to which they sentence nonconforming adults and youth. In these centers punishment and awards are administered to them while they are imprisoned far from the support of their families and friends.

Brainwashing is the process by which individuals are forced to do something that contradicts their beliefs — like spitting on their country's flag or making statements against their country. After someone who loves his country and his flag is forced with physical torture to do this kind of an act for awhile, he or she faces a dilemma. Either 1) the act has to stop, which is difficult because the torturers will do everything they can to force the individual to continue doing it, 2) the individual has to change his beliefs to conform with the act, or 3) the person has a serious mental breakdown. The objective of the brainwashing torturers, of course, is to induce the individual to change his or her beliefs so that they conform to those desired by the torturer. Some individuals' values are so strong that they refuse to commit the acts for which they are severely tortured until they nearly die or are actually killed.

Brainwashing then, involves the creation of stress, physical and/or mental, on an individual forcing him or her to do something that violates his or her beliefs with the expectation that the desired change in those beliefs will be achieved. The stress created ranges from the ruthless torturing of individuals as done in the Christian inquisition of the Middle Ages and in the communist dictatorships and religious fundamentalist countries of recent years to the subtle but effective indoctrination of youth by educators.

In nations that have existed for several generations, parents will relay to their children the values that support the type of government they are used to and have accepted. A truly democratic government with full freedom for its people does not operate as smoothly as does a government that restricts both thinking and acting of its citizens. Those who disrupt things under the restrictive government, that is, those inadequately socialized as far as that government is concerned, are imprisoned or killed so that they no longer can cause trouble or stimulate doubts in the minds of the others.

Because of fundamental human characteristics, it is less stressful, and therefore easier for people to change from believing in dictatorial, communistic or theistic governments to democracies than it is to change from democracy to other types of government. Similarly, it is more difficult for people in societies with religious totalitarian control to change to democratic values than for those in communist totalitarian dictatorships to accept democratic values. Individuals under any other type of government, however, do adjust to democratic forms of government, especially when they realize how their own efforts in a free market economy can produce economic and social improvement in their lives.

The control of values is not done deliberately by the government in a democracy. Thus, citizens in a democracy can complain about actions of their government and continually try to influence government policy and how it is carried out without fear of being arrested, imprisoned and punished as long as they do not disrupt government or citizen affairs or destroy property of the government or of citizens. They also can appeal decisions of their government, including the courts, by seeking a review of them by a higher court up to the highest national court. If their appeal is turned down by all the courts, they can strive to have the legislators they elected pass laws appropriate to their way of thinking.

Democratic governments today vary from one another in organization and style of operation. In one there may be a queen or a king who is tolerated or respected because the role of such a person is ceremonial with the governmental decisions left to elected officials. In another, the citizens elect representatives to a parliament whose members remain in their legislative positions for a stated number of years or until it is difficult for them to reach decisions on issues because they disagree with each other or with the elected or appointed Prime Minister. When parliamentary legislators feel that they cannot function well, an election is scheduled. In still other countries, people elect representatives on a regular basis for terms of one, two, four or six years.

The judicial system also varies among democracies. For example, in the United States, any law or act judged to be unconstitutional by the courts is illegal, and, therefore, canceled. In Great Britain where decisions of Parliament depend on action by the House of Commons, the House of Lords and the Monarch, there is no real division of powers between the legislative and judicial. The Lord Chancellor as Speaker of the House of Lords heads the judicial function with the House of Lords being the final court of appeals. All laws have to be approved by the Monarch while their interpretation is by judges who base their decisions on the "rule of law" derived from acts of the Parliament and agreements as far back as the Magna Carta agreement between the barons and the Monarch in 1215 as well as on prior judicial decisions.

D. Summary

The objective of this chapter is to provide an understanding of what a government is without glittering generalities or political jargon. Government, therefore, is depicted here as the relationships with each other that humans have invented, arranged and maintained for working and living in proximity to one another. If the function of a government is to provide a favorable environment for human potentialities of all citizens to flourish, democracies have demonstrated their superiority in moving toward the accomplishment of this objective.

Some democracies that, according to recently accepted definitions of democratic republics, are governments in which citizens elect legislators to represent them in law-making, have been in operation for more than 200 consecutive years. This long history makes possible detailed descriptions of them as presented in Section B of this Chapter. These characteristics of democracies include a Constitution, the written instrument that codifies the creation, organization and definition of the three significant functions or branches of government and delegates to each certain powers along with stipulations on how each limits control of the others. Some of the other characteristics presented are the guaranteeing of the sovereignty of the people; the assurance of religious freedom and freedom from religion; the maintenance of military subservience to the civilian government; and the provision that there be one language across the nation.

It was pointed out that variations in governments, including democracies, are to be expected because the citizens that establish and continue them are not alike. Each individual has a unique personality that originates in their families, families that exist in their particular society with its ways of behaving and methods of government. The acquisition of sets of values foreign to an individual involves mental stress, especially for adults.

It is easier for people whose beliefs support dictatorial, communist, or theistic governments to change their thinking to support democracy than to change from believing in democracies to the other types of governments. It also is more difficult for people living under religious totalitarianism to accept democratic values than it is for those living under communism.

****

Chapter II.
The Essential Bond between Democracy and Free Enterprise

A. Introduction

People who are free to develop and operate their own enterprises as they see fit, to buy from and to sell to whomever they want to at whatever price they choose, cannot tolerate a repressive government that attempts to limit their freedoms. Similarly, a government that is controlled by its citizens will have citizens who also control their own economic destinies. ***A repressive government that expects to control the economic system with central planning and government ownership cannot tolerate a people free to speak, write and openly discuss the government.***

The bond between individual enterprise and democratic government is necessary for both to prosper. An advanced democracy requires an economic system among its citizens that fosters growth in the amount of goods and services produced, called by economists, the "Gross National Product." These products of human endeavors must be directly related to the desires of the people. It is free enterprise with free markets that achieves this continued increase of goods and services, and it is this continual expansion that improves the quality of life for the citizens. ***Political freedom and economic freedom are so interrelated that it is almost impossible to have one without the other.***

B. Capitalism as an Economic System

The economic system that much more than any other, meets essential requirements of democracies is capitalism. Capitalists have beliefs about human activity that include continual striving to increase their income beyond that needed for the necessities of life. They do this by working hard to earn money and then by spending less than they earn. The money they save is used to obtain additional money by investing it in businesses or from interest for the use of it that is paid by banks who invest it. The objective of people who own businesses in a capitalistic society is to increase the size or scope of their businesses with the profits from their endeavors rather than to spend it all on consumer goods and services.

The critical difference between capitalism and other economic systems, therefore, is that a major proportion of the excess of receipts over expenditures is used to increase the size of the business that produced it or to improve old or install new equipment to increase production. Thse uses of funds produce the economic growth from which support for democratic government operations is obtained. At the same time, use of the material products and services of capitalism improves the quality of life of people in the producing nation as well as in many other countries.

Because citizens of democracies control the government, they tend to demand an ever increasing amount of services from their government. The pressure for additional services from citizens is difficult for the representatives they elect to ignore. Therefore, the trend in democracies is a continual increase in government expenditures and thus the necessity for more financial support from the people. When capitalism is functioning well, it provides the economic expansion that can support a government that also is growing at the same rate.

Since human behavior evolved, some men and women have been able to achieve great wealth. Some have accomplished this accumulation of resources by inflicting extreme suffering on people, as in the buying and selling of men, women and children to be used as slaves or by profiting directly from the free labor of slaves they own along with minimizing the amount and quality of food, housing, medical care and other necessities of life allocated to their slaves. Others become wealthy by acquiring the property of others through confiscation or the eradication of its owners. Still others achieve wealth through the use of their knowledge and skills in inventing new products desired by others or by improving the usefulness of old products and increasing the efficiency of producing them under a free market capitalistic society.

Being rich is not in itself an unsuitable attribute. On the contrary, individual wealth can enhance the quality of life of others. The effect of individual wealth, however, depends on how it is utilized in every country. And this applies for any amount of goods or money ranging from the few kopecks of a small farmer to the millions of pounds or dollars that some factory owners or bankers may accumulate.

Among the historical diversions of income from increasing the productivity of the society is the spending of <u>most</u> of one's income to:

1. maintain a splendorous life style;
2. purchase products harmful to one's health;
3. build individual and family edifices;
4. patronize the arts extensively;
5. support religious organizations lavishly;
6. maintain military establishments and finance campaigns;
7. expand non-productive property holdings; and
8. finance government bureaucracies.

Although all of these uses of wealth result in jobs and

thus income for people, none of them produce growth in the number of jobs beyond those necessary to carry out the immediate tasks. No matter how much it may be admired, a luxurious home costing five million dollars, is quite a different investment in terms of the economic return to the country than a factory that produces farm machinery. When the home is built, it does not produce income. The factory, however, can keep on producing income that can be used to expand it or build other factories for the next generation if it is carefully managed with a resulting improvement in the level of living of the people.

Political leaders promoting democracy call for free markets. ***Just having free markets, however, does not result in a democracy or in itself indicate that one exists or that the economic system is capitalistic.*** Many nondemocratic societies have markets to which people bring their goods to sell or barter for other goods. Each participant in such a market applies all the skills he or she possesses to obtain the most favorable deal for himself or herself. The buyers and sellers in many of these markets are there to obtain products they can use. They are not there to make much money. Making money by itself is not their primary goal. If they do receive extra money they are likely to spend it for something they need right away. It is not put in a bank to earn interest for them, that at the same time makes it possible for the bank to lend it to businesspersons and it is not used to purchase many more products they can sell. Thus, their endeavors are not capitalistic.

There is another significant difference between the trading that has been occurring for thousands of years and the buying and selling under free enterprise in a democracy. It is the relationship between buyer and seller. People have always traded, but trading relationships were typically between enemies. When buyers are obtaining products from their enemies and sellers consider buyers their enemies, each feels justified in cheating the other. Under democracies with free markets, the buyer and seller tend to treat each other as friends. Prices no longer are haggled over but are the same for each purchaser. Businesses try to please their customers and tell their employees "the customer is always right." Customers who think the prices are too high, take their business somewhere else. They do not try to destroy the business or assault the businesspersons.

Immigrants to democratic countries from areas without a history of free enterprise, along with citizens of democracies who were inadequately assimilated, may have the attitude that businesspeople are their enemies. Although treated fairly, they may with slight provocation destroy the businesses on which they have depended by rioting, looting, smashing property and burning buildings. That is why hard working Koreans and other storekeepers in Los Angeles, California of the United States witnessed their customers stealing from them and wrecking their businesses. This occurred when less assimilated people reacted to news that a representative of a minority was supposed to have been mistreated by the police. Similar incidents have happened in England and other countries.

This belief by people that those they were selling to or buying from are their enemies also leads to serious confrontations between the two groups in countries changing from controlled state-owned businesses to privately-owned businesses. With prices determined by demand and supply, instead of being set by the government, merchants are condemned for their prices, beaten or killed, their goods stolen and their facilities destroyed. This has happened in Russian cities, especially when the sellers are from distant parts of the country even though a continuing supply of their agricultural products or other goods for sale were desperately needed by the destructive buyers.

C. Economic Growth and Capitalism

Capitalism produces economic growth when correct business decisions are continually and consistently made by the capitalists and the government does not restrict their endeavors with unnecessary regulation and excessive taxation. To make correct decisions, members of the capitalistic society require complete and timely market information. Communication of such data has to be among a multitude of individual businesspeople, each free to make decisions as to what, how much, and when to grow or manufacture products. Capitalism tends to be flexible in that it adjusts to actual demand because it is governed by multiple decision-makers close to the action. Each capitalist produces what he or she thinks can be sold and not what someone orders to be produced. Democratic governments provide capitalists with the freedom to take risks. It is the businessperson's individual fortunes that are at risk. If he or she wants to continue in business, unwanted products can not be allowed to pile up in storage. Capitalists' success depends on how well they can deduce current demand or predict future needs and then how quickly they can produce what is demanded.

In capitalistic societies, it is not just the businesspersons who have the values that make capitalism successful. Most of the people also follow the principles of capitalism although they may not realize it. Many employees in industry, clerks in stores and teachers in schools, for example, dream of saving enough money to invest or to start their own businesses and they work hard in an effort to accomplish that objective. Even scientists tend to tailor their efforts to conform with sources of support that will produce the greatest return for their labors. The savings of these capitalistic employees are not kept at home, but rather deposited in banks and/or invested in enterprises run by others. Thus, their objective is to continually increase their income and wealth to the point where new businesses can be launched. Meanwhile, their funds are being used to finance and expand already existing enterprises or to develop new ones.

Because it is to the advantage of the capitalist to increase demand for products, considerable effort is devoted to increasing consumer aspirations for products by making the products available where potential purchasers can see them and by advertising them, that is, providing information about the products that can be heard or seen by those who may want to buy them. Advertisements may be printed in different forms and displayed where they may be seen, or mailed to potential consumers or placed in newspapers and magazines. Advertising also may be read on radio or displayed on television programs. Directly correlated with the advertising process is an increase in the level of living of consumers as well as an improvement in their knowledge because they expand the amount of products and variety they use.

D. The Importance of Free Trade in Democracies

The capitalist is always looking for larger markets for products. This means that products must be sold outside of his or her local community and frequently in another country. Thus, capitalism results in greatly increased trade along with an increase in essential banking, transportation, storage, and communication services. Trading, both exporting and importing, helps build a strong internal economic system.

It is essential for businesspeople to have access to all the information about what products are needed and how much of a supply or potential supply there is of the product, if they are to be successful. With these data, they must have the ability to prepare analyses that provide them with valid conclusions about the possibilities of making a profit if they were to manufacture or process a product or even to stock an item made by someone else in order to sell it.

Also it is necessary for businesspeople to be free to buy and sell anywhere, both within their countries as well as outside of them. An effective national economic system can not be achieved when trade is restricted within a country and between its business people and those of other countries.

The greatest error in the advancement of human societies has been restrictions placed on the processes of supply and demand. The most effective forces in economic development are free markets and free enterprise when these stretch across the boundaries of families, tribes, and nations, uninhibited by beliefs, ethnocentric loyalties, cultural biases, quotas, tariffs, subsidies, or taxes. When trade increases — the free movement of people, goods and services across boundaries — the ever so critical infrastructure is improved and expanded. For example:

transportation systems develop;
storage facilities are built;
refrigeration and other means of protecting and preserving products are constructed;
accounting methods and management skills are improved;
banking services and investment are multiplied;
written and spoken languages become more uniform, as do currencies;
a much better understanding and greater tolerance for cultural variations occur;
the standardization of equipment, products, and measurements takes place to the extent that each person involved in trading transactions knows that the equipment purchased or transported fits his or her requirements as well as the quality desired;
the quality of products greatly improves;
individualism and healthy competitiveness develop with a resulting improvement in respect for human life;
agricultural and industrial means of production increase; and
business receipts over expenditures become more prominent, thus leading to reinvestment in needed enterprises. These business earnings, in turn, result in modernized efficient production and distribution systems,

thus speeding progress in all of the
advantageous changes just listed.

Although free trade is essential in democratic nations, adjustments may have to occur in the economy to compensate for some of the effects of the free flow of goods. Competition may be increased regarding some products in the country such as imports being available at a lower cost than those made in the country. If traditional production methods in a country result in a higher cost and/or lower quality product than can be obtained through trade, improved production methods for old products have to be devised or else different products may have to be grown, processed or manufactured. These changes may require extensive training of entrepreneurs as well as workers.

Because capitalism demands efficiency, it lifts the burden of production and transportation from the heads and shoulders of men, women and children and transfers it to machines. More and more people, therefore, are employed in occupations requiring them to use their minds rather than their backs.

By using machines instead of human hands, production, processing, storage and shipment of products, as well as service tasks, can be done quicker and better. This increased efficiency with the use of machines results in shorter working hours, a higher return per hour worked in real money and improved diets and health.

Along with these changes comes a substantial increase in formal technological and scientific learning and adjustments upward in the quality of life desired and obtained by people. Similarly, voluntary family planning takes place that limits population growth without which possibilities for economic advancement are devastated. Furthermore, the efficient use of human resources and capital provides more discretionary funds to satisfy the accompanying increase in both the variety and amount of products demanded by consumers. This machine caused human efficiency results in more leisure time, along with surplus funds to pay for formal education and for the absolutely essential scientific research that produces the innovations that fuel and refuel the whole economy. (There is a further discussion of the population issue in Chapter IV, Section M and Part B, Chapter XIII, Section B in this book.)

Under the capitalistic system, money accumulates, but it is quickly transformed into further means of production. With the capitalist concentrating on expanding income producing enterprises, instead of spending a large proportion of income for those activities already designated as "diversions of money" from reinvestment opportunities, wealth can multiply in a geometric manner. That is, an amount earned over expenditures when reinvested in the enterprise will, along with that already invested, produce more than that produced with the initial funds. When earnings are repeatedly reinvested, the size of the enterprise and/or the number of enterprises supported grow rapidly.

Because capitalists' objectives are to accumulate wealth, some may become ruthless in seeking that goal. As is emphasized in Chapter VI, the government must not stymie capitalism with needless regulations. On the other hand, it is essential that the possible excesses of capitalists be controlled. That is, capitalists as individuals or together must be prevented from obtaining a monopoly by which they can burden consumers with prices for products or services that result in returns on the capital investments of the providers far beyond that which is considered normal. For example, owners of a manufacturing firm may control all of a special type of metal needed to produce their product and thus keep other businesses from being established to make the product. To prevent this type of monopoly, the government may have to restrict their control of the metal to allow some for others or it may have to limit the firm's profit. Likewise, if a firm is given the right to provide an essential service such as supplying electricity, natural gas or water, the right has to be accompanied by a limitation on the profit for the owners as well as on the amount paid as salaries and expenses to the management staff of the firm.

Capitalism is a method of distributing wealth among

the people of a country. This distribution has to be fairly divided between owners for providing their capital and management skills and workers for their labors. As a means of achieving a satisfactory share of the returns from capitalistic enterprises, those who work for capitalists, from management personnel to laborers must have the right to organize and negotiate their wages. They must, however, be subject to the same type of government controls that prevent owners from obtaining monopolies. Worker organizations cannot be allowed to develop a monopoly of employees or potential employees. A type of humanistic capitalism should be achieved in which the financial returns for owners make it worthwhile for them to invest their funds, while at the same time their workers receive sufficient income, job security and benefits to support a satisfactory quality of life.

It is feasible for owners and workers engaged in a capitalistic enterprize to achieve a balance in the returns received that is agreeable to each. Modern owners recognize that higher productivity of quality products results when workers are treated fairly. Similarly, most workers today realize that to remain in business, owners must receive an excess of receipts over expenditures to pay the cost of capital invested as well as to meet expenditures for the research and technology that keep the enterprise competitive.

E. Summary

As Figure 1 illustrates there is a direct relationship, and a dependency, between democratic governments and capitalistic economies. Both democracy and capitalism require citizens to value their independence in thinking and acting and insist that it be protected. The freedom required for capitalism is inherent in democracy and capitalism generates the funds by which democratic governments can operate.

Figure 1. The Interdependence of Democracy and Capitalism

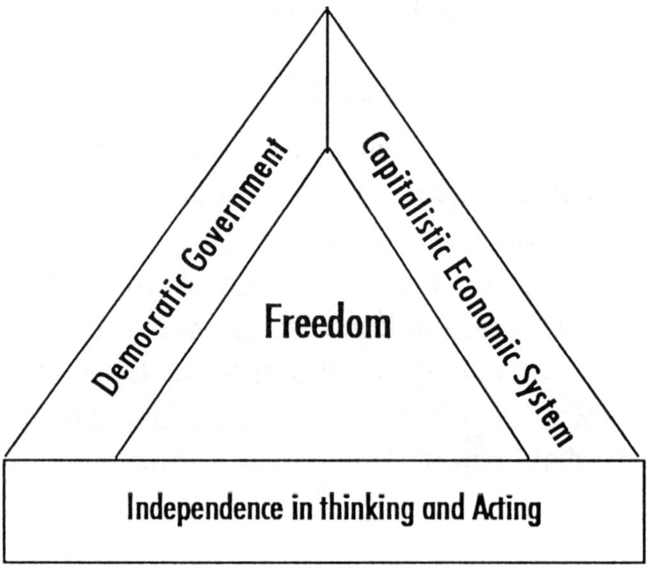

****

Chapter III. Maintaining the Subservient Role of the Military

A. The Necessity for Civilian Governments to Completely Control the Military in Democracies

The most dangerous and destructive force for new democracies is a military that elected leaders do not completely control. Men and women in new democracies who are trained and organized to instigate and carry out military operations have the guns and other equipment to counter democratic endeavors. To prevent this from happening the supreme commander of the military must be elected by the people, thus causing the commander's allegiance to be to the citizens. ***Civilian control of the military must be one of the strong values held by all citizens in a democracy.***

In older democracies, like Canada, Australia, Great Britain and the United States, the basic beliefs of members of the military regarding the necessity for civilian control of the military are the same as those of nonmilitary civilians.

Thus, members of the military seldom strongly object to having their top officers under the authority of civilians. The aspirations of men and women in the military for positions outside of the armed forces when they decide to leave the military or upon retirement is further evidence of their acceptance of civilian control. To reinforce this attitude about the desirability of a second career in the civilian sector upon retirement, they should be permitted to serve no more than 20 years, except when their country is at war.

The essential orientation to future nonmilitary pursuits is especially true for those who have become famous because of their actions while in military service of the older democracies. They strive to enter business, education, community organizations or seek elected offices. Many generals and admirals desire to become elected to the presidency or prime ministership of their countries and some are elected. Those who are elected, even to head their governments, do so as civilians and not as military leaders.

For example, the commander of the World War II Allied Forces in Northern Europe, General Dwight D. Eisenhower, was sought after by the political parties in the United States to become their candidate for the Presidency. They wanted to utilize his popularity to influence people to vote for him and their party in order to win an election. Eisenhower did seek and win the election for the Presidency, but not as a man who emphasized his leadership in war. As

President, he became the Commander-in-Chief of all the Armed Forces, but as President and not as General Eisenhower. While President, he even warned his fellow Americans that the "powerful military-industrial complex" could be a danger to their democracy.

What Eisenhower meant was, that if the military insists on continued increases in expenditures of government funds for equipment and materiel and if the industrial sector that supplies it presses legislators to approve the funds, a significant proportion of the nation's economy would be dependent on the military and armament industry. This would lead to insufficient attention to civilian needs and subsequent shortages of civilian goods. In addition, it could result in a dangerously powerful military establishment.

In the older democracies, whenever a military leader attempts to ignore his commander, he is demoted or dismissed from his position. This type of removal has happened in the United States with top generals a number of times. An example that stands out because it was publicized in many newspaper articles and on radio and television news programs, involved General Douglas MacArthur. During the Korean War, General MacArthur of the United States acted as if he were independent of his Commander-in-Chief, the President of the United States. Because he openly violated a fundamental law of his democracy, by rejecting his civilian commander and setting his own policy during the war, he was stripped of his command and then he retired from the military.

The interesting aspect of this case was that many United States Senators and Representatives at first forgot how important this principle is in their democracy and condemned their President for being Commander-in-Chief and preserving their democracy by relieving General MacArthur of his command. Later, most legislators accepted their President's action as being necessary and correct in a democracy because military leaders must be subject to the authority of the civilian head of the government.

B. The Usual Reason Military Dictators Give for Taking Control of Civilian Governments

Civilian control of the military too often is not a characteristic of governments. Being elected president, a national legislator or judge in a country does not have much significance in terms of governing if the military is independent of all three. If the military leader or leaders feel that the president, legislators, or the judiciary are impinging on their power, all they have to do is to depose the president and abolish the legislature and the judiciary. Any resistance to this action is quickly overcome by the military who arrest the elected officials. To the rest of the world the military leader tries to justify such action by condemning the elected officials and the judicial as being corrupt beyond redemption. Therefore, that type of leader states that the military government is the only way the immediate problems of the people will be solved.

Military dictators who take over governments from duly elected civilians justify the drastic action they take in the name of democracy. Military takeovers are nearly always accompanied by promises that democratic elections will soon take place, but the date they suggest when this will occur keeps on being changed or is ignored completely by them. When an election is allowed, it likely will be controlled to ensure that the military's candidates win.

C. The Parliamentary System of Government and Military Takeovers

New governments that follow the "parliamentary" system tend to be more subject to military takeovers than those in which the electoral process is the direct means by which the decision is made as to who will run the government. In the parliamentary type of government, voters elect members of their parties who then appoint the head of the government, usually called a "Prime Minister." Parliaments subject to the dictates of a monarch or another type of dictator, are not democracies even though members of the parliament are elected by the citizens. On the other hand some parliamentary systems headed by a monarch, in reality, are democracies because they have monarchs who have only a ceremonial role in the government. Therefore, they pose no threat to democratic processes.

The reason the parliamentary system is more subject to abolishment by individuals intent on dominating a country is because the terms of elected legislators, although for a stated maximum numbers of years, frequently are terminated quickly or shortened by party leaders when they cannot agree on important issues or maintain a majority vote on issues they favor. Under these circumstances, the government is considered to have collapsed because of a policy disagreement crisis and as a consequence, the prime minister resigns. Although the length of time legislators in parliament serve can be shortened, it is not uncommon, during national emergencies such as wars, for them to lengthen their terms. Normally, citizens select representatives for the parliamentary legislatures for a specified number of years by voting in an election. Therefore, when terms are lengthened in this manner, citizens lose much of their direct influence on the decisions of their government.

Under the parliamentary system, when the legislators cannot agree and they decide to have an election, the bureauracy of the executive branch keeps functioning. Although the bureaucracy may still be under the influence of the former elected leaders of the parliament, the government is operated by employees in the bureaucracy rather than by elected representatives of the citizens until an election takes place and representatives are elected or reelected.

Under a parliamentary government, a dictatorial leader, especially if that person is able to control the military, can dismiss the legislators and operate the government himself or herself. With the bureaucracy under their administration and the military protecting them, dictators can put down almost all democratic efforts to restore the government to the people. At first, this dismissal of the legislators may not seem too unusual to citizens under the parliamentary system, but rather, they may consider it just another instance of the government collapsing. Later, the citizens who might not have been too concerned about the changes in their government often come to the realization of the dictatorial aspect of this takeover with its loss of citizen control.

Therefore, it is suggested that leaders and citizens in new democracies become cognizant of the possible inherent weakness in the parliamentary system just discussed when types of democratic governments are being considered for their country.

D. Is a National Military Force Necessary?

Founders of the United States feared a standing army

because they knew how such military forces had been used for centuries by leaders of European nations to control their own citizens as well as attack other countries. A standing army can be a threat to peace among nations and a force to suppress citizen's freedom. This strong belief of United States leaders during the early history of the country prevented the military of this democracy from ever achieving decision-making power over the government and the people.

Just as was true when the United States was formed, the question as to whether or not a national military force to protect the nation from other nations is necessary at all should be given serious consideration by those working to form new democracies. With current communication technology, the armaments of one country can become known to others. If it is accepted that such a military force exists to protect the nation from other countries and is not to be used against its own citizens, then the necessity for it has to be justified by fear of neighboring nations. Seeing a military force being increased in nations on the other side of their borders will be interpreted as preparation for attacking them.

A fear of neighboring nations may not be justified in many parts of the world. For example, a number of nations that have chosen not to have national armies, such as Costa Rica, have existed in peace with their neighbors for many years.

The absurdity of one nation building a major military force to protect it against another is evident when that action produces a similar increase in armaments by its neighbors. This escalating process becomes even more ridiculous when major world powers justify their subsidization of the military of small nations to "achieve a balance of power among nations in a region." If it is a balance of power that is desired, then the world powers should expend their efforts in inducing countries to reduce their arms. This reduction process would achieve the balance of power objective argument they use to justify the buildup of arms in countries.

E. Forces Influencing Expansion of the Military

Unfortunately, there are two variables working to increase armaments rather than to decrease them in nations. One of these is the desire on the part of individuals to make money producing and/or selling arms to their own government or to other governments. In nations with government owned industry producing military products, the leaders use this method of obtaining income. The money-making sale of munitions by the citizens of one country to enemies of their own nation also occurs, either directly or indirectly through dealers in a third country. The sale of arms often endangers a previous balance of power between nations and may result in devastating conflicts.

The production of munitions in a nation for its own military can be controlled by legislators by limiting the budget for operating the military. Whether the arms are produced for internal use or for export, their production may be a significant factor in the economy of the nation. Because of this economic factor, legislators may be reluctant to limit such production. For the same reason, legislators may not want to restrict the exporting of munitions except to nations that pose a threat or potential threat to their country. International agreements limiting arms sales can have some effect on exports, even though some countries will not respect such restrictions.

The second variable is the mindset of military leaders whose values are oriented toward increasing the size, amount and technical capability of their armaments rather than reducing them. This desire is no different from that of leaders in non-military organizations who also work to improve their organizations by increasing their own capability to carry out their objectives whether they be government agencies, foundations or private businesses. Leaders in democracies must obtain, on a continuing basis, full information on the size and type of their country's military organization and weapons and limit them by legislation, to what is necessary.

The need for a national military force is enhanced by real or imaginary external threats to the sovereignty of a country. It should be recognized, however, that there is a direct relationship between the need for a national military and the rewards, in terms of promotions in rank, advancement in salaries, and increase in social recognition for military personnel that accompany military preparation for action. Conversely, the lack of promotions, the stagnation of salaries, and the lowering of prestige, characterizes an inactive peace-time military. Therefore, to improve their social rank and increase their personal income, military personnel tend to seek additional financial and moral support from their governments by emphasizing the necessity to be prepared for possible conflicts with other nations. When considering the preparedness argument of the military, legislators must understand their use of it to increase the military budget and discount it in accord with reality.

F. Possible Effects of the Practice of Visiting Dignitaries Reviewing the Troops

The practice of "reviewing the troops" whereby a visiting dignitary, such as a president, from one country walks across in front of expensively dressed, expressionless soldiers alongside the president of the country being visited, emphasizes the importance of the military. A "twenty-one gun salute" honoring a visiting official is a similar military expression.

What these ceremonies achieve, therefore, is contrary to what is desired in a democracy where the military is de-emphasized. In fact, the special soldiers of the nation being reviewed, usually referred to as the "elite guard," may quickly come to be considered by the host president as his or her own personal troops. This special elite guard may be a step toward full military control of the country by that president. The presence of these well-disciplined troops in the past, when the reviewing the troops practice began, constituted "saber rattling" which is a display of arms and thus a somewhat friendly, but nevertheless a threat to the visiting dignitary.

G. Military Structure, Organization and Objectives in Relation to Democracy Development

To understand the negative influence of the military on the development of democracies, the structure, organizational relations among military personnel and the objectives of the military should be analyzed. To begin with, the structure of the military organization is rigid. Every member must behave according to his or her rank. Each must obey those with higher rank and may not initiate a conversation with someone of higher rank without first securing permission from that individual. Infractions of such rules result in penalties against the person of lower rank.

This behavior contrasts with the structure and functioning of democratic organizations where everyone is supposed to be equal. The differences in status that exist in democratic organizations do not prevent a person of lower status, that is someone who possesses fewer goods and services of the society, from speaking to one of higher status. For such an act there is no punishment. Moreover, the lower status individual does not have to obey the higher one. In fact, a lower status person can at times order the higher one to do something if his or her position justifies it. One example is that police or fire officers can order people of any rank to move away from dangerous areas. Similarly, operators of buses or trains and pilots of airplanes or ships are in authority over passengers while they are in the airplanes or ships. In non-military organizations such as large businesses and government agencies, however, people in the lower positions also are expected to obtain permission of their immediate supervisors to talk about their work with administrators still higher in the structure.

Another difference between the military and democratic organizations relates to the values placed on human life. For the military, the loss of life of military personnel as well as civilians who may be in the areas to be attacked or defended, is one of the risk factors influencing military decision-making. For the military, human life is expendable. In a democracy, the military usually plans its operations in such a way as to keep the number of people killed and wounded as low as possible. Unfortunately, however, some military commanders, oriented toward achieving a goal at any cost, have ordered their personnel to attack or defend an area knowing that a large proportion will become casualties. This was done without adequately evaluating whether or not the loss of life justified the military objective.

There is a critical difference between the military organization and democratic organizations regarding the value of human life. In democratically operated organizations the life of every individual is supposed to be sacred. Many people in democracies consider the sacredness of human life violated for criminals where capital punishment is the policy and where the withdrawal of life-supporting equipment is permitted for individuals whose brains, because of accidents or disease, cannot and never will function. This principle is adherred to by leaders of the armed forces of democracies. Of course during wars, national officials, both military and civilian, must accept the fact that some lives of military personnel are expendable.

During actual wars, military officers tend to concentrate on objectives such as having their forces take a hill or an island from the enemy. The need to succeed in accomplishing the objective can become an obssession with them because it will affect their immediate status as well as their career advancement, whereas failure will hinder it. Therefore, to give sufficient consideration to the number of human lives that may be lost in these types of military operations in relation to the significance of the military objectives, there should be nonmilitary input in the decision-making.

H. Techniques of Military Leaders to Enhance Their Power and Wealth When They Control a Nation

With the actual power they have over people and the feeling of superiority this power engenders, military leaders controlling a nation can easily engage in a variety of activities to enhance their power and their wealth. A few of the techniques they may use are to monopolize supplies of commodities and other necessities of the people in order to sell them at high prices, to trade in arms, to traffic in drugs and to launder money.

Because they realize that their dictatorial military control may be limited in time, dictators usually transfer large sums of public funds to bank accounts in their names to another country, usually a democracy, to ensure that they will be wealthy if some other dictator, or the people, overthrow their rule.

I. Summary

In this chapter, it was observed that the most serious defect in a number of countries professing to be democratic is the uncontrolled power of the military. ***The military has to be completely dominated by the civilian government or***

the nation can never be a democracy. The civilian authority over the military cannot be by just one branch of the government, such as the executive. Instead, civilian control has to be a basic tenet of the Constitution and policy of the people with authority vested in more than one branch, and it must include the elected legislature.

Also, it was suggested that the parliament type of government, because it requires a clear majority of elected legislators to agree on critical issues such as who is to head the executive branch before an effective policy-making government can operate, may be more vulnerable to being taken over by a dictator in new democracies than democracies with elected presidents who head the executive branch of government. Another reason for this possible vulnerability is that the terms of legislators in a parliamentary government may be ended when agreement on issues can not be reached whereas those in non-parliamentary democracies remain in office for their full terms. A dictator can dismiss the legislators until an election and then never schedule it.

It was suggested that a national military force should never be established and maintained for use against citizens of the country. To have an army to protect the country from other nations may not be justified, as has been demonstrated by countries without armies like Costa Rica. Where there are national armies, the structure, organization and objectives of the military may conflict with democratic procedures.

Military dictators strive to enhance their power and wealth with a variety of methods illegal in democracies. The military establishment in democracies during peace-time, however, seeks increases in funding from legislators on the basis that the nation must be prepared to defend itself. Also it was emphasized, that in democracies the elected representatives of the citizens must understand the tendency of the military to want to expand and control this with budget restrictions or budget increases in accordance with policies they establish for the country.

****

It [Calvinism] established a religion without a prelate, a government without a king.

—*George Bancroft*

. . .personality is primarily the product of social experience, not of heredity.

—*F. Ivan Nye and Felix M. Berardo*

Whoever serves his country well has no need of ancestors.

—*Voltaire*

Democracy is less a system of government than it is a system to keep government limited, unintrusive; a system of constraints on power to keep politics and government secondary to the important things in life, the true sources of value found only in family and faith.

—*Ronald Reagan*

Chapter IV.
Religion, Family, Population and Democracy

A. Introduction

As will be discussed in this chapter, there is a direct correlation between systems of beliefs of people and the number of children they have as well as the type of government they can support. There also is a relationship between population density in a country and the capability of the resources to support the people above a subsistence level of living. The initial source of peoples beliefs originates with the family into which they are born. In many societies, parents' beliefs are derived from, and/or reinforced by, the dogma of their religion.

An effective democratic government requires full citizen participation from the smallest neighborhoods with their clusters of families to the national level. It is extremely difficult for a country to be transformed from another type of government into a free enterprise capitalistic, democratic country when the population is so large in relation to resources that individuals and families must devote all of their time and energy in efforts to sustain themselves at a subsistence level. Similarly, religions that require adherents to devote most of their time not used in making a living, limits their participation in democratic governments.

In an attempt to provide an understanding of how democracies may be established or improved, it is essential that the interaction of religion, family, population and democracy and their interrelationships be understood. That is why they are discussed in this chapter.

B. Evolution of Humans that Made it Possible for Them to Seek Answers to Questions about Their Origins, Current Existence and Future

The evolutionary process resulted in the superior brain capacity of humans. This development gave humans the ability to consider their relationships with other humans and thus the types of government desired. With this power of reasoning, individuals also were able to think about themselves as an organism. ***To continue to function effectively, it became necessary for each person to have an explanation that is acceptable to himself or herself as to how humans originated, why they are here and where they will end up after their life as a living organism is completed.***

These are vital questions because answers that are not accepted or deemed unsatisfactory to individuals frequently result in abnormal behavior and sometimes, even suicide. Belief that a supernatural power or an individual with charisma, frequently considered to be "God," endowed humans with sacred characteristics is widespread throughout the world. Although such systems of thought, or religions, vary from one another extensively, they all provide the sought after answers about the past, present and future for the vast majority of humans. Many other individuals, however, have a set of beliefs about their origins, existence and future that is satisfactory to them even though it does not include a supreme being.

Attempts have been made, primarily in communist controlled countries, to eradicate God from belief systems in order to transfer people's loyalty, devotion, and energy to a cause or national interest such as socialism. When people are converted to socialism, or children are indoctrinated by communists, what actually may take place is the substitution of another individual who may be the current communist leader, or his predecessor, for God. In promoting such a person as a hero to be worshiped, charismatic characteristics will be accorded him or her. Such a mortal being soon becomes immortal and is worshiped as a God by those accepting the propaganda.

The answers to basic questions about life are sought by humans in several ways. The most widespread manner is through religious beliefs. Under socialism, belief in the superiority of the state is promoted as furnishing the answers, and leaders considered the founders of communist governments may become revered as Gods. Still another process that provides satisfactory answers for many people is reasoning unrestricted by religious or communist doctrine.

C. Religious Functions and How They Sometimes are Subverted

Religions serve an essential function for humans. They are, however, subject to the same forces that affect all other group endeavors. Religions become the means by which some of the adherents, and sometimes nonbelievers pretending to be believers, secure for themselves power over others. The primary function of religious officials ought to be to assist members of their churches, the congregations, to learn church doctrines, to guide them in conducting rituals, to help them understand and appreciate the meaning and significance of religious values and to help them through difficult and stressful periods in their lives, and not to control nations.

Regardless of how much brotherly love and tolerance original religious founders and their scriptures professed, these can be subverted by religious leaders if they seek power over people and personal status and wealth rather than providing services for the well being of their members.

It is essential for humans to respect themselves as well as the small groups or larger organizations in which they interact. Overemphasis of the importance of self — egocentrism, or of the group — ethnocentrism, leads to conflicts with governments, particularly with democracies. A religion can be an easy way to develop one's self importance — one's ego — to the level where an individual will allow no one else to share the prestige and the decision-making power at the top of a hierarchical pyramid. Similarly, individuals can become so ethnocentric, so devoted to their organization that they do not want any other group to be permitted to function.

All religions have a system of ethics and rules of behavior that are taught to youth. Children and adults in religions whose members support democracies learn that:

human life is sacred,
people must be tolerant of those who differ from them,
their government and their church should be maintained separately,
they must respect law and order,
independence and individualism is important at the same time that cooperation with others is essential,
individuals can and should improve themselves by working hard, and

democratic processes are the way to solve conflicts.

D. Religious Leaders Who Sometimes Control Societies in a Totalitarian Fashion

Some religious leaders, especially those who head governments controlled by their religions, justify their superior status by claiming to be God-chosen. Individuals who challenge a leader who claims to have received his or her omnipotence from God, are considered to be against God by the leader and therefore so evil and wicked that condemning them to death is deemed justified.

Similarly, some religious leaders attempt to justify their desire to monopolize human emotions by claiming to represent the chosen religion, as the only true religion. Statements are made by leaders of such religions like these: "I am right." "He or she is wrong and a heretic." "We are right." "They are wrong and must be stopped." One outcome of these beliefs, if the group is still small and a minority in a society, is that the members move to an isolated area either within their own country or to another one. If, however, they are large in number and are in control of their nation, anyone who challenges their religious leader or the power of the group must be banished or killed to prevent them from converting some of the leader's adherents to another set of beliefs.

This type of religious philosophy, this leadership, is antithetical to democracy. The same type of philosophy, but justified by love of a motherland, a fatherland, or a secular leader, with the same degree of intensity of leadership on the part of a government is antithetical to religion. Conflict results between representatives of those religions or governments and people promoting democracy.

E. Religious Tyranny That May Result When Religion and Government are United

When religion and the government are united, that is, when the religious hierarchy is the government, extreme tyranny can be the result with non-believers and non-conformists tortured, killed or banished. When religious fundamentalists, whether they be Islamic, Jewish, Catholic, Protestants, Buddhists, Hinduists or any other, achieve control of a nation they can establish a benevolent government or a murderous totalitarian regime that destroys individual freedom and technological progress.

A totalitarian theocracy can eliminate those among its citizens who have acquired knowledge beyond the narrow confines of fundamentalism and carry on a reign of terror to prevent the entrance of what they believe to be nonacceptable knowledge and behavior. Frequently, religious rationalism is used to sanctify torturing and executing of nonbelievers who are considered enemies of the fundamentalists.

One technique religious zealots are using in an attempt to obtain international attention is terrorism. By placing bombs in passenger airplanes or in locations where innocent people will be killed, they obtain great personal satisfaction along with praise from their cohorts and religious leaders because of the publicity about their horrible acts. The approval of such despicable techniques to promote a religion by religious fundamentalists leaders and the formal training of terrorists in their countries is endangering the development of democracies as well as violating human rights. Religious tyranny requires the international cooperation of nations. Therefore, countries promoting terrorists, whether they provide a protected home for, or actually train and furnish them with destructive devices, must be combated.

F. A Balance of Influence Between Government and Religion in a Democracy is Essential

A democratic government requires considerable freedom of thought and action on the part of its citizens. To tolerate each other, a religion and a democracy each must limit their control of people. The leaders of each must accept the other's right to coexist and they must not prevent, or resist in any way, the practice of other religions among the people. The policy of each must be a positive attitude toward the others, even to the extent of encouraging the others, with the expectation that this attitude will be reciprocated.

G. The Evolution of Ancient Grecian and Modern Democracy

Democracy began to evolve when Greek citizens succeeded in developing governments by representatives quite free from religious constraints. The Greek leaders' love of oratory and freedom of expression fostered a type of democracy, but one that was limited to a select minority authorized to be citizens and one that provided special material benefits to those who were privileged to debate and decide governmental issues. Although eventually, luxurious living and lack of non-citizen residents' support led to the downfall of this experiment in democracy, the concept was preserved in the literature for later generations to ponder.

Modern citizen participative democracy began its development when north European church scholars, like Martin Luther, in 1517, objected to the strict control of all phases of life by the church and to the luxurious life styles of the top leaders. Luther advocated that people have a direct relationship with their God, and did not need intermediaries, as had been customary in Christianity. This new approach opened the door to freedom in thinking and acting by Christians. As a result, Christians began forming their own branches of the church with local leadership structures and interpretations of the original doctrines.

With church leaders no longer having a monopoly on

contact with God, an adherent did not need to ply them with wealth to get them to assist him or her to achieve the goal of joining God in heaven. To answer the question as to how a church member could assure a place in heaven, these religious people deduced that some must be more acceptable than others because they were better off economically. This apparent blessing by their God became a desirable objective with people concentrating on accumulating wealth through hard work and thriftiness in using their earnings. They continued to support their churches and were admonished by religious leaders to share their wealth with those less fortunate, but, only a small part of their income was used for these purposes.

H. Protestantism and the Development of Capitalism

Protestants who believed that their ultimate destiny was heaven, and who no longer depended on their churches for passage to it, saw no reason to transfer all of their wealth to the churches. This independence, combined with the belief that those better off must be chosen by God, led to the reinvestment back into their businesses of the earnings in excess of what they needed for the expenses of a moderate lifestyle. Thus, their enterprises produced even more income. This type of Protestant reasoning about Christianity, begun in the sixteenth century, led to capitalism.

This initial capitalism produced the industrial cities of Europe and the commerce among them and with other trading centers around the world. It is capitalism that produced the resources from which democratic governments drew their essential moral and financial support.

It also was these commercial centers that attracted the rural poor and provided the means by which their numbers expanded as they crowded into the sections of the city near the manufacturing and business enterprises where they worked, thus generating areas of poverty in cities. The commercial centers also produced a wealthy minority of owners, along with a moderately prosperous middle class of expediters, such as clerks and administrators.

It took more than 200 years before democratic processes, especially the right to organize labor unions, led to the reduction of the poverty of factory workers. Workers who had moved from agricultural areas to urban centers to be near the factories could no longer obtain some of their living from farms or gardens. Without this supply of food, the low wages paid by the owners and managers of manufacturing enterprises were insufficient for them to maintain their families above the poverty level. Labor unions they formed made it possible for them to bargain successfully with their employers for better working conditions and higher wages.

In Chapter II of this book, the essential relationship between democracy and capitalism was discussed. In this current chapter, it has been shown that capitalism evolved out of the Christian religion when the realization was accepted that people could have a direct relationship with their God. Thus, they did not need to use the majority of the results of their labors to pay church leaders to serve as intermediaries between them and their God. This deviation from Christianity as it had been practiced at that time, provided freedom from religious control for people who became known as protesters of the traditional Christian doctrine, or Protestant Christians and it led to the development of both capitalism and democracy.

A Protestant religion, however, can be just as rigid and just as tyrannical as others when it is in control of a government. Because Protestants believe they can follow sacred ways of behaving acceptable to God by themselves, however, they are not united in one organization. Many leave Protestant churches they feel restrict their freedom or whose practices and doctrines they consider too conservative or too liberal, in comparison with their own beliefs, and form other Protestant churches. Thus, it is unlikely that one Protestant church will become so powerful that it can dominate a whole nation.

I. The Importance of Religion in the Formation of the United States Democracy

Although the Christian religion did not become a restrictive force in the formation of the United States democracy, perhaps because a number of the founders were not religious, Christian morality and ethnics had a very significant positive influence. As has been indicated, democracy evolved because of Christian Protestantism that had incorporated in its doctrines the independence of thought and action necessary for people to design a government that they could control and one that would provide them with the freedom to present their ideas in open discussions and publications. Also recognized as being essential by the protestants of various demoniations, both before and after the United States was established, was the importance of the individual, tolerance for cultural differences among humans, and cooperation among people rather than conflict.

This religious influence in the American democracy continues today. It is reflected in the patriotic songs and numerous ceremonies, including "The Pledge of Allegiance to the Flag of the United States of America" to which the phrase "Under God" was added in 1954. Similarly, the significance of religion is acknowledged when the Bible is used as a symbol of truth and loyalty. This happens when the President and other officials pledge to support their government and its Constitution while their right hand rests on a Bible.

It is not the religion or God that is significant in the American democratic tradition, because people who pledge allegiance to their country and place their hand upon the Bible do not have to be religious or believe in God. They do, however, accept the morality implied in the religious references as well as recognize the importance of the values associated with it in the formation and operation of their government. On the other hand, a person who considers that the reference to a God or the use of the Bible conflicts with his or her beliefs, does not have to refer to a God in the Pledge of Allegiance or have the Bible used when accepting a public office.

Religion in another nation, Poland, had a significant positive role in overthrowing the communist oppression of citizens and control of the government. The Catholic religious leaders did this by providing political advice along with spiritual support to the striking workers and their leaders who united in a solidarity movement. Predominately a single religion country, this assistance by the Church helped make the restablishment of Polish democracy possible. At first, the Church exerted a major influence in government affairs. Government leaders, elected by vote of citizens, soon objected to excess church control with the result that political and economic decisions then were made by the elected officials without consulting church leaders. Although most Polish people are Catholics, other religions are not prohibited in Poland. Thus, many citizens are members of a variety of religions.

J. Characteristics of Religions that Inhibit Democratic Processes

Religion can be a positive force in the establishment of a democracy, as it was in the formation of the United States of America more than 215 years ago, or in the strengthening of one already existing; but it also can be a serious deterrent to the development of democracy. Some of the characteristics of religions that inhibit or prohibit democratic processes are:

1. Absolute control of the government by religious leaders.

2. A mutually supportive and cooperative relationship between religious and military leaders in a country.

3. Religious policy that requires a substantial amount of the time of followers or that takes from them much of their earnings beyond what they need for bare subsistence, thus preventing

them from improving their economic status or from investing in capitalist enterprises or that inhibits their active participation in democratic processes.

4. Religious doctrines that induce families to have children regardless of their ability to feed, cloth, house, educate, or provide them with adequate medical care, thus preventing the families from advancing their level of living from generation to generation and inhibiting their participation in democratic processes.

5. Ethnocentrism that prevents followers from gaining experiences from outsiders that would improve their endeavors or keeps them from entering into contracts for business with nonadherents.

6. Beliefs that the answers to all problems are in the scriptures or sayings of religious leaders, thus inhibiting them from trying new ideas that could increase their productivity and, along with it, their level of living. Level of living is measured by the type and quality of the goods and services of a society an individual or family possesses.

7. The necessity to curtail productive activities while preparing for and during an inordinate number of "holy days" (up to 155 days in one year in some traditional societies in Asia and Africa) or the expenditure of most of adherents' income on pilgrimages to distant holy sites.

8. Rules and practices that violate acceptable sanitation, thus endangering the health of other people.

Some people who are members of religions that have a rigid hierarchy with policy decisions flowing from the top to the lay members at the bottom, tend to be able to accept the centralized planning and control of a dictator or communist controlled, socialist government easier than they can a democracy with its freedom, independence and individualism. This acceptance is especially true if the dictatorial rulers allow the religious leaders to continue to function as heads of their religious organizations.

K. The Role of Women and Democratic Governments

When people have full freedom, as in an advanced democracy, the role of women is no longer fully concentrated on the production and care of children. Life for both men and women becomes one of self-fulfillment in which potential endeavors are evaluated before they are undertaken. Objectives in life and how they are achieved become individualized rather than controlled by forces in the government, religion, or family of origin. Thus, restrictions on women and men who wish to limit the number of children they have, or who do not want to have any children, are out of place in democracies as are government regulations limiting the number of children families can have or at what age youth may marry.

Some government officials, both elected and appointed, tend to believe that action must be taken to force people in their countries to conform to the officials' values. That is, if the officials are opposed to having women in combat roles in the military, are against abortions, or feel strongly about some other issue, they will seek ways of mandating the behavior they favor regardless of whether or not a majority of the citizens desire it. They may attempt to achieve their objectives through government regulations even though the rules they promulgate might conflict with stipulations of their constitution. In a democracy, moral issues never should be settled through legislation. ***Because emotionally involved legislators or regulatory staff try to impose their values on others, the jurists in the courts must be diligent in their efforts to insure that constitutionally guaranteed rights of individuals are not violated.***

L. Family Size and Citizen Participation in Democracies

Democracies require considerable time and effort of their citizens. Citizens who are overburdened by the responsibilities of many pregnancies, along with providing the necessities for many children, can have serious difficulties in participating in democracies. Similarly, their interests can tend to be focused on obtaining the bare necessities of living for themselves and taking care of their families rather than spending their limited time working on political campaigns, voting in elections or seeking and holding elected offices. Therefore, promises by a variety of nondemocratic leaders that they will solve the families' economic problems for them quickly can sound much more attractive than would be true in a democracy where families are expected to help solve their own problems.

When belief systems in a country are based on religions that stipulate that a woman's duty is to populate the world for her God and that it is a sin to use any means of preventing pregnancies, the change from that status to the individual independence of a democracy can be very difficult for women and men. Most democracies, nevertheless, do contain some families with such beliefs. Because of the freedom that individuals have, however, most eventually give up those beliefs or do not practice them fully.

A goal of democratic governments to have their citizens achieve prosperity, or at least be free from want, is often difficult, or impossible to achieve, by those members of the population who do not limit the size of their families. Unlimited population growth can prevent adequate enculturation of the youth in democratic values as the educational and other services of a democratic government have insufficient resources to perform well. This also is true in nondemocratic countries where the disparity between the resources available to individuals and families is severely limited because of the necessity to spread them among a large number of people. Because neither families nor the government is able to care for and educate them, thousands of young children in urban areas in a number of countries live on the streets where many survive by resorting to crime.

Among the freedoms in democracies are the freedom from want and the freedom to prosper. These, however, are not attained by all the citizens for many reasons, including the large number of children they have, the lack of desire, unwillingness to work hard enough and to postpone pleasures until resources have met other more immediate needs, illnesses, accidents, limited formal education, unwise diets, misuse of drugs such as alcohol, nicotine and narcotics, or a combination of any of these.

The democratic form of government is most successful when there is a substantial middle class of citizens. It

is difficult to establish effective representative government when there are two strata, a small number of very wealthy people and a very large number of people living in poverty. Strict religious beliefs and practices and restrictive economic systems frequently support a two strata society and prevent expansion of the middle class. It is belief in the importance of all humans, based on religious independence of individuals and a free enterprise economic system, that leads to a predominace of middle class citizens and a minimization of the number of both the very wealthy and the very poor.

M. The Natural Occurrence of Family Size Limitation in Successful Democracies

In a democracy that is functioning well with free enterprise capitalism, parents who are directly involved in business and government limit the number of children regardless of the formal doctrine of their religions or their own basic ideological beliefs as a means to improve their own economic status. A minority, however, who have not learned or accepted those values of the society, continue to have large numbers of children, with many of them born out of wedlock and this inhibits for many of them their ability to become full participants in the democracy.

In some countries where governments are becoming democracies, overpopulation is not a problem because their citizens already limit the size of their families. For many countries, however, the challenge is to determine how to establish democratic governments along with capitalistic enterprises and keep them functioning until the values of a majority of the people are such that democratic processes are supported by them. It may take more than one generation before most people will acquire the work ethic and the values associated with it, such as saving part of their earnings and investing them, and planning for children and providing them with the knowledge and skills needed by businesses.

N. The Family as the Foundation of All Human Societies

The family, whether the basis for it is the union of one man and one woman or the marriage of more than one person to the same spouse, is the foundation of all human societies. It is the means not only by which individuals are added to the society, but just as importantly, the process by which the values of the parents are imparted to the young. A democracy is a government that stimulates change because of the freedom of its citizens and its free enterprise economic system. Information flowing to the youth because of the formal education they receive as well as from people they associate with in their communities prepares them to accept change as desirable as well as to become innovators themselves. There needs to be a recognition on the part of parents that youth in a democracy, because of their formal education and their associations outside of their families, will differ from their parents in their knowledge and understanding of issues and ways of solving problems.

On the other hand, professional educators must recognize and appreciate the family values of their students. A college professor who tells the aspiring teachers in his class that their future students' parents will be their enemies, as one did in a major university, needs to learn the important function of family values in the society. Similarly, professional educators who oppose instruction of children by their parents before children start their formal schooling and later after school hours, should realize how harmful their opposition is to children. For example, families that teach their children to read at an early age, give them a head start in education that can last throughout their school and college careers. Also, children whose parents help them learn while they are going to school, learn better than the children not helped by their parents.

Because the knowledge and the beliefs received from the family by the child and youth may differ significantly from those received from other sources, conflicts frequently occur between the young and the old. If the parents have not implanted their basic values solidly in the minds of their children, the youths' beliefs and actions may be transformed into anti-family and anti-society beliefs as well as activities distasteful to the parents and destructive to their community and country. If, on the other hand, the parents have implanted their values well in the minds of their children by serving as positive examples themselves and through relationships with them based on friendship, love and respect, they will successfully resist the pressures of other children in their schools and communities with different values as well as the forces of change from adults, including teachers and professors.

Many college students who refuse to change their beliefs about subjects such as socialism to conform with a professor's support of Marxism, manage to complete required college courses by making believe they agree while they are in the class. It would seem that Marxist philosphers and economists would wonder why it is that most college graduates in democracies become successful participants in the capitalistic system after having completed their courses. They may not realize that they as professors were duped by students who passed their courses without being indoctrinated.

In the democracy and free enterprise climate of change, the ***family values transferred to youth must include the flexibility of acquiring new knowledge and ways of solving problems***. This force for change requires the parents to broaden their own prospectives of life as their children mature.

O. The Possible Negative Effect of Government Programs that are Supposed to Provide Economic Support to Families

Although families at times may need financial and advisory assistance from their government to survive, ***government programs for children, mothers and families, too often weaken and destroy family bonds instead of strengthening them.*** "Mothers" allowance programs in which money is given to the mother in accordance with the number of children she has, and welfare programs for mothers in which the amount of support is reduced if the child's father or another man lives with the mother, encourage single parent families. This lack of two parents inhibits adequate transfer of family values to children, a deficiency that may continue from one generation to another in the same family as each mother in the single parent families fails to receive values that would cause her to have the discipline to insist on having a husband father her children. Of course, even though it can be difficult, some mothers and some fathers are highly successful in rearing their children without the other parent.

Government programs of support for families that need it are essential, but requirements must be such that families are strengthened. Actually, the emphasis should be on the importance of moral values of two-parent families rather than on the acceptance of motherhood without husbands as normal. There is a need for parental instruction on the responsibilities of having children and raising them so that the children become men and women who are productive members of their democracy. Similarly, children should be taught that having a baby is one of the most significant events in their lives that effects their future and for which both father and mother must be prepared to accept long-term child raising duties.

P. Summary

As indicated in this chapter, ***both the capitalistic economic system and the democratic representative form of government evolved from the Protestant religion.*** The Protestant religion advocated the importance of the individual along with the freedom to be independent from religious leaders in choosing the type of government as well as in the use of the products of one's labors. This independence of thought and action made it possible for people to cooperate with one another in establishing representative democracies as well as to become capitalists.

It was pointed out that the minimization of rigid religious control is achieved best where many denominations of Protestantism, along with the Catholic Church and Judiasm and many other religions exist together. This happened in North America when the United States' democracy was established, and is still true. A number of the founding members of the American democracy who wrote the Declaration of Independence, the Articles of Confederation and later the Constitution of the United States were not religious, yet these critical works reflected their Judeo-Christian moral values and orientations.

It is difficult for women and men to participate adequately in democratic governments when their time, energy and resources are devoted to meeting needs of large numbers of children. Therefore, there is an inverse relationship between rapid population growth in a country that already has a surplus of people in relation to its resources, and the degree of success of capitalism and democratic government in that country. Democracies prosper when a middle class of citizens predominates and there are small numbers of very wealthy and very poor citizens. The increase, decline or stabilization of populations depend on what the people value, and this is directly related to their religious beliefs. Thus, the interrelationships of religion, population size and democracy are emphasized in this chapter.

****

Aristotle maintained that the political leader or statesman, the politikos, to be an elected official, should be subject to a limited term , usually a year of office, answerable in a popular assembly and the popular jury-courts for the conduct of his office, and invested even in time of war with far less than absolute power. The citizens he led were not his inferiors in legal status or rank but equal and like.

—*Aristotle*

Few men have virtue to withstand the highest bidder.

—*George Washington*

No man is good enough to govern another man without that other's consent.

—*Abraham Lincoln*

Anyone entrusted with power will abuse it if not also animated with the love of truth and virtue, no matter whether he be a prince, or one of the people.

—*Jean de La Fontaine*

Power intoxicates men. When a man is intoxicated by alcohol he can recover, but when intoxicated by power he seldom recovers.

—*James F. Byrnes*

Chapter V. Overcoming the Human Urge to Control

A. Introduction

The freedom that exists in democracies for individuals to act independently can lead to some attempting to control other people economically and politically. In totalitarian nations, anyone not part of the governing clique who attempts to exert control over people is quickly stopped with harsh punishment or is killed. In democracies, individuals must be free to improve the quality of their lives through hard work and the application of their knowledge. Citizens, however, have to be diligent to insure no one acquires sufficient power to overthrow their democratic government or hinder democratic processes.

The discussions in this chapter call attention to possible sources of dangerous power and provide an understanding of how and why they can arise and become destructive to democratic processes.

B. Competition Among Animals for Social Advantages

To emphasize that competition for control is natural among animals, including humans, this anecdote about frog behavior is given.

The author and one of his brothers spent a happy half-hour or so one warm summer afternoon observing male frogs wrestle with one another for leadership positions in the frog hierarchy. It was the dry part of summer so that water in ponds was low. This dry period resulted in a tendency for frogs not known to each other to concentrate in the remaining water.

We sat on the bank and listened and watched as a frog on one side would utter his croaking challenge to all others. This signal was followed by a croak of a competitor on the other side of the shallow water. Soon they started toward one another, meeting in the space between them. As they came close to each other in the shallow water their noses would touch. Because their back feet could touch the bottom, they exerted pressure on each other until their pushing raised their heads and front legs out of the water.

The shoving continued until they were standing on their back legs facing each other with their front legs wrapped around each other. The one whose back feet had firmer mud to keep him from slipping, or who was stronger, or who was able to bluff better, soon pushed the other over backwards, or at least off at an angle sideways, and won the round. Then both usually retired to their former positions on opposite sides of the pond.

This round would be followed by another frog's croaking challenge being met by a competitor. Frequently several wrestling bouts were going on at the same time. You can imagine how much two people, familiar with the attempts of other animals and birds to move upward in the pecking order of their societies by inflicting injuries on their enemies, enjoyed the spectacle when they saw small creatures act like larger animals and small boys, in a way that damaged them socially but not physically. Needless to say, we used a lot of energy laughing at their natural antics. Our presence did not deter them because they had more serious business to take care of— their competion for advantage and survival.

C. The Evolutionary Process That Produced Humans and The Methods Used To Control Others

Competition for things they want, whether it be food, water, shelter, territory, sex or social position, is just about universal among creatures, including humans. The evolutionary process, however, produced humans with an extensive language and a brain that provided for the storage and retrieval of vast amounts of information. This improvement in the brain evolved because members of the early ancestors of humans who did not happen to inherit improved brains were unable to solve the problems they faced in their environments and thus did not survive long enough to produce children. Those inheriting more effective brains were able to pass this trait on to their children. With their improved brain capability, humans developed not only extensive usable knowledge they could store in their brains but also beliefs intermingled with it that determine how they evaluate situations they encounter, and how they react to them.

Both the extent of the urge to control others and the means by which it is done, therefore, are determined by the information that has been acquired by the human brain. Whether or not a man or woman uses brute force or reasoning and social maneuvering to dominate others is thereby determined by the values acquired since birth. Parents with one set of values may train their children to be belligerent with their fists and/or with weapons. Others may teach their children that physical means of asserting oneself is never acceptable.

During a visit by the author to two university campuses, the behavior of the students was found to be quite different. The young men and women on one of the campuses acted much more like ladies and gentlemen than on the other. They acknowledged each other's presence as well as those of visitors to the campus with a polite greeting as they passed and encouraged others to enter doors before they did, whereas this did not seem to be true on the other campus.

To be a lady or a gentleman like the young people on the first campus was a strong value transferred by parents to children in many traditional American families. It meant that the child was polite to others and acted in a calm sensible manner and kept their emotions under control. A famous American general gave his definition of a gentleman that is quoted here because it is directly related to the topic of this chapter, "Overcoming the Human Urge to Control."

"...the manner in which an individual enjoys certain advantages over others, is a test of a true gentleman. The power which the strong have over the weak, the magistrate over the citizen, the employer over the employed, the educated over the unlettered, the experienced over the confiding, even the clever over the silly; the forbearing and inoffensive use of all this power or authority, or a total abstinence from it when the case admits it, will show the gentleman in a plain light. The gentleman does not needlessly and unnecessarily remind an offender of a wrong he may have committed against him. He cannot only forgive, he can forget; and he strives for that nobleness of self and mildness of character, which imparts sufficient strength to let the past be but the past. A true man of honor feels humbled himself when he cannot help humbling others." (General Robert E. Lee)

Parents in whatever country they live should again emphasize to their children the necessity of becoming ladies and gentlemen. By so doing they can reduce the drive to control others unfairly both while they are children and later as adults.

The predominate lesson learned by most children in democracies is that issues can best be solved when individuals are honest and cooperative with each other and willing to adjust their needs and desires to accommodate those of others. Unfortunately, when democratic leaders with these typical methods of solving problems confront leaders from other countries not having those values, they are at a great disadvantage. This happened in the late 1930's when French and English statesmen faced Germany's Chancellor Adolph Hitler and believed him each time when he indicated that his interests in Europe were limited to one additional land area.

During World War II and just afterward, Prime Minister of Great Britain, Winston S. Churchill, and Presidents of the United States, Franklin D. Roosevelt and later Harry S. Truman, reacted to the head of the Soviet Union, Joseph V. Stalin, as if he were honest and wanted to solve territorial areas of influence on a fair and peaceful basis. After much of East Europe was incorporated into the Soviet Union through agreements made with Stalin, these leaders of democracies realized that Stalin had taken advantage of their honest and sincere method of solving problems.

One reason the democracies do not have wars with each other is the similar system of values of their leaders. They resolve their differences by discussing the issues in a straightforward and honest manner and are able to arrive at decisions because each makes concessions to the other. On issues such as trade barriers, the discussions and negotiations may take several years before solutions satisfactory to the countries involved are reached. During that time world conditions may change or be changed by the participants, to make agreement possible.

D. Competition in the Enculturation of Children and Youth

The process of enculturation, which is the transferring of the beliefs and ways of behaving of society to children and youth, involves competition among a number of forces. Children are influenced by parents, older children, adults in the community, school and college instructors, officials, leaders and members of religious organizations and youth groups both formally and informally. Some of these seek to implant their own ideas in the minds of young children and youth. While their children were living at home, whatever parents thought they were impressing upon them may either be reinforced or counteracted by their offsprings' contacts outside the family. Peer pressure to get them to substitute the values of the group they wish to join for those they had acquired earlier, along with the influence of teachers and other adults they come to respect and trust can result in significant changes in children's thinking and behavior. Other major influences are radio and television programs, movies, performances by popular musicians, and books and articles glamorizing individuals with bizarre ways of behaving.

This difference between what they wanted their children to be like and how they turned out is illustrated in the violent behavior of some children. For example, statements made by inner city youth imprisoned for using weapons to get what they desired and to compete with others, indicate that they consider the weapon to be an essential extension of their egos. With a knife or gun, they feel superior and they use it to acquire that status — to become the most powerful person in their area. Some youth may behave like this in spite of most parents and other adults in their neighborhoods deploring this type of behavior and wondering what went wrong in their training at home and in school that turned their young people into criminals and even murderers.

At the same time, however, these adults, who would never use a gun to win dominance, still may support the concept of punishment by killing those members of their society who have murdered people. In the older democracies, citizens have some convicted murderers executed by their government. Executions for murder, although the result of sound judicial procedures from a constitutional viewpoint, unfortunately may transfer the message to youth that killing is an acceptable way to demonstrate one's superiority, especially when it is applied to someone in their neighborhoods or communities.

Mass media coverage of a person who has murdered another, can impress youth with the prominence of the murderer even though society regards the murderer as repugnant. The negative effect on youth of the message from the media may be enhanced further if a trial leads to a sentence of death that is followed by numerous widely publicized appeals during the many years they may take before the execution. In fact, some women and men are so enthralled by bizarre, brutal and/or multiple murderers that they visit the murderers in prison, fall in love, seek and sometimes are permitted to marry the criminals.

In England and some other countries, the media do not publicize murderers in dramatic fashion unless they have had important positions in the government or business or have high status in society. Because of the free press in democracies, some publishers like to print stories about murders because they think people want to read about them and will buy their papers. Those publishers concerned about the negative effect of such news items, minimize the importance of murders by placing items about them on inside pages of the paper instead of keeping them on the front page. Most newspaper editors, however, favor negative stories rather than positive ones. Although they might not want to admit it, this should be brought to their attention with the hope that they would consider changing their approach to news reporting.

The absence of one or both parents and/or the failure of parents to socialize their children in a way that prevents them from committing acts against the society is a very serious phenomena especially in many urban communities. Most children, however, do not use a weapon to obtain the things they desire because they have learned from their parents, older children, teachers, and other adults they know that acquiring knowledge in school and college and/or participating in activities such as clubs or sports will result in rewards that are much more valuable and lasting than are obtained by delinquent or criminal behavior. They compete with each other by studying and learning or by becoming skilled leaders in their groups or performers in sports.

E. Conspicuous Consumption; A Method of Gaining Control

Intermixed with all of the ways the urge to control is manifested is the attempt some people make to impress others with their social standing. They do this by "conspicuous consumption," that is, they openly exhibit the luxury products of their society by making sure others know that they drive expensive automobiles, live in large luxurious homes, wear high fashion clothes, jewelry, or shoes and use the latest computer games, recreational vehicles or other equipment. They do this even though they may not own them, or have much equity in them. Their expectation is that through these practices, they will be given special privileges by others such as loans of money, credit for purchases, high paying jobs, dates with attractive partners, and even the freedom to violate rules of behavior and laws. Although some of those engaging in this practice succeed in fooling people for awhile and do secure the things they desire without deserving them, their success is usually limited to a short period of time and many fail to achieve any of their objectives.

There are many additional ways followed by adults who wish to control or be superior to others such as threatening to use political or legal action against them. Many of these produce positive results for people who use them whereas some of their methods have extremely negative effects. The objective of those striving for power is to acquire more status, more money, more property, wider recognition, and/or a larger organization than others. Associating with higher status individuals is used to gain favors with still higher ones through the process of "name" and "situation" dropping to impress others with one's supposed superior connections to important people and involvement in important activities. Furthermore, as already has been noted, wealth may be displayed in a conspicuous manner such as with a home or two homes, an expensive automobile or other property even though these may be mortgaged heavily or merely rented.

Exhibiting possessions conspicuously is quite different from accumulating wealth in a capitalistic manner. That is, working hard to earn money and then investing much of it in enterprises that return still more income, instead of spending it all on non-essential goods and services. This work-oriented philosophy permits expenditures for personal training and education as well as school and college education for one's children.

F. Variations Between Messages Children Receive From Adults and Adult Behavior They Observe

In a free society with its capitalistic economy, competition is essential. This concept is taught to children by parents at an early age. They are told to study hard, play hard, work hard, and to be better than other children. They are told not to cheat in their studies, to play fair, be a good team player and to turn in an honest day's work. At the same time, they may hear and see evidence that their parents and other adults are not following these doctrines. For instance, a boy who had been taught by his father that he should always tell the truth, objected when he heard his father lying to a neighbor, only to be told to shut up. The lesson he learned was that what adults actually meant when they told him to tell the truth, to work hard and be honest is quite different from what they say and do themselves.

For example, children first learn from school or college publications written by adults that the purpose of athletic programs is to build character by teaching sports-personlike behavior. When they take part in sports, however, they discover that their parents and their coaches want them to win even though it may require behavior unfair to their opponents. A football coach may tell the players to hit an opposing player so hard that he will not be able to finish the game. A basketball player frequently is told to commit a foul on an opposing player, that is to bump into or to grab the arms of the player, in order to prolong the game. Because this type of behavior is not permitted, the referee will stop the game and award the offended player one or two attempts to throw the ball in the basket. The team members committing the foul hope that the ball will not go in the basket and they will have another opportunity to obtain the ball themselves. The message players receive in team sports is to never let the other team get the best of them even though it may be necessary to play somewhat unfairly.

In the business world, youth may learn indirectly from adults that it is all right to behave unfairly or immorally. For example, to make money by producing and selling inferior products or providing poor services; that it is acceptable to agree with business associates that there is nothing really wrong in promising high quality goods and services with no intention of delivering them; that it is appropriate to put the best apples on top of the basket; that it is fine to design a fake bottom in packaging so the products look larger to the purchaser; that it is wise if you have a competitor, especially one with fewer resources than you, to lower your prices below your costs until your competitor is forced out of business and then you can raise your prices high above your costs and make lots of money; or that you may use your financial resources to illegally buy a legislator's support for your endeavors.

G. Bureaucratic Control

A method used to gain power and control over people by bureaucrats in government, industry, and other organizations is to demand additional staff by stating that the job can not be done without more workers even though this may not be true. For example, in a mental health clinic, a psychiatrist administrator demanded more staff to evaluate patients because he said "we cannot handle the work. We are swamped." A review of the patient records, however, showed that there usually was only one patient a week to be evaluated and that the clinical psychologist, psychiatric nurse and psychiatric social worker virtually had nothing to do except meet with one another to discuss patients. By acquiring more staff and the larger budget to support them, the psychiatrist's own status and salary would be increased. He knew that in a bureaucracy, whether it be in government, business or other organizations, the status and power, as well as the amount of salary of each person is determined by the number of people in the hierarchy under them. (Bureaucracies are discussed in greater detail in Chapter VII).

H. Participative Decision-Making

The philosophy of leadership in democratic societies has its foundation in the equality and freedom of the citizens. Whether it be decision-making in government, business or education, leaders cannot retain their positions or the loyalty of their followers if they consistently fail to consider the desires of the people in their organizations. Similarly, the successes of their organizations are related to their leadership style. That is, those leaders who share the decision-making with subordinates and treat them as colleagues rather than as inferiors, accomplish more than those who keep the control all to themselves. This participative management is about the only effective leadership technique in the long run. Democratic governments enhance the use of participative management whereas dictatorships do not.

It may be obvious that citizen's participation in decision-making is not allowed in totalitarian governments, but it is not as clearly realized that the participation of employees in decisions supervisors are supposed to make violates operating principles of a bureaucracy. When this unwritten rule is followed, it is very difficult for a bureaucracy, whether it be in government, business, education or research, to have its procedures improved.

The changes necessary to increase efficiency in organizations can best originate with the people who do the work because they are the ones who know what is wrong. The farther up the bureaucratic hierarchy an employee is, the greater the distance from the actual work that the bureaucracy was set up to perform. At the bottom the employees work with tools or carry out the services themselves. Supervisors above them work with the people they supervise while those still further up work with paper. Although they may be far from where the organization's work is done, and may not be cognizant of what the worker at the bottom faces, it is the administrators who make the decisions about what should be done and how it should be done.

As Ross Perot, a highly successful international businessman and candidate for President of the United States in 1992, has maintained, workers on the production line in factories do not have as much control of product quality as is claimed by economists. This is because product design, equipment and tools used in the production process are designed by engineers and technitions and not by the workers.

Many government administrators and supervisors run inefficient organizations that fail to accomplish their objectives but continue in operation because they are part of the government. On the other hand, many business administrators and supervisors who do not understand and/or accept participative management techniques, cause their organizations to lose money to the extent that the business fails. The difference between business and government is that the government organization keeps on functioning while the business fails and is closed.

If government and business administrators and supervisors practiced this simple principle that the practical knowledge of how to do things rests with the ones who do it and therefore, it is from them that methods of improving the work can come, both the efficiency and quality of the service or product would be greatly improved. The McCormick Spice Company's president initiated a program involving workers in management decision making in the early 1930's that continues today. As a result, the McCormick Company was profitable all during the great depression.

To adopt methods that allow people at a lower level in a bureaucracy to take an active part in decision-making all the way to the top is difficult for egotistical individuals who consider people below them as subordinates. On the other hand, those dedicated to doing a better job find it easier when they treat fellow employees as their equals regardless of where they are in the organization's structure.

I. The Peaceful and Quick Transfer of the Powers and Responsibilities of Offices by the Incumbents to Newly Elected Officials

It is very difficult for some officials to allow another person to replace them even though that person is better qualified than they are to handle the responsibilities. Also, some incumbents do not want to relinquish an elected office to a newly elected official when their term expires. This peaceful and timely transfer of the authority of leadership is a serious problem in new democracies because usually there has not been a long history of leaders giving up their positions to someone who has just been elected to replace them as there has been in older democracies. For example, in the Central American countries of Panama, Granada and Haiti, newly elected leaders were not allowed to govern by former dictators or leaders who controlled the military in those countries. The democratic leaders in Panama and Granada quickly received military support from the United States and other countries and were able to reestablish democracies. Elected officials in Haiti did not receive such aid and the country is still under control of a military dictatorship.

In on-going democracies, children learn at an early

age that when they elect new officers in their organizations, the old officers let new ones run the organization as soon as their terms begin. This quick and friendly transfer of responsibilities is the traditional action for them while they are young as well as when they become adults. It is almost never questioned. When someone refuses to give up a political office at the time that his or her term is over, this undemocratic action is considered abnormal behavior and it becomes a newsworthy event. Journalists who publicize such an infrequent event severely condemn the culprits. This negative publicity almost always causes the holdout to turn the office over to the new official. Therefore, in new democracies, anyone not willing to transfer the duties and status of an office to the person just elected should have that behavior made known to the public along with a statement of how it violates stipulations of the country's constitution.

It is frequently necessary for leadership of a democratic government to be transferred not only from one elected person to another but also from one political party to another. For example, on January 20, 1993, Republican Party leader President George Bush relinquished the Presidency of the United States to Democratic Party leader William J. Clinton in a ceremony at the Capitol building in Washington, DC. Not only was there a change in the Presidency but also for more than 100 Senators and Representatives. Similarly, thousands of state and local elected officials were replaced by newly elected individuals throughout the country. Regardless of who won and who lost in the elections, the transfer was a routine peaceful procedure.

J. The Corruption of Some Democratically Elected Leaders

In relation to the control of nations, some national leaders who profess democratic values, perhaps sincerely while campaigning for office, become corrupted after being elected. Because of the power they have acquired, it becomes easy for them to feel that they are superior and should continue in office beyond their elected terms. Any means to retain their leadership office becomes acceptable to arrogant leaders who may identify themselves as the state and thus above the law.

There are many ways these, as well as other, dictatorially inclined leaders accomplish their goal of staying in charge such as by:

1. controlling who is allowed to vote;
2. postponing or canceling elections;
3. declaring a state of national emergency and giving themselves "war powers" or by declaring "martial law" (war powers and martial law are used by leaders to justify actions that violate stipulations of

constitutions because they maintain that the conditions in the country justify these extreme measures);

4. dismissing legislators and the judicial branch;
5. canceling the constitution; or
6. killing or imprisoning opponents.

Remaining in power regardless of the method, provides continual self gratification and glory to the leader as his lieutenants honor him in order to obtain rewards of power and wealth for themselves.

K. Treatment of Citizens Who Resist Totalitarian Government Leaders

In nations where people do not control their governments, whether they be run by military, religious or socialistic dictators, anyone resisting the government, or even considered to be a possible resister, is severely punished. To remain in control, dictatorial leaders either have to devise an economic system by which the masses of people receive sufficient income to survive, such as through government employment, or they have to convince citizens that they are protecting them from a worse evil. The evil is usually an external force such as another country the leaders maintain is bent on destroying them. But, it can be internal such as a group of people with a different religion or who advocate a change in the government. For example, Fidel Castro in

Cuba uses the United States as the enemy while Adolph Hitler in Germany used Jews, other minorities, and capitalist bankers as justification for his rule.

The individual, events, and/or processes that dictatorial leaders indicate are preventing the citizens from having ample food, housing and other necessities must be defeated, according to them, at all costs. Therefore, dictators maintain that it is necessary and right to torture and kill anyone who is considered to be part of the opposition and thus, an enemy of the state. Not only does this rationalization result in much suffering and loss of life of people who are seen as enemies, but it also provides an opportunity for supporters of the dictators to subject their fellow citizens to severe punishment, frequently through a justice system they devise that is unfair to the accused. When the dictators' agents, such as prison wardens and guards have abnormal personalities, the punishment of the accused can be sadistic in such a manner that it provides the agents with personal enjoyment, sometimes even bizarre sexual gratification.

An excellent example of the extent to which innocent people can be accused and condemned was Czechoslovakian communist government's treatment of the air heroes of World War II who risked their lives, with many of their fellow flyers losing theirs, to fight for their country against Hitler. Soon after they returned home to their beloved country they were arrested and sentenced to prison by committees of three men sitting as a court. As part of the process, they were tortured to get them to confess actions against their country. As prisoners they were subjected to torture and to death by sadistic prison wardens and guards.

Why were these war heroes accused, convicted, and punished? Although they had made a significant contribution to defeating Hitler's military machine that occupied their country, they had served in the west as members of the Air Force of England. That association with a capitalistic society, although temporary, was enough to condemn them in the minds of communists. Taken from their homes in the middle of the night with no warning, they disappeared from their families for many years, or forever. Similarly, the Soviet as well as other communist governments, arrested, tortured, banished to distant slave labor prisons and/or killed those citizens who members of the ruling government wanted to get rid of. This was the same type of treatment that Hitler's officials had followed in Germany, Poland, the western part of the Soviet Union and other countries Germany occupied.

The killing of tens of millions of people by Joseph V. Stalin who ruled the Soviet Union from 1927 until his death in 1953 were justified, according to former Soviet Foreign Minister Vyacheslav Molotov. Molotov defended Stalin's use of terror against Soviet citizens in an interview published in the Russian book, <u>One Hundred Forty</u>

Conversations. He said that “without terror, we wouldn’t have gotten through the pre-war period and after the war we wouldn’t have had a more or less stable situation in the country.” With the fall of Soviet communism, this harsh treatment of people has ceased in most of the countries that were part of the Soviet Union and few current leaders in those countries would condone such Stalinistic behavior.

L. Bribery as a Method of Obtaining Influence in Government

Regardless of the type of government, there always are people attempting to obtain favors from its leaders including the privilege of being part of the ruling class. Some of them want to protect themselves and their families from persecution by the government and others are intent on preserving their property or businesses. The favorite method to obtain favors is to bribe the leader or leaders with gifts, accompanied by praise and pledges of support.

In democracies where free elections take place, candidates may buy advertising in newspapers, print information about their qualifications and what they will do if elected, purchase time from radio and television stations and rent space for offices and meetings. To do all of this they may hire professionals as well as have unpaid volunteers help them. Expenses of a campaign for offices in a large city, a section of the country or the nation can be too large for the candidate to pay from personal funds. Therefore, funds are solicited from individuals who believe that the candidate to whose campaign they are contributing, will do what they want when elected. Just because they want a particular candidate to be elected, however, some people contribute money and services without being asked and without expecting a return for their contributions other than having an honest and fair representative in government.

The fact that legislators have the power to make laws that favor special interests or prevent laws from being passed that inhibit activities of organizations or individuals with special interests, has resulted in the profession of lobbyists. Lobbyists attempt to influence legislators as well as officials in the executive branch to do what they want done. To achieve their objectives they use all sorts of techniques, including supplying their targets with whatever they want such as money, free trips, vacations, dinners, parties, liquor and sex. Their most effective method is to convince the elected legislator that they can deliver sufficient votes to elect or reelect him or her and/or to furnish sufficient funds to assure election.

Lobbyists yield power over legislation and government programs for the individuals, businesses, educational institutions, other types of organizations and foreign countries they represent while the interests of unorganized voters who make up the majority of citizens are neglected. These lobbyists form an "extra branch of government" that poses a serious threat to democratic government. Because lobbyists are protected by the free speech stipulation of constitutions, they can be controlled only by statespersonlike legislators and honest government employees who place needs of all constituents over those of special interest groups.

The competition for major political offices has resulted in elaborate and expensive election campaigns with candidates aided, or even managed, by high salaried campaign professionals. This results in opportunities for bribery in the form of contributions of funds to these campaigns. In the United States, laws have been passed to limit the amount that individuals and organizations can contribute to a candidate for a national office and to prohibit contributions from certain organizations such as corporations, labor unions, and non-profit groups. Some local jurisdictions also have similar laws for their elected offices.

To thwart these laws, Political Action Committees (PACs) have been formed to which large sums of money can be contributed. This money is used to support the candidates favored by the contributors to the PACs. PACs also join together to provide huge sums to those candidates they decide will vote for proposed laws favoring their interests or against proposed laws that would hinder their interests.

A candidate may receive 90 percent of the money for a campaign from PACs and 10 percent from the people in his or her district or state. If a candidate who a PAC had not supported wins, the PAC may quickly send money to him or her after the election. The PACs contribute the money because they want the legislators to protect their interests. The candidates accept the money with the knowledge of what the PAC wants. This type of bribery is such a serious threat to the future of democratic government in the United States that many citizens are concerned. Their concern may lead to legislation that limits or prohibits PAC type contributions to campaigns. Legislators are resisting such a restriction because they benefit from the PAC money.

There also is a $1,000 limit on contributions of individuals to persons seeking to become President of the United States. To circumvent the $1,000 limit, the contributor can give money to the political party of the candidate as well as to the PAC that supports the candidate. Again, this way of bypassing the law, eventually may be prohibited by law because it provides the opportunity for people and organizations with money to exert more pressure on legislators and potential legislators than can be done by people with little money or by those not wanting to participate in any possible type of corruption of officials.

M. The Risk of Leadership

Considering all of the issues involved in leadership discussed in this chapter, the question may be raised as to why so many people who want to serve their communities and their country do seek elected offices. The answer is that they believe in democracy and are willing to subject themselves to the stress that accompanies campaigning and serving in office because of those beliefs. Also the rewards of special status that come with winning an election and representing fellow citizens is important to them. They hope to personally improve their society by being elected. They may realize that they, as elected representatives, are the only voice in government for the unorganized citizens. The possibility of having a direct role in decisions that are important to them and their friends is a significant reason for others.

Unfortunately, some of those who win elections in democratic countries and are honest and sincere about serving their fellow citizens, decide not to seek reelection after they have experienced one term in office. The constant demands of people with special interests who think their concerns are more important than those of others, the necessity to obtain funds for campaigns, the lack of interest in the issues to be decided on the part of legislators serving with them, and the necessity to consider inadequate or inaccurate data about issues, contrast with their own objectives of being in office. Also they may feel that their own honesty and integrity will suffer under the pressures they face and decide that the risk is more than they care to take.

N. Summary

The discussion of actions and beliefs of youth and adults illustrates the means by which variations occur in how the urge to control others is manifested among people. Because human behavior depends on what has been learned, the extent to which individuals attempt to control others varies from the type of person who lets everyone order him or her around, to one who must always be giving the orders. Similarly, the methods utilized to control people vary from polite persuasion to methods used by arrogant totalitarian dictators who attempt to dominate people by ruthless torturing and killing of competitors and objectors.

A successful democracy cannot be a nation of followers, but it also cannot be a nation of bullies—people who force others to obey them. There must be people willing to take the risk of leadership in industry, business, science, education, professions and government. Both controlling others and not allowing oneself to be controlled by others is a necessary attribute of leaders. How control or prevention of control is handled relates directly to whether the individuals are acting in an autocratic, dictatorial or democratic manner. The technique of participative management in which individuals at every level take part in decisions about objectives and methods of achieving them should be understood, accepted and practiced in all organizations.

The critical issue in older and new democracies is how children can be enculturated to accept leadership or fellowship roles in appropriate situations. In the new democracies, how adults who have been dominant over others for years can be encouraged to give up or share leadership is a serious issue. Intensive adult education programs to increase understanding of democratic principles of leadership and to change attitudes, as is emphasized in Chapter VIII, along with constitutional stipulations of the rights of people, are essential.

****

Chapter VI.
Government Regulations and the Decline of Democratic Principles

A. Introduction

The substance of this chapter involves the conflict between the theory that the less government there is the better the government is and the belief that the proper role of government is to force all of the population in a country to conform to standards set by a few of the people. In any type of totalitarianism, the solution to this conflict is straightforward forced conformity by all citizens not in governmental positions of control to dictatorial rules. In a democracy, however, although it is necessary for individuals to relinquish some freedom in respect for the rights of others, citizens must not be stripped of most of their freedom to live independently of government control.

An attempt is made in the sections of the chapter to provide an understanding of how government regulations are generated and then extended until they begin to strangle democratic principles. The contest between government officials who regulate and people being regulated is a one-sided battle because the officials have secure positions with ample tax funds to support them and their legal counsel while the people must depend on earnings from their enterprises that they may be prevented from operating. Thus, the healthy advancement of businesses along with innovations in technology can be curtailed by regulators. Not only do unnecessary government regulations hamper businesses but they also have a negative effect on the economy that produces the taxes that pay salaries and expenses of the regulators. Because the number of government employees is seldom reduced, the tax rate has to continuously be increased or debt incurred by the government to pay for them.

B. The Bond Between Citizens and Elected Officials in a Democracy

Legislators and other government officials in a democracy are elected because the voting citizens believe that the person they vote for will represent them and their interests better than his or her opponents. The bond between voters and elected officials should be strong. Because the official is elected by many people whose desires vary, however, one citizen or a small group of them must not control the official to the extent that wishes of other voters are ignored.

Legislators face a dilemma because they are supposed to represent interests of all the people in their districts yet are faced with demands from an individual or group of citizens who made it possible for them to be elected and whose help may be necessary in the next election. If legislators want to stay in office, they may have special relationships with large contributors of funds to their campaigns, with citizens who can make their demands known by organizing demonstrations, and with members of the media who can provide positive or negative information about legislators to the voting public.

Thus, people who want a law passed regulating something others are doing that they do not like will be supported by the legislator if they can provide substantial campaign funds, organize a highly vocal group supporting their views or stimulate the media to emphasize their demands. As subsequent discussions in this chapter will indicate, it is difficult for legislators to fulfill a statesperson's role in judging whether or not the government should regulate each specific activity that they are requested to consider.

C. Origins of a Regulation

When people are free, the experiences they have had, the education they have received, the environment in which they live and their behavior will vary from one person to another. These differences are reflected in what they expect from their legislators, including what they want regulated or not regulated. For example, one may keep a cat or two, another may strive to keep cats away from birds, and still others may not care whether or not cats are around. While the cat lovers may want freedom for everybody's cats, the cat haters may want stray cats done away with and the other cats restricted to their owner's property. Many other people simply would prefer that cat lovers and cat haters quit fighting over cats and apply their energies to something more worthwhile, like picking up trash from the sides of roads.

Shown a cat-mangled bird by the cat haters, a legislator proposes a law to restrict predatory felines. The possibility that such a law might be passed really stimulates cat lovers to make their feelings about cats known. They come to meetings to talk about the value of cats and bring with them their cute children hugging beautiful placid kittens. The newspapers, radio stations, and television channels carry the cat story. This exposure brings cat lovers from all over the land to protest restrictions on their cat friends and their children's loving pets. They are faced by the cat haters from across the country, who like their opponents, feel deeply that it is their duty to save their country by fighting for or against the cat law. Having nothing better to do until another issue comes along, they can spend a lot of time on the cat problem. In the meantime, because they are so emotionally and physically involved, they may be neglecting their children and spouses in their own homes.

Faced with this type of pressure, what is the legislator to do? First, the legislator, along with his colleagues, could transfer the cat problem to a legislative committee to consider whether or not anything should be done about it. Second, the issue could be assigned to an already existing government agency to come up with regulations. Third, it could be put off until a public hearing is arranged where citizens would be invited to give their opinions on the cat problem. Fourth, a cat law could be passed requiring cats to be kept at their owner's homes or tied to their owners by a leash when they are taken out. If the legislators consider this issue important to a substantial number of their constituents, the legislators are quite likely to hire their own cat specialists, or designate members of their staffs to become experts on this subject.

When a law is passed — and it probably will be because legislators know that is what they are supposed to do — it will include penalties against cat owners for disobeying the law. A law does not meet the intentions of those who passed it unless it is enforced and those disobeying it, penalized.

This cat story, although used to illustrate that regulations originate in the thinking of people concerned about an issue, is quite realistic, as may be noted in this article in a newspaper that appeared after this description was written:

Fur flies over cat licensing

PITTSBURGH, PA. USA — Hours after the City Council president introduced an ordinance to license cats, opponents pounced on it.

"People think there's already too much government control, that it would be another bureaucracy." Councilman Don Onorato, who is undecided on the measure, said after the Council was inundated with complaint calls.

Council President Jack Wagner's proposal, introduced Monday, would require cat owners to obtain licenses similar to those now mandated for dogs. The annual cost would be $5 for spayed or neutered cats and $12 for other cats.

The city picks up about 2,000 stray cats a year. Mr. Wagner said he wants to reduce that number. No licenses are currently required for cats.

Mayor Sophie Masloff hasn't taken a stand on the issue, said her aide, Joseph Sabino Mistick. "We're going to sit back and watch the fur fly over in Council," he said.

D. The Initiation and Expansion of a Regulatory Bureaucracy

As Pittsburgh Councilman Don Onorato indicated, to administer a cat law a government bureaucratic agency would need to be organized, staff hired, facilities rented, and equipment purchased. The first thing the staff would do if a regulatory law were passed is to determine what they think the law is supposed to do. There are a lot of questions they would spend time discussing like: What is a cat? Does the law apply to kittens? When is a kitten a cat? Is a neutered or spayed cat still a cat? Does the law apply to rural as well as urban cats? And if the cat is taken for a walk, how short must the string tying the cat to the person have to be?

To carry out the law, the staff would decide it needs to know where the cats are. Therefore, they might decide that the cats have to be registered and their owners issued permits for them. The forms to be filled out by people wanting cat permits would have to be designed and printed. One draft after another of the cat forms may have to be made as the staff continues to grow and new members insert their ideas into the form-making process resulting in longer and longer forms. Because cats do not have social security numbers or another type of identification, each would need to be given a number and a plastic tag to wear.

By this time, there can be forms to record:

1. When a kitten is born;
2. The transfer of a cat to a second owner;
3. When the cat receives its immunizations against diseases;
4. If it is lost or stolen;
5. Neutered or spayed cats; and
6. When a cat dies.

All this would require many jobs for government workers. Thus a significant bureaucracy would evolve which is a pyramid type of organization with layers of employees, one above the other, with specified supervisory or other duties, as illustrated in Figure 3 on page 143 of Chapter VII. Employees would have to be recruited, evaluated to make sure they are qualified, tested for cat lore, hired and then trained about the law and the forms. There would need to be supervisors to make sure that every employee does his or her job according to their specific job descriptions and not what someone else is supposed to do. There would have to be administrators to keep the superordinate/subordinate structure functioning and to talk with outsiders, including representatives of legislators, who by this time would have their own cat staff. Trainers would be hired to prepare workers for their jobs. Added to these positions would be veterinarians, legal counsel, public relations specialists and people to make sure that equal employment laws are followed, that is, minorities of many types are hired.

All this activity would produce a set of regulations with a hierarchy of government employees to enforce them. Eventually, the cat lovers and cat haters and the legislators would have other issues of concern to themselves, leaving the government workers in the hierarchy to run the show the way they want to with taxpayers paying their salaries and expenses. Anyone who discovers that his or her freedom to act is unduly limited by the cat laws, even beyond the intentions of the original legislators who enacted the laws, will have a difficult time having any grievance heard by anyone in the government agency. They may have to resort to a court of law to gain attention to the problem they feel the cat law has caused.

Although the cat law regulation used for illustrative purposes was reported to have stemmed from citizen concerns and action, most regulations evolve from the work of the regulators who seek to expand their controls.

This review of the process by which government regulations can come about sounds like a lot of fuss and bother about cats, and it is. What it illustrates, however, is that a seemingly trivial problem can produce an expensive and burdensome bureaucracy that functions on its own to control human behavior. Multiply this by thousands of issues decided by thousands of laws in a large country. Now consider those issues that are complicated, such as, education, defense, air and water pollution, food production and packaging, and drug manufacturing. The number of government employees placing restrictions on individuals' freedom in these issues become immense.

These are real issues fought for or against by people operating primarily on the basis of their emotions rather than objectively derived facts. These concerned people are listened to by legislators who cannot be competent in all the fields, but who want as many votes as they can get in the next election. When legislators begin to feel that the way the law is administered does not conform to their intention when they passed it, and consider repealing it, they are faced not only with the cat people but with a force that can be much greater — that of the government employees who want to protect their jobs. Employees who have had the training and who have the time, the organization and the money will fight for their "job rights." Legislators listen to them because they know that the employees, members of their families and their friends all vote and that the media will support the government employees.

E. Restrictions on Freedom Imposed by Regulations

Government money spent for regulators who impose restrictions on private enterprise, and in the case of environmental regulations, actually shut down those they deem not to have met their stipulations, amounts to an enormous sum on a national basis. It exceeds by far the amount private enterprises can spend to devise ways to produce the goods and services in the manner demanded by the regulators. Yet it is the taxes paid by the enterprises that pay the cost of having the regulators.

The restriction on the freedom of individuals and their businesses by ever expanding government regulations threatens to destroy the foundation of democracy in many countries. For example the extent of federal regulations in the United States is indicated by the "Federal Register" that lists them. In 1987, seventy-two thousand pages of 8 1/2 by 11 inch paper were needed to print the federal regulations for that year. Although the instigation of regulations was slowed by the administration of President George Bush, 52,000 pages were still required in 1991. Another indication of the regulation phenomena is that just to write procurement rules that had to be met by firms doing business with the United States after 1984, required a staff working for five years who spent 50 million dollars to complete the project.

Every time regulations are changed, such as the size and type of substances that manufacturing plants can release into the air or water, the manufacturers have to develop and install methods of meeting these new requirements. Because many do not have the economic resources to make these changes, or to build new plants, they must terminate their businesses.

Regulations have an adverse effect on individual and family activities. For example, if a married couple decides to build a house in which to raise a family, they soon learn that there are a lot of government employees — regulators — making decisions for them about their house for which they will pay the cost of construction. This couple cannot build a house unless it conforms to regulations such as: location, type, size, height, color, type of building materials and construction, electrical wiring, plumbing, water supply, waste disposal, entrance from the street or road and safety devices.

Each law that is passed to regulate something infringes on the rights of individuals, their businesses, or other activities. In a democracy, citizens generally recognize that they have to give up some of their own freedom to accommodate the needs of others. They accept the fact that they cannot be free to engage in activities that negatively affect the health, safety and enjoyment of others, for example. When, however, restrictions by government regulations dominate nearly every part of their lives, democracy gives way to governmentocracy — rule by government employees — and freedom is reduced, as illustrated in Figure 2 on the next page.

F. Governmentocracy

With an immense, arrogant and unresponsive

Figure 2. Effect of Government Regulations on an Individual's Freedom

A. Before regulation

B. One set of regulations displacing some freedom

C. Several sets of regulations displacing considerable freedom

D. Many sets of regulations severely limiting freedom.

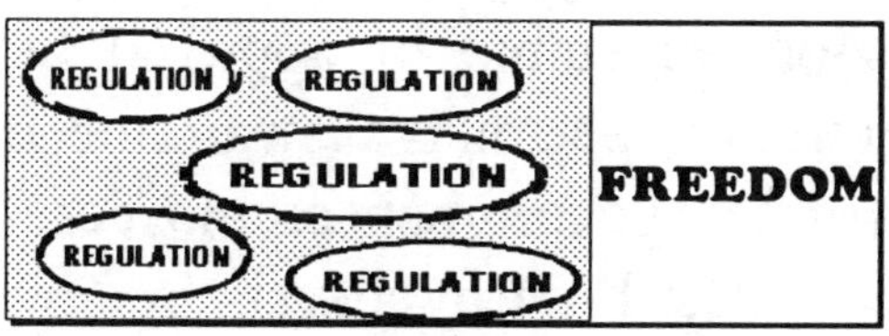

governmentocracy, an iron damper is put on technological progress and a tremendous increase in the cost of producing goods and services occurs. Consequently, a great economic burden must be carried by the consumers with a damaging effect on the level of living of the citizens. Level of Living is a measure of the quality of life of individuals and families. It is an accounting of the goods and services available to them — those items that are necessary for them to survive at a comfortable level, as well as luxuries that help make their living easier and more enjoyable. It includes the furnishings of their homes, their means of transportation and communication and educational resources such as telephones, radios, televisions, magazines, books and personal computers.

Governmentocracy has long characterized nations controlled by the various types of dictators — military, religious, socialistic, communistic or monarchical. It is essential in those types of societies for the ruling class to maintain complete control of the actions of citizens. This type of control is not necessary in a democracy.

The vicious tool of the governmentocrat is the permit, with his or her stamp of approval required. The authority of granting a permit is a law or rule, or more often, interpretation of it by government employees. The power of enforcement is carried out by arrests by government employees, police or summons to their offices or to courts of law. The punishment, which may be severe, varies from having to cease the nonpermitted action or conform to permit requirements at great cost. Significant fines and penalties frequently accompany failure to adhere to permit requirements in democracies while in totalitarian dictatorships, imprisonment, or torture and death may be the penalties for serious offenders.

Governmentocracy is a condition of dictatorships and a disease of democracies. For the dictators, that type of control is necessary for the rulers to stay in power. For the democracies, the source of regulations can be traced primarily to special interest organizations who put pressure on legislators to pass regulatory laws. After such a law is passed, and employees are hired to administer it, the expansion of regulations beyond what was intended by lawmakers is due to the inherent characteristics of bureaucrats. Bureaucrats tend to enlarge their empires by increasing or broadening their mission and adding staff and supervisory layers to carry out the additional responsibilities. Also they tend to satisfy their own egos by assuming that their decisions as to what should be controlled under a law and how it should be done, are supreme.

G. The Difficulty Citizens Have in Attempting to Control Governmentocracy

Under dictatorships there is not much that can be done

by citizens to overcome governmentocracy unless they can overthrow the dictators. In a democracy, it is extremely difficult to combat this same self-perpetuating, self-expanding power over citizens' lives. It is difficult to prevent government regulations from being put into force, and more difficult to reverse them after they are enacted because their proponents argue that they are necessary to preserve or improve the quality of life of the people.

If representative democracy is to survive, however, legislators must become statesmen and stateswomen and control governmentocracy at its source. A decision as to whether or not a regulation is necessary has to be based on the effect of having or not having it on the quality of life of all the people who would be affected by the regulation.

For example, the cat problem discussed near the beginning of this chapter should have been evaluated objectively rather than having its solution depend on the interpretation of the pressures exerted on legislators by cat lovers and cat haters. Research has shown that a free roaming cat kills an average of one bird a day. Therefore, the loss of birds and the frightening of others is one consideration. Also, cats carry one of the HIV viruses that may be shown to be harmful to humans. Any health risk, however, would be greater to the cat owners than to people near where the cats roam. Cats can serve as valuable companions to some people, particularly elderly ones, and their presence may help them live independently for a longer time than if they did not have cats. The economic factors must be included in the evaluation to determine whether or not the cost of initiating and administering a cat law along with the cost of complying on the part of citizens justify having such a law. Of course, an objective appraisal would have taken more time and effort than it would have taken to decide on the basis of opinions of people.

Results of scientific research and analyses should be the primary evidence utilized in the evaluation of regulatory issues by legislators. Unfortunately, promoters of regulations, particularly those affecting the environment, present "research" of their own that supports their positions. Their self-serving arguments appeal to the emotions of legislators as well as to the hopes of regulators that they can have larger organizations and more regulatory responsibilities. It frequently takes many years for scientists to have findings of their research accepted and the "research" of the proponents discredited.

This delay between when claims are made about the need for a regulation and when basic reliable research is accepted has been especially true in relation to the resolution of the lead contamination problem that was alleged to cause mental retardation of children as well as to the exaggerated harmful effect of all types of asbestos on the health of people. The results of research of one person who claimed to have shown that small amounts of lead caused children to be mentally retarded were accepted by legislators and used by regulators to justify strict lead control programs. It took more than a decade before the conclusions of scientists that the strong causal relationship did not exist and that the original research was not as reliable as had been thought were accepted. Similarly, billions of dollars were spent by governments and citizens in western countries in an attempt to eliminate relatively small amounts of asbestos from buildings before it was accepted that the expenditure for this was not warranted by the low level of possible risk to the health of humans. In many situations the disturbance of the asbestos during its removeal was more hazardous to health than if it had been left in the building.

H. The Necessity for Essential Regulations

In technologically advanced societies people expect to have a high quality of life. They want to breathe clean air, drink water free from natural or human produced pollutants, be able to work and relax in environments where they are protected from loud noises, unpleasant smells, high or low temperatures, and from being physically injured. Because the causes of many of these hazards to their well-being are beyond their own control, they realize that to eliminate or reduce them, their government has to be involved.

Therefore, they demand that their government prevent environmental polluting and protect them from dangerous circumstances at work and in their communities. Similarly, they seek protection from unscrupulous people who attempt to sell them harmful products or worthless investments. As a result, many regulations are legislated that are essential to the maintenance of modern high quality life.

When the effect of essential government regulations are evaluated, their success is the result of a combination of regulations and the cooperation and active participation of many people. One of the best examples of this is a law permitting hunting of game animals and birds during specified periods of time that are obeyed by nearly all hunters. The result is that game birds and animals like the American wild turkey and the white tail deer have multiplied to where the hunting periods have been extended. In fact, white tail deer have increased in numbers to where they are adversely affecting their own environment. This example of the result of fine participation of citizens in carrying out a government regulation may be somewhat unusual, however, because American hunters tend to have rural backgrounds. They are people who strongly value their independence from government interference, but at the same time are highly respectful of the laws of their country.

Not all citizens are that participative in environmental or other regulatory efforts. Some who seek laws to prevent the pollution of lakes and rivers by industry, still continue to pollute the water themselves by discarding wastes that wash into the lakes or by using gas powered boats that discharge oil into the water. Although nature is the greatest polluter of water, because moving water carries a tremendous amount of soil and debris into lakes and rivers — especially during storms, human settlements cause pollution that is more dangerous to their quality of life. People need continuing education about their personal responsibilities to keep their environment clean.

As a result of essential government regulations the quality of life has been greatly improved in the older democracies. Essential regulations are those that have been shown to be needed through objective analyses of the risks to all forms of life on which they are focused, along with the actual effect of the regulations on reducing those risks. In many newer democracies, the quality of life requires much improvement, but it is expected that it will be improved rapidly as each country's economy is enhanced.

The emphasis should be on providing incentives to individuals and businesses to conduct their affairs in ways that protect the rights of others and preserve the quality of the environment. Instead of expensive regulations requiring a huge government bureaucracy, corporations can be given tax incentives to modernize their production facilities to reduce air, water and soil pollution, and develop substitutes for harmful products. This type of cooperative action will result in necessary innovations more quickly and much lower costs than will regulations and their enforcement.

I. Summary

The discussion in this chapter has shown that a major activity of governments of all types and at all levels is the regulation of citizen activities beyond those necessary to improve their quality of life. Although necessary in countries with repressive governments if their leaders are to remain in power, government regulations also are restrictive in democratic countries to the extent that some basic freedoms have been lost. The imposition of regulations tends to result in the establishment of large bureaucracies. The society thus becomes ruled by governmentocracy rather than by elected legislators. Incentives, such as tax benefits were suggested as a better method for inducing individuals and businesses to voluntarily find ways and means to protect the rights of people and improve the quality of the environment.

The effect of governmentocracy on the lives of citizens in all countries must be recognized and minimized by legislators as statesmen and stateswomen if democracies are to continue as nations where the individuals' freedom is sacred. At the same time, essential regulations along with active citizen participation in meeting their objectives have greatly improved the quality of life of people. Instead of relying on emotions to determine whether or not a regulation is necessary, however, decisions must be based on objective data derived by scientists qualified to do research on the specific issue being considered.

****

However wretched a fellow mortal may be, he is still a member of our common species.

—*Lucius Annaeus Seneca*

The foundation of American freedoms is in the structure of our Republic. The major features of that structure are the separation of the powers of the national government and the limitation of national power to preserve a large degree of autonomy in the states.

—*Robert H. Bork*

The fourth [concern is] the proliferation of government bureaucracies and the danger that comes from delegating them power. As Frankenstein delegated power to the monster, so do we to impersonal, self motivating institutions operating on a dynamism of their own.

—*Eugene J. McCarthy*

Chapter VII.
Bureaucratic Dangers to Democracy

A. The Necessity to have Government Employees

When people began to live together in groups larger than single families, it became necessary to have rules of behavior toward one another, thus government. When the rules begin to be enforced, the individuals designated for those responsibilities by the people, or who assume them, become the government officials. From then on they make decisions that result in jobs to be done. These jobs, whether they involve building a defense system against enemies or potential enemies in neighboring communities or nations, road building, or teaching children, can be done on a voluntary unpaid basis by members of the society only when it is quite small. For larger groups, a staff has to be hired to carry out the tasks and to see that they are completed well and in a timely manner.

B. The Bureaucratic Organization

As the number of people in the community or nation increases, the size of the staff of their government also increases. An efficient way to organize employees is to create a bureaucracy. A bureaucracy consists of a series of positions so related to one another that a person in one position has the right of authority over those below him or her and is, in turn, subject to the authority of the person in the position above. These levels of authority are arranged in a pyramid type of hierarchy as is shown in Figure 3. If responsibilities of a government are numerous, they will be divided into departments or bureaus, each with its own bureaucracy.

A bureaucrat acquires leadership by satisfying the requirements of the position he or she is to fill. These prerequisites are usually a certain amount of formal training and experience. Both the requirements and duties of the position are written down so that anyone can learn what they are. Bureaucratic leadership positions may be filled by anyone meeting the requirements and obeying the rules.

As was noted in Section B of Chapter I on page 6, in democracies, as in most governments, the major responsibilities are carried out by three branches of government, the legislative, judicial, and executive. In the legislative the laws are made, while in the judicial, decisions are made as to whether or not the laws are in accordance with the nation's constitution. The executive branch has the responsibility of organizing and administering the programs authorized by the laws. This is accomplished by building bureaucracies.

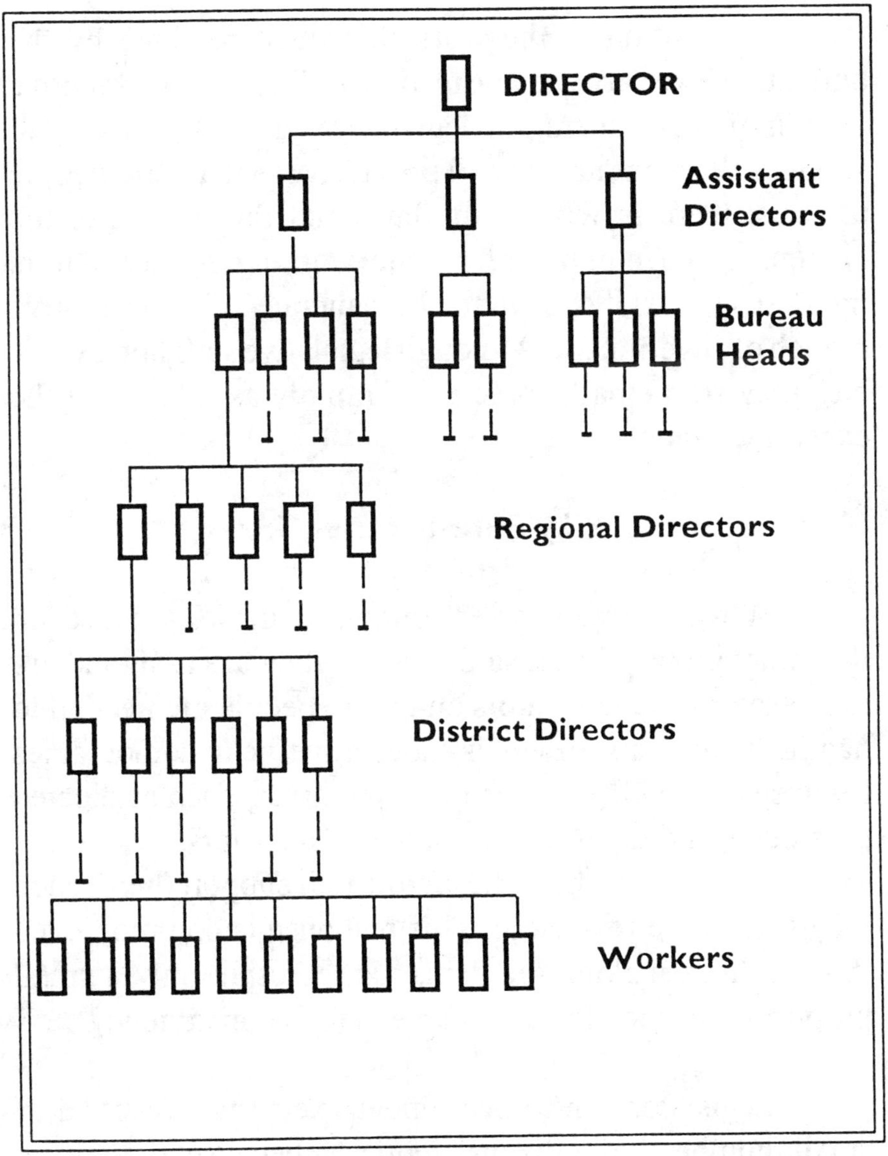

Figure 3. A Bureaucratic Type of Organizational Structure.

In addition to the work that must be done by the bureaucracy to carry out the responsibilities of the executive branch of government, the legislators who determine what services the government will provide, also may hire people to assist them in writing the laws and responding to the citizens. The number of people working for legislators increases just as it does in the bureaucracy of the executive branch of government. Although legislative staff bureaucracies may start small, some grow rapidly as they do in the executive branch.

C. Why Bureaucracies Grow

Why do bureaucracies continue to grow? One reason they may grow is because the duties they are assigned are increased by the legislators and more people are needed to handle them. This growth is especially true in democracies because elected legislators and executives, such as elected presidents and town, city or country managers, respond to demands of those whom they know will support them when they seek to be reelected. This response is common even though those making the demands represent only a small proportion of the citizens in an elector's constituency.

Legislators and government executives respond to small numbers of citizens' requests because they form special interest groups and organize forceful campaigns to impress legislators and mass media personnel. As discussed in Section L of Chapter V, political action committees called PACs have been provided with large sums of money by special interest groups of people to finance political campaigns of legislators. This is done to induce them to support the laws desired by the sponsors. By using PAC funds and well organized pressure techniques small numbers of citizens have a greater influence on issues of concern to them than the proportion of the population their numbers would justify. This influence produces a type of monopoly by the minority in terms of the attention and action of the law-making representatives of the citizens.

For example, a person may be concerned because a child living near an electric transmission line is afflicted with cancer and blame the disease on the electrical field generated by the flow of electricity in the wires. Other people living near electric lines, or who have lived near them, whose children have cancer, hear about the first case of child cancer and join the adults who blame it on the electrical transmission lines. Because there are such lines near many residences, and some children do have cancer, the number of parents blaming the disease on electricity becomes quite large with grandparents, friends and neighbors of sick children and other people who do not know the cancer stricken children, but feel sorry for them, joining the group.

Together all these people demand laws to prevent the building of power lines and to have some of those already in existence moved. Because their appeal is so emotional in that it involves sick children, legislators respond to them. When public health authorities present data indicating that the rate of cancer among children living near electric transmission lines is no different than the rate for children living elsewhere, they are accused of misleading the public. Regulations that control location of electric lines may have been passed and begun to be enforced before the truth is accepted.

New demands for services that are needed as well as regulations increase the number of government employees. The rapid growth in bureaucracies, however, comes about because of the nature of the bureaucracy itself. One cause of this expansion is the promotion and compensation system. A bureaucrat's status and salary depends on the number of people under him or her in the pyramid.

To the complete bureaucrat, the primary emphasis is on doing only what is required by the position he or she has, while watching for opportunities to add people underneath or for openings above. Anyone who does more than other members of the bureaucracy deem is right may be criticized by fellow workers, as the author was while working in government as a scientist. He was told by a senior bureaucrat that he was not being fair when he worked hard, because he was taking a job away from someone who could be hired to do that work.

Bureaucrats multiply not only because there are new programs to administer but also because of the characteristic of bureaucracies. In a study of a health agency, it was found that even though the number of people actually providing the services — like sanitary engineers, public health physicians and nurses declined, the number of those involved in managing the program — the bureaucratic staff, increased significantly. This phenomenon has also been quite obvious in public school systems where large decreases in the number of students or small increases have been accompanied by very large increases in administrators at the same time that there was a decrease in the number of teachers.

D. The Socialistic Tendency of Government Employees

The reasoning of government employees tends to be socialistic. A new employee soon accepts the values of those already conditioned to believe that the goals of their government agency are right and that it is the employee's responsibility to protect the agency from interference by nongovernment organizations or individuals who are considered to be the enemy by government employees. Loyal to their agencies, they use the power they know they have to control their own destinies. The preservation of their agency, and thus their jobs with extensive benefits, becomes a primary focus of their attention. Some also tend to assume the authority of the elected official for whom they work as this comment of an aide to a mayor indicates in the news article about a possible cat control law that was given on Section C, Chapter VI on page 120:

> . . . Mayor Sophie Masloff hasn't taken a stand on the issue, said her aide, Joseph Sabino Mistick. "We're going to sit back and watch the fur fly over in Council," he said.

Changes in the system of values of college graduates hired by the government were observed to take place rapidly as they went through an orientation program. Arriving with an idealism that government employment provided a wonderful opportunity for concerned individuals to become hard-working servants of the public who would dedicate themselves to public service and devote their skills to a good purpose, their interest soon became focused on the benefits due them. They insisted on being paid for every minute of time they spent in work related activities such as returning to their home from meetings. Similarly they used every day of sick leave. They took advantage of opportunities to travel with their expenses for food, lodging and transportation being reimbursed to them at the highest rate allowed.

These new government employees did their work

well, but obtaining job benefits became their prime objective rather than their contribution to fellow citizens through carrying out the duties of the job. It should be noted that those new college graduates observed, were in the bureaucracy planning unit of their agency. Similar trainees in the service units may not have changed their outlook in the same manner although some of their orientation also was done by the planning personnel who emphasized the benefit programs.

Fortunately, there are many exceptions to the bureaucrat typified herein. Some government employees work very hard, seldom take long vacations, and are conscientious people dedicated to performing high quality public service throughout their working careers. Some of these devoted employees, however, are not rewarded for their contributions to meeting the goals of the government agency in which they work. Under promotion systems and employee award programs they may be passed over because they spend their time and effort handling their responsibilities rather than in self-promotion.

Another belief developed by many government workers is that private ownership is undesirable. To people employed by the government, it may seem right for the government to own enterprises because they feel private owners cannot, or will not, conform to the standards the government has established for their operations. The independence of businesspersons irks some government employees who have to obtain supplies and equipment from them. Government employees further try to justify government ownership, because according to them, the government can do the required job not only better but also cheaper than anyone else. In justifying their cost argument, however, they neglect to include the administrative overhead of government programs.

E. Private Ownership and the Failure of the Socialistic Government of the Soviet Union

The issue of whether government or private ownership of business enterprises is better for the people was answered by the admission of leaders in the Soviet Union that the socialistic system of government ownership had failed miserably. For a considerable number of government employees, however, the collapse of communism in Eastern Europe and the Soviet Union, as well as in some African countries where the government owned the bussinesses, has not been accepted as the final answer as to whether private ownership of property and businesses is superior to government ownership. This lack of acceptance of private ownership may be because of training they received in schools and colleges where private enterprises were depicted by some of their teachers as evil. It also may be due to the ethnocentric feeling they developed as government employees that their agencies can carry out tasks better than any other organization.

When government staffs compute the expense of providing a service for citizens, the costs of the capital investment are almost never included nor is the loss of taxes that private owners must pay the government on the property they own and on the income the activity produces or the taxes paid just for the permission to operate a business. Similarly, administrative expenses usually are not included or are understated when they compare government owned and run enterprises with those that are private.

Public versus private education is an example about which tax-paying citizens usually base their comparisons of costs on the tuition students pay. Education at a private college with an annual tuition of $10,000 is considered to cost much more that the $3,336 at a nearby public college, for example. Computed in the tuition of the private college are all costs incurred in giving the education such as for staff, faculty, academic supplies, capital construction, debt service, and property maintenance. For the public college, however, capital costs are not included nor is the major part of the budget that the college receives from taxpayers. Due to much larger staffs and much more elaborate and newer buildings in many public colleges, the actual costs of private colleges are many times lower than the cost of public ones.

F. Bureaucracies in Private Enterprises

Bureaucracies also grow in private enterprises, especially large corporations. The number of administrative and clerical employees in some corporations has increased to the point where formerly healthy, vigorous and profitable firms have collapsed into bankruptcy. To survive, some firms abolish hundreds and sometimes thousands of management positions. The theory advocated by management consultant firms and graduates of business schools, that supervisors should have a limited number of subordinates, has often caused firms to fail when they formed an expensive superstructure of managers. The salaries, expenses and overhead of all the vice presidents, assistant vice presidents and assistants to the assistant vice presidents and their staffs may require more money than can be earned from the products of the workers below them. The money spent each year just on exorbitant administrative expenses for a few of the corporate executives, could have been better used in purchasing new technology needed by the workers, to keep the manufacturing or processing plant competitive.

G. The Danger to Democracies of Bureaucracies

Government employees make it possible for governments to function, but they can and do prevent some democratic processes from occurring. They know they have a number of advantages over elected legislators and executive branch officials. Because many legislators work part-time and have to be concerned with getting reelected, they do not take time to determine how the bureaucracy is functioning. Also legislators cannot be knowledgeable or skilled in all the fields of responsibility carried out by government employees. On the other hand, the bureaucrats hold their positions over a long period of time, most on a permanent basis. A technique bureaucrats utilize to control legislators is simply to delay responding to legislative requests or in carrying out legislative mandates with the expectation that the legislator will be replaced in the next election or else lose interest. They treat the appointed directors of their agencies the same way.

Members of the bureaucracy are taught by more experienced ones just how to thwart legislators and the elected head of the administrative government who may expect the agency to achieve objectives not desired by the regular employees. In fact, senior members of the bureaucracy in the United States government are encouraged to attend courses on how to work with legislators in Congress and with the staff of the President. In these courses, they actually can learn techniques for controlling members of congress and their staffs as well as ways to control the President's staff. Bureaucrats protect themselves from losing their jobs whether they are under democratic governments or those run by monarchs, religious leaders, military dictators or communists.

Government bureaucracies also are a danger to democracies because their continual growth requires a tremendous amount of money that legislators have to obtain through taxation. In addition, studies have shown that many programs designed to help people with needs, actually benefit those operating them to a much greater extent than those in need. The report of one such study is entitled "Who Benefits from Federal Intervention." This carefully conducted and documented research focused on the Head Start Program that was supposed to help preschool-children prepare for school. Its author concluded that it was not the children who benefited the most from the Head Start Program, but rather the individual who was hired to operate it.

For government programs where the interest of citizens the programs are supposed to help is low, suggesting they may not be needed to the degree that was expected, the bureaucrats running the programs resort to extensive advertising to entice people to take part. This procedure was carried out by the administrators of the United States food stamp program. Another technique used where the administration of government programs want a larger number of people to participate, thus justifying the program and their jobs, is to change the requirements for participating in the program so that more people will qualify. For example, the food subsidy program for people with low incomes, just mentioned, induced more "clients" to apply both with an advertising campaign and by increasing the amount of income families and individuals could earn and still qualify as being "low income" and thus receive the government support.

Bureaucrats also may add to requirements in accordance with their own interests. When they do, additional personnel are needed to administer the program and thus, a larger budget. Special interest organizations also may pressure legislators and program administrators for changes that benefit them. A prime example of this is when citizens and professionals promoting mental health lobby for a government mental health department independent of the regular health department. This may double the number of personnel working in the same geographical area. With one health department, public health nurses could attend to all health problems of a family. When a mental health department is added, a public health nurse no longer could be concerned with mental health problems because that became the responsibility of a mental health department staff member who also had to visit the same family.

Another serious danger to democracies is the interpretation of legislation by bureaucrats. Organizing the programs legislators have approved and operating them is the responsibility of government employees. This responsibility gives them many opportunities to promote their own ideas of what is needed by interpreting the laws as they see them. After a bureaucracy is organized its staff is almost immune from examination from outsiders including the legislators who authorize its program. A bureaucracy prevents the assessment of responsibility and performance of its personnel. Nor can its specific objectives be clearly evaluated in relation to the type and number of its staff. Legislator sponsors of laws frequently are astonished when they learn that what is actually being done by the bureaucracy is much different from what was intended by the legislation.

Democracy requires that citizens have a right to object to the government and its programs. They can petition the government about their grievances. It is this right that bureaucracies are very expert at preventing. To begin with, staff members are the "gatekeepers" through which protesters must pass. If a citizen wants to talk with a legislator or an official in the bureaucracy by telephone or in person, it is necessary to talk first to someone else who determines whether or not the meeting should be scheduled.

H. Bribing of Government Employees

One way citizens can catch the attention of the official they need to see is by bribing the gatekeeper and/or the official. Bribes are always destructive in a society and can come in many forms. They may be money, contributions to election campaigns, or a variety of gifts and favors. The bribe, however, may simply be status association. That is, the person seeking entrance has sufficient status in the society or is so wealthy that the gatekeeper desires to acquire some of that status by informing others that he or she has an association with the visitor.

Governments always take a protective role. That is, they make rules and regulations to make citizens conform to things the legislators conclude are correct or to keep them from doing things legislators believe are harmful. The enforcement of government rules provides many opportunities for government employees to be bribed so they will be less stringent in enforcing rules. Some employees seek bribes by hinting that they will go easy on the person or firm seeking their approval. Because they have the law backing them and because time is on their side, citizens who must convince the government official that they are satisfying government regulations are at a great disadvantage.

If a newly constructed residence is required to meet electrical, plumbing, zoning, environmental and several other requirements, those who are to inspect the property and certify that it has met the requirements, thereby giving a permit authorizing the home to be completed and/or stating that it is ready to be occupied can be subject to bribes. The house builder or the family that has built a house, are in a stressful position if the sale cannot be concluded and/or the family cannot move into it until all inspectors approve it.

An effective technique is for an inspector to decide that a small adjustment is necessary, like a hand rail, before he will approve the structure of a house. The hand rail is installed the next day but the unbribed inspector does not come back for a month or so. On the second visit, a water heater is deemed a few gallons too small and it is changed. Months later another minor fault is found. Meanwhile costs of maintaining the house continue to increase along with interest on the money it took to build it. The inspector, on the other hand, continues to be paid his salary and benefits. To get the house approved so that a family can move in, the builder or owner finally may decide to pay a bribe, especially when they learn that the experienced builders consider this a normal part of the cost of building a home. Some people, however, decide not to pay the bribes and wait until the approval is given even though they finally have to sell the house at a loss.

Obtaining the necessary permits for building or for starting a business thus can be very time consuming and costly. The freedom of citizens to act is also dampened by the mass of papers that must be filled out. ***Democratic principles can be defeated by forms***. When the permit obtaining process is considered, it is easy to realize how difficult it may be for honest and sincere administrators in the bureaucracy to prevent misuse of the power of permit givers and inspectors. Although, in some countries, bribes must be paid to government employees before they will provide the service they are paid to perform, in the democracies that have been in existance for many years, this illegal activity also occurs sometimes but is not considered a normal procedure.

As this news article states, a government employee in charge of issuing permits had received $30,000 in bribes from builders before his illegal activities were discovered. Apparently, his deeds were so obvious that he pleaded guilty and undoubtedly will spend time in jail for violating the trust placed in him by the public.

City official admits taking bribes

The city's former director of permits has pleaded guilty to receiving $30,000 in bribes from builders over a four-year period.

Prosecutors are recommending that he receive concurrent 18-month sentences in federal and state courts.

He is expected to plead guilty to six state bribery charges in the county circuit court.

He was assistant city engineer for

> 10 years when he was promoted to director of the city's permits and code management office.

One of the techniques honest government officials use to prevent members of inspection units from accepting bribes is to obtain satisfactory salaries for them and then to supervise them carefully. Policemen in one city who were paid very low salaries collected "protection" money from each merchant on a regular, although illegal basis, while those in a nearby city who were paid well did not seek or accept bribes. Furthermore, the higher salaries in the second city attracted individuals who had completed more formal education and training for the positions.

I. Government Procurement Issues

Another area where government employees are subject to special pressures involves procurement. The necessity to obtain numerous products, some in huge quantities, to carry out the responsibilities of their agencies, provides government employees with considerable power. In many countries it is necessary for the supplier of goods and services to the government to pay individuals who control purchasing for that privilege. Unfortunately, even with numerous controls on the procurement process, there is still some bribery in the awarding of contracts in the older democracies. If the contracts involve large sums of money, and the bribes paid are substantial, this illegal behavior is usually discovered and the guilty individuals, both those receiving the bribes and those paying them, are punished with fines or imprisonment.

A special type of misconduct in the awarding of contracts for government business, concerns one friend helping another to receive contracts for work to be done without having to compete with others for the business. This type is more difficult to discover than the direct bribes. As one official stated, "We have to buy a lot of insurance. The cost of insurance is about the same from each company so it really doesn't matter which company supplies it. So I give the business to my friends."

In a democracy, everyone is supposed to have an equal opportunity to produce and sell goods and provide services needed by the government. The procurement process is about the most difficult government function to maintain in accordance with democratic principles. It is absolutely necessary, therefore, for democracies to develop an effective method of monitoring the entire procurement process. As part of the process, the government must make available the technical specifications for the product or service to be purchased and then request sealed bids from all potential suppliers by a certain date. The government must indicate how much the decision as to whom the contract will be awarded will depend on how well the specifications are met and how much on the price. These bids should be opened and rated by individuals selected for their knowledge and experience and not by the government employees directly involved in the purchasing.

J. Summary

In this chapter, the focus was on the danger to democracies of government bureaucracies. The number of government employees is a significant proportion of the employed population in most countries. Bureaucracies continue to grow because the salaries and power of government employees depend on the number of employees they supervise and because bureaucrats come to believe that their organization can do things better and cheaper than nongovernment organizations or private individuals. Bureaucrats use many techniques to preserve their jobs and agencies including delaying action and restricting information about the need for their services and about their activities that are needed by legislators if they are to make objective decisions.

One of the serious problems faced by all types of governments is the possibility that people seeking assistance from the government will resort to bribes to obtain what they want. An objective and fair procurement system is required if citizens who desire to provide services and products to the government are to be treated equally.

One of the most difficult challenges for existing democracies is how to subject bureaucratic encroachments on individual and organizational freedom to continuous control by the legislators and the courts. Although authorized and established by legislators, bureaucracies soon become almost independent of control by legislators. When this loss of control happens, the citizens are subjected to rule by governmentocracy that seriously inhibits their freedoms whether they live in a democracy or in countries ruled by dictatorships.

****

What government is the best? That which teaches us to govern ourselves.

—*Johann Wolfgang von Goethe*

To solve our problems, we must first understand them. And understanding begins with truth.

—*John B. Anderson*

Politics I conceive to be nothing more than the science of the ordered progress of society along the lines of greatest usefulness and convenience to itself.

—*Woodrow Wilson*

I know no safe depository of the ultimate powers of the society but the people themselves; and if we think them not enlightened enough to exercise their control with a wholesome discretion, the remedy is not to take it from them, but to inform their discretion by education.

—*Thomas Jefferson*

We aren't educated until we come truly to find democracy not just in the machinery of government but in the hearts of men.

—*James M. Spinning*

Chapter VIII.
The Essential Learning Process in Democracies

A. Introduction

The thesis that has been presented in earlier chapters of this book is that the specific type of government that people have is not a naturally occurring phenomenon. Instead, each type is an adaptation that came about through a learning process. People who condone a government controlled by their religious leaders, or by a monarch, a dictator or communist leader, or by elected representatives, do so because they have been conditioned to consider it acceptable and the way government ought to be. Those individuals who have had experiences with and/or obtained knowledge of how types of governments function that differ from their own country's, however, may favor another type if they have not been completely conditioned to believe that theirs is the only type acceptable.

B. The Learning Process and Governments

The learning process all through the lives of citizens

must be influenced by leaders in each type of government if they want their government to continue to exist. For example, those government leaders who restrict freedom and subdue human rights cannot allow communication of information about governments under which freedom is enjoyed and prosperity fostered to flow into their countries. If they do, the possibility that the people would rebel against them would be greatly increased. With modern day technology, however, maintaining an effective barrier against the knowledge of how people in other nations are living is very difficult to accomplish. The inability of the former Soviet Union to stop the flow of knowledge about the freedom and prosperity enjoyed in the democratic nations was one of the important factors in the collapse of its socialist system of economics and communist government.

C. The Enculturation Process

The means by which infants of whatever country they are born into are transformed into effective adults and changed as they encounter new situations in their lives, is an enculturation process. This process will now be described to enhance an understanding of what has already been presented in this book as well as to underscore the importance of early and continuous education and practical experience in fostering a democratic type of government.

An infant, from the anthropological point of view, is

an amorphous being that has the potential of becoming a contributing member of the society into which it is born. Progress toward adulthood is achieved by changes in the infant, child, and adolescent brought about through interaction first with the mother, father and other family members and later with many other individuals and groups.

Small informal groups, starting with the family, become the medium for enculturating the infant and child as Figure 4 illustrates. The young human acquires a system of beliefs or values and a pattern of behavior from individuals in the groups who transfer some of their knowledge and beliefs to the child deliberately and some without knowing they are doing it. This store of knowledge, rules of behavior and beliefs that reach each individual through others is the "culture" of the people. Culture makes it possible for the individual acquiring it to proceed through life adjusting to each new experience.

In order to comprehend how this culture is transmitted from the family and others to the infant and growing child and how they utilize it in their lives, "interaction" needs to be understood. Interaction is the response of one person to another. It is a meaningful type of contact between people. This communication may be a spoken statement, a nod, or some other type of gesture. Contacts between people during which one does not react to the other would not be

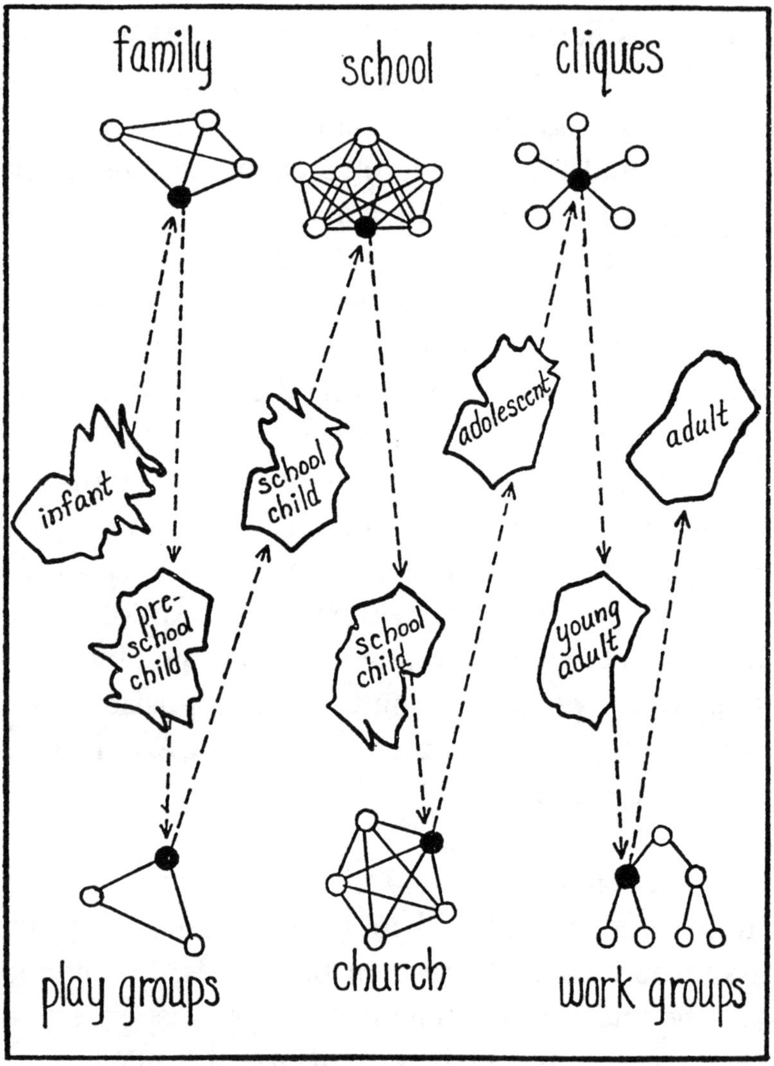

Figure 4. The Enculturation Process

Figure 4 illustrates how the personality of a newborn infant is shaped through interaction with individuals in vaious groups as it progresses through childhood and young adulthood.

considered interaction. Making of a suggestion by one person or giving a command are obvious types of origination of communication on the part of that person, whereas following a suggestion or obeying a command by another is an obvious response.

Many times the origination of action is much more subtle, like the stern glance of a mother toward her misbehaving child that makes him or her stop that behavior, or the movement of a finger by a participant recognized as a signal by an auctioneer that he is making an offer to buy the object the auctioneer is selling. Because interaction is a two-way process, one can originate repeatedly and still not interact with another unless the other responds.

The most important gesture in interaction is the vocal one, which for every human society existing today takes shape in a complex of significant sounds called language. Without the complicated language in interaction, the beliefs, or values, and ways of behavior that accompany them and the culture would not have been possible. Similarly, the widespread variations in human societies and their governments, as we know them, evolves because of the languge capability of humans.

D. The Significance of Human Interaction

When people interact with one another over a long

period of time, either continually or intermittently, they each know how the other thinks and from this they can predict what the other will do or say under most circumstances. The ability to predict the behavior of others takes the strain out of living by reducing the number and seriousness of conflicting actions. After people associate with one another in the same social system for some time, they will accept their own and each other's behavior as proper to the extent that actions of anyone outside their group will appear strange. This feeling of being correct in contrast with others who do things differently is called "ethnocentrism." It applies equally well to small and large groups. Family members, club members, political party members, religious adherents, inhabitants of a city, or citizens of an entire nation who share the idea that no other family, club, religion, city, or country is equal to their own, have developed ethnocentrism.

The most important need of a newborn infant is to have people around it. Relationships of an infant with parents and others are life-giving because through them not only are physiological requirements met, but also personality characteristics that can determine how he or she will function as a member of society during the rest of his or her life. This need for other people continues through childhood and adulthood, because security-giving relationships with other people are necessary for the child to develop into, and remain, an adequately functioning member of a society and to have physical and social wants satisfied.

E. How Children Learn Democratic Principles

Children tend to copy what those a little older do. In a military controlled society, or one during which military activities are emphasized, they will pretend that sticks are guns and pretend to shoot one another. In a religion controlled society, they will tend to play the roles of religious leaders more than they would do in nonreligious societies. In a free market democratic society, even preschoolers will attempt to operate a business like their parents or other adults by setting up a stand to sell lemonade or other items to neighbors. They will put on plays and ask older children and adults to buy tickets if they want to see and hear the plays. In socialistic countries where people are restricted from most activities that would produce extra income or profits for themselves, some children still will try to sell items to obtain money, especially to visitors from outside their areas, even though this activity may be prohibited by their government. Their parents may secretly do the same things on the "black market" that the children do more openly due to their age.

Children also will form organizations to associate with each other as playmates. In representative democracies, even at a preschool age, children will agree on rules of behavior to be followed and criteria to be met by those wanting to join in their activities. When they enter schools, teachers will help children formalize the free and secret election process of their country by having elections for class officers.

As children in democracies advance from entrance level in schools to the last year of their studies, the election process becomes more complicated as student candidates for class offices carry on campaigns to induce fellow students to vote for them. If later they attend college, election to student leadership positions for many youth becomes an important part of their college experience and education.

All through school youths form or join organizations in their neighborhoods and wider communities in which constitutions or bylaws are written for their organizations and democratic election processes are followed. These youth organizations expand to become city or countywide and some state and nationwide. Thus, not only does their formal education foster democratic practice, but it prevails in their social, athletic, and work related activities outside of schools and colleges. Also, it continues into adulthood and senior citizen status.

When children are inadequately trained and/or supervised, the activity of members of groups they form may be destructive in the communities. Such groups, or gangs as they are labeled by law enforcement personnel, have leaders and followers like any organization. In addition, they have a geographical territory such as a city block, several blocks, or a section of a city. Gangs of youth, uncontrolled by adults are especially prevalent in areas where significant proportions of the population are migrants or immigrants who have not yet been assimilated into the society and where one or both parents are absent or do not control their children. Some of the gangs center their attention on constructive activities such as athletics or music, while others focus on antisocial or criminal pursuits.

Many programs have been designed to guide youth into constructive activities such as providing facilities for them to meet and play that are clean and safe with adult supervision. Similar programs for gang members that are not so domineering that the young people refuse to participate is a continuing necessity in most countries. The problem of destructive gang behavior is more serious in urban areas than in rural because rural youth usually are kept busy assisting their parents in their vocational endeavors.

The process of brainwashing, already discussed in Section C of Chapter I, occurs in varying degrees in many training programs for children and young adults such as in education, social work and mental health in democratic societies as well as in others. For example, when a professor of education tells prospective teachers that their worst enemy is the children's parents, that professor is attempting to force his or her values into the personalities of the college students and then have them, when they become teachers, react in that way to parents of children in their classrooms.

The professor has the power to do this because he or she determines whether or not they pass the course and thus whether or not they become teachers. The stress created is the necessity to obtain the professor's approval. The student's worst fear is the threat of disapproval and failure to qualify for the profession the student desires to enter. It can be enough to cause students to do things that violate their beliefs or that they know are incorrect until they exchange their values for the professor's doctrine.

Frequently, the educational or training program in which brainwashing techniques are used prepares people for employment in the social welfare and mental health services. If they are to obtain the required degrees and job experience approval, applicants must conform to the methods of providing assistance to "clients" advocated by their professors and those under whom they receive their field experiences. The brainwashing stress applied is the threat of disapproval and failure to qualify for their profession.

Ways that individuals govern their behavior in groups learned during childhood and young adulthood become part of the system of values of people whether they be in a society ruled by dictators, monarchs, religious leaders or elected representatives. For example, Americans, soon after rushing to gold mining areas in unsettled parts of their country, formed elected governments similar to those they left behind. The miners may have been rough and tough men with little formal education but they still carried the plans in their heads for self-government. In some locations, those not as well socialized in democratic procedures set up criminally controlled governments that eventually were overthrown as the number of democratically inclined people increased in their communities.

F. The Decision-Making Process

Decision-making ranges from the autocratic type of leader's orders to be obeyed by the rest of the people after policy is decided by the leader, to decisions reached through extensive discussions and agreed to by all participants before the action is taken.

In the older democracies, individuals win elections because they receive more votes than other candidates. Issues are decided on the same basis. The principle involved is that the action most people desire should be taken. The smaller number of people who do not agree, need to accept it as being the democratic way to resolve issues.

People in a democratically run group can be on the losing minority side of an issue but be on the majority winning side of the next issue discussed. For example, some may not want to change the time of day when they meet from 7:30 to 8:00 PM. When the majority of members vote for the change, those not wanting it accept the decision. On the next issue, whether or not they should go to a sports program, some of those who voted against the time change, might favor having their group attend the sports event and vote for it. With most members also wanting to go, the number voting for it is more than the number against it. Individuals who were against the first issue and thus part of the minority become part of the majority if they vote for the second issue.

In at least one society, the manner of reaching decisions started with a general discussion type of debate with everyone participating who cared to, and ended with a unanimous decision after those disagreeing with the solution left the group. In fact, although it is very unusual, sometimes individuals who disagree with the outcome of discussions about an issue in democratically operated organizations also resign from them. By leaving the group, their viewpoint is no longer represented and they lose any further opportunity to persuade members of the group to accept their view, but they are not participating in an activity of which they disapprove.

Another type of decision-making is based on a consensus of opinions among participants. A decision reached by a consensus of opinions of members of organizations or governments on an issue may seem different from basing a decision on what a majority wants. With the consensus method, however, the decision is still dependent on more people wanting it than wanting another solution. The difference between the consensus method and a majority vote, particularly a secret vote, is that the higher status individuals, or those with the best debating skills involved in arriving at a consensus, may keep people desiring a different solution to the issue from expressing their views. Consensus decisions, therefore, may not represent the actual opinion of the group, as might the results of a secret ballot.

G. The Importance of Normal Enculturation

The enculturation process is the means by which all types of behavior are produced. For example, it is the responsibility of fathers to claim their young sons for manhood by treating them as males and doing male activities with them. The father who, upon learning his wife has given birth to his son, immediately tells his friends that he already has hunting boots on him, meaning that the father intends to teach his child to be a male, reflects a very significant attitude toward the child. With the male variation in the society's system of values transferred to the boy, it will be difficult for others to change him into a "she-man," which was what some Native Americans called a man who took a female role in their society.

When boys and young men learn to be sexually

attracted to other males rather than females, this abnormality is due to the failure of parents, along with other adults in the society, to transfer male values to their sons. The same process takes place on the part of girls who focus their love emotions on other females rather than males. Their mothers and older women in their lives along with their fathers have failed to transfer female values to them. In this learning of gender in relation to sexual relationships, both parents play an essential role in that the father not only must treat his son as a boy but also must react to his daughter as a girl. Similarly, the mother must respond to her son as a boy and her daughter as a girl.

It also is the responsibility of adults to claim their children for their democracy from the time they are born through childhood. To do this, parents must provide the security-giving relationships essential for children to develop into productive members of their societies. An effective democracy requires that its members have respect — respect for each other and the rights of others, respect for cultural variations in personalities of individuals and how people live in groups, respect for law and order and democratic principles, respect for property and respect for flora and fauna of the natural environment. Successful parents impart their values to their children, which influences how they react to events and people throughout their lives. Parents transfer their beliefs through language and by their actions.

When fathers were the main wage earners in families and mothers spent much of their time at home with their children, mothers had a major responsibility for character formation in children. It was the mother's character, reinforced by the father's, when fathers were home, that tended to result in honest, hardworking and productive young adults, characteristics they carried with them through life. With most fathers in the older democracies spending less time in employment now and more with their families, they have a more significant role in the formation of sound character in their children. This will also become true in the newer democracies as their economies improve resulting in an increase in citizens' levels of living.

To counteract the effect families have had on young people while they were children, the communist government of North Vietnam gave the sons and daughters of village leaders in South Vietnam scholarships to retraining schools in the North. By isolating them from their parents and friends and treating them well, they were able to transform them into devoted communists who then were returned to their villages where they took the leadership away from their elders. When East Germany was under control of communists, youth who participated in protests against the government were confined to prison away from their parents and made to work 12 hours per day, seven days a week while living on cold, watery soup and bread for every meal. Without the reinforcement of values provided by families, some youth could be influenced to cooperate with and accept communist values when their captors promised to relieve them from this punishment. Many continued to resist their communnist captors, however, and some managed to escape from the prisons.

H. The Importance of Two-parent Families

When babies become a by-product of sexual behavior by individuals who have no intention of getting married or of serving as viable parents, prospects for the children produced to become law-abiding, productive members of the society are greatly reduced. When the sexual partners are "still children" themselves, the children they produce are even more unlikely to become effective adults. A society that through its public media, especially television, and government educational and welfare programs, condones, rather than condemns behavior that results in illegitimate children, will have serious problems. Children, youth and adults in such a society may not fit into the mainstream. Without adequate parents, street gangs tend to take their place and antisocial and criminal behavior become the accepted way of life rather than a legitimate, useful occupation that supports the society and its democratic government.

The seriousness of the need to provide children with good character in democratic countries can not be over-emphasized. Character consists of those facets of each person's personality that determine his or her behavior. It involves the qualities of honesty, integrity, courteousness, self respect, recognition of the importance of good health practices for one's own body, willingness to devote one's energy and time to self improvement, the tendency to work hard and diligently while pursuing careers, eagerness to carry more than a fair share of responsibilities and labor, tolerance for others, reverence for all sacred aspects of society whether or not they are personally sacred to the individual, use of reason and sound knowledge in arriving at decisions, persistence in solving problems, openness to new ideas and knowledge and to the changes in opinions and ways of handling problems the new information suggests, eagerness to help people in need and to share one's knowledge and skills, ability to know right from wrong, respect for law and order, and love of country.

Many more character traits could be added to this list to describe a person whom others judge to be noble because of his or her character. ***None of these traits that nice human beings possess include the amount of power over others or the extent of their wealth. Therefore, no one has to be excluded from acquiring good character.*** Unfortunately, however, many people are excluded because they were not provided with the foundation as a child and youth of beliefs and ways of behaving that make up good character. A review of the list of desirable characteristics suggests that it is not an easy task to inculcate these in an infant, child and young adult who's mobility brings it in contact with many types of people.

From the time a child is born its character begins to form. It is its parents who have the first and most important opportunity to initiate a strong foundation upon which a sound character can develop. What is necessary is the establishment of security-giving relationships between parents and child. The child needs to know that the parents care about him or her. It is not enough just to have food and other physical needs met.

Although a single parent can accomplish this difficult task, it is much easier for two parents. With a mother and father who have a loving relationship with each other, the child knows their object is to have a happy home for the whole family in which each parent has a role. Some single parents frequently have quite different objectives in that they may be seeking social and sexual partners outside the family. Also they may have to spend a significant amount of time away from the child earning a living. Finally, they provide only one sex role.

Compounding the difficulty of parenting is the use of narcotics and alcohol by parents, older siblings and adults in the neighborhoods where the families live. When a single mother is an addict, attempts by grandmothers and others to help nurture infants and children may not be effective in forming good character in the children.

In addition to parents, a number of organizations such as religious ones, Four H Clubs, Cub Scouts, Boy Scouts, Girl Scouts, Boys Clubs, Girl Guides, Campfire Girls and Kiwanis Key Clubs emphasize sound character. Character development also should be a goal of schools from the first level to the last. This can be achieved through the advocation of study and recreational habits. Heroes recognized for their outstanding character should be put forward as role models for children. Only those entertainment and sports stars with lifestyles that demonstrate highly moral and unselfish behavior should be held up as examples.

If children are provided the security-giving relationships by caring parents who want them to become good human beings, they can resist the temptations of meeting those needs by participating in anti-social and criminal cliques and gangs nor will they seek social status by emulating criminal leaders in their neighborhoods and communities.

I. Democratic Values and Formal Education

Citizens in a democracy, because they control their government rather than being slaves to totalitarian rulers, must be well-educated. Their learning has to include an understanding and appreciation of democratic procedures along with scientific, technological and management knowledge. They must learn to use their brains to persuade others to agree with them as well as to adjust their thinking about issues in accordance with the reasoning of others.

If democratic values are to be transferred to the young, the formal educational system must be oriented toward that goal. When a copy of a painting of the first President of the United States, George Washington, hung on the walls of many grade schools in the United States, children had a reminder that honesty would lead to greatness. When they were taught the last words of another hero, Nathan Hale, who said to his English captors as they prepared to kill him during the American Revolutionary War, "I regret that I have only one life to give for my country," the youth knew how noble it was to love their country to the point of giving their lives for it. The stories they read about heroes who overcame poverty and hardships through self-improvement and hard work, stimulated them to follow in those heros' footsteps by learning how to pursue useful occupations and be involved in improving themselves as well as their communities.

J. The Necessity for Immigrants to Learn Democratic Principles

With rapid and efficient communication and transportation, along with relaxation of laws restricting immigration, democratic nations that have prospered because of their democratic values emphasizing free enterprise, must be concerned with large numbers of people coming to live in their countries. This is because immigrants usually do not arrive with the same culture as the people in their new country. Their way of reasoning and behaving frequently is different from the citizens who have been born in the country they have entered. This disparity of beliefs and behavior results in a serious problem in democracies when the newcomers do not understand or appreciate democratic principles. This is especially true regarding their relationships with each other and with people already living in their new country. Democracy requires a give and take relationship among people as well as a respect for those differing from one another.

The United States came into existence because of immigrants to North America from Europe. For the millions of immigrants who settled on its vast lands, the government had an effective "Americanization" program during much of its history. The objective of this Americanization effort was to teach new citizens the English language, if they did not speak and read it already. In addition, regardless of where they came from, they were taught the history of their new country and how its government functioned. This adult education process did much to transform most of the immigrants into Americans, while the public schools taught children the English language and American values.

In 1886 France gave the United States the Statue of Liberty pictured on the cover of the book, to honor the friendship between the two nations. It was erected on an

On Ellis Island near the Statue of Liberty, the large and beautiful building pictured on this page was constructed as a reception center for immigrants. Between 1892 and 1924 12 million people disembarked from the ships that brought them across the Atlantic Ocean. Perspective citizens entered this building on their way to their new homeland.

island in the harbor of New York City and is today recognized as a symbol of liberty throughout the world. It has been seen by millions of immigrants to the United States. To them, it indicated the special country that would become their new home.

In the United States, government policy regarding immigrants has changed during the last few decades from encouraging and assisting them in becoming Americans to aiding them in maintaining their original language and culture. The extensive welfare and medical care, as well as public education in the immigrants' languages, enhances their becoming wards of the government and inhibits their transformation into independent and productive citizens. Also, this welfare process has produced conflict between law-abiding democratic, free enterprising citizens and those among their new neighbors who have not understood or accepted the responsibility of citizenship in a democracy.

Although the effective Americanization program has been jeopardized recently by people who want bi-lingualism and cultural diversity emphasized, fortunately, many immigrants are ignoring that tendency and obtaining the training themselves. Contrary to what multi-culturalists insist, many of the immigrants want to become "Americans" to the extent that they pay for and attend English classes themselves and sometimes even Americanize their names. They work hard to overcome their cultural backgrounds as well as to improve their level of living, including starting their own businesses as capitalists.

Problems generated by large numbers of immigrants are occurring in many democracies as it becomes easier for people to move from one country to another. European countries, especially Germany and England, are attempting to solve their immigration problems with programs to assist new residents and citizens. They are, however, as is Japan, restricting the number of people, with specified characteristics, allowed to immigrate to their countries. In most countries the restriction or quotas that limit the number of immigrants from a country are not very successful in keeping more than the allowed number from moving where they want to live. It is too easy for immigrants to just enter by airplane, boat, motor vehicle or by walking across borders.

Because of military conflicts in some nations and the repression of individuals opposing totalitarian leaders, the world has serious refugee problems. People become refugees when they leave their homes to avoid persecution by government leaders for their political beliefs or actions. To protect political refugees, many countries have accepted them as immigrants. This has resulted in many nonrefugees attempting to have themselves declared refugees in order to immigrate.

Regardless of how they arrived or how long they have

resided in them, all nations, especially new democracies, need to encourage the integration of all of their citizens through educational programs that reduce bi-lingual and multi-cultural differences. ***It is highly advantageous to have bi-lingual individuals as well as people with different subcultures, but dangerous to have a bi-lingual and multi-cultural nation.*** This diversity is dangerous to the country because it can lead to ethnocentric feelings that become so strong that citizens cannot tolerate each other if they have different languages and ways of living.

K. The Importance of Local Control of Public Schools

During the first 150 years in the United States most public school teachers were hired and controlled by the parents of the children living around the schools. This relationship slowly changed during the last 60 years until today the teachers are "professionalized" and controlled by "professional" educational administrators. Parents no longer decide who is hired or what is taught. Although citizens in some areas may select members of school boards by voting in school elections for those they favor, the school board members usually can appoint only the head of the school system and make a few decisions about the curricula. Their decisions are restricted in that their choice of someone to direct the school system must meet qualifications determined by professional educators on a state or federal level.

Similarly, the curricula must be approved by the same professionals. Parents who try to influence the curricula in the schools of their children usually fail in their efforts. As one superintendent stated, when he was faced by parents who requested courses be included in their schooling that would prepare the children for jobs, "no ###damn parent is going to tell me what to do."

Leaders in developing nations striving to improve the formal education for children must make sure they do not follow advice from professional educators in the older democracies that has caused the decline in the quality of instruction and learning in those countries. For effective formal education at the elementary and secondary school levels, the curriculum needs to be a combination of courses that are useful to the students in their communities, and courses that prepare them for a technologically advancing society. They must have courses that help them become knowledgeable and effective participants in their democratic government and free market, capitalistic economy. Children must be taught to think effectively and to solve problems.

As Dr. Edward C. Stewart has stated, the professional educators have changed the goal of schooling from performance to sensitivity. No longer is the emphasis on learning the school subjects well. Rather, the most important achievement is how well children get along with other children. To be judged successful by the professional educators who control school requirements, the student must love all other students and adults regardless of how repugnant their life-styles might be to him or her. Among the kinds of people children are expected to respect are individuals with a wide range of behavior and beliefs. For example, children who have been taught by their parents and religious leaders that homosexuality, learned by a few of their classmates and some adults with whom they must associate, is abnormal, are supposed to change their beliefs. It is not enough for the children to accept the abnormal behavior but they must consider it normal. The result is a conflict between the school personnel and parents. When parents lose this moral battle, their children may change their own normal behavior to correspond with the abnormal behavior the educators support.

Control of schools by parents of the children results in parents' active involvement in their education. When local control is tempered by nationwide standards, the quality of the schooling can be improved. Therefore, a balance between the desires of the parents and the requirements of the nation has to be achieved. Section E. of Chapter XIII in Part B of this book contains further suggestions about a practical school curriculum.

L. Sharing of Freedoms in a Democracy

In Chapter I of this book, government was defined as the means by which the relationships between and among people are arranged and maintained. ***In an "ideal" democracy, the responsibilities, duties and limits of government are determined by its citizens.*** Although the freedom of citizens with a democratic government may seem unlimited to people under dictatorships, there are many limitations to their freedom. Because they share control of their government with others whose systems of values and patterns of behavior vary, they must give up some of their freedom so others can have some freedom.

For example, members of a family who enjoy repairing motor vehicles at home have to consider their neighbors who are bothered by the noise and the inoperative and unsightly vehicles left to be repaired, including some that are abandoned. Therefore, if automobile mechanics live in residential neighborhoods they must give up the freedom to repair automobiles they do not own at their homes so their neighbors will be free from what they consider an unsightly environment.

This giving up of some freedoms to live in harmony with other citizens must be learned by children as well as by immigrants in a democracy. In teaching about democratic governments, the educators must help people understand

and appreciate this mutually advantageous surrender of some freedom that makes a democratic government successful. The self-centered, egocentric view has to be overcome by this other-concerned ethnocentric attitude.

At the same time that people are adjusting to each others' needs, they must be watchful that the government agency charged with ensuring that the agreed upon rules are followed does not impose its own requirements. Democracies are characterized by individualism. The importance of the individual and the preservation of his or her rights must be kept sacred even though somewhat restricted through consideration of other individuals.

M. Summary

Information in this chapter concerned the learning process that produces an effective adult from the newborn infant — learning that is necessary if the child is to become a healthy, normal human being in any nation. Because behavior in democracies is much more fully controlled by the citizens themselves than under other systems of government, it is essential that special attention be given to the type of enculturation of the child. Two-parent families can be much more successful in transferring sound values to children. Families must be encouraged to produce youths and adults who can assume responsibility for the democratic governing process as well as become successful participants in the free market, capitalistic economy.

Children must learn the type of respect that results in people giving up some of their freedom to make it possible for their neighbors who differ from them to share with them the rewards of freedom their country has made possible. Public media and government educational and welfare programs for families must encourage two-parent families and assist them in transferring the principles of self improvement through hard work and free enterprise that make democracy successful. Immigrants need special attention to help them learn how to function successfully in a democracy because their beliefs and patterns of behavior usually differ significantly from those of other citizens in democracies.

****

Part B

Practical Suggestions
to Achieve an Ideal Democracy
or Improve The One You
Now Have

The object of government is freedom.

—McGeorge Bundy

The rights of free expression of opinion and of freedom of organization inhere in the very concept of government by consent.

—1951 Planning Commission of India

We have a system that was shrewdly designed to be strong enough for leadership, but in which power was diffuse enough to assure liberty.

—James Reston

[In setting up three branches of government, the founders] purpose was not to avoid friction, but, by means of the inevitable friction incident to the distribution of the governmental powers among three departments, to save the people from autocracy.

—Louis D. Brandeis

The power to tax is the power to destroy.

—John Marshall

Chapter IX.
A Review of the Objectives of This Book

The first objective of this book is to assist readers in understanding democracy along with some of the relationships between democracy and the variables that are so critical to its success. The second objective is to provide suggestions as to how democracies may be established in countries that do not have this form of government, or how to strengthen and maintain democracies in those countries already having some form of democratic government, including the older democracies. The discussions in the first eight chapters in Part A are designed to highlight the issues faced in democracies that affect the success or failure of democratic processes. Part B contains practical suggestions for developing the essential government and business structures of a democracy as well as for establishing the system of beliefs and way of life needed by the citizens in a democracy.

It is indicated in Part A of this book that ***an ideal democracy cannot exist without free enterprise and that capitalism and democracy reinforce one another.*** Dangers to democracy in the form of an uncontrolled military, excessive government regulations and an ever-expanding bureaucracy are discussed as are the issues of religion and population size. The problem of overcoming the human tendency to control others and the necessity for people without democratic experience to learn what democracy is and how it functions are presented.

Although ideas and suggestions about how to build new democracies and improve those already in existence may be gleaned from the presentations in Part A, more specific recommendations are given in this Part of the book. What is presented are suggestions as to what may be done to speed the transformation to a democracy from other types of government and to improve older democracies. Included are some of the actions that should be avoided along with possible problems that have to be solved. These suggestions are provided to enable those working to establish or improve democracies to obtain ideas that will prove helpful to them. The real value to those promoting or strengthening democracies, however, may be for recognizing opportunities already present for overcoming obstacles and to take advantage of positive factors in their countries that can come from reading this book.

It is the adaptation and adjustment to the special social and economic conditions found in their own countries where the concepts presented here will make the most significant contribution to their efforts. With adequate knowledge of what is involved in promoting democracies, the citizen leaders of each nation can make a difference in the designing and/or operating of a successful and long-lasting, participative democratic republic.

****

The will of the people is the only legitimate foundation of any government, and to protect its free expression should be our first objective.

—*Thomas Jefferson*

The whole purpose of democracy is that we may hold counsel with one another, so as not to depend upon the understanding of one man, but to depend upon the counsel of all. For only as men are brought into counsel, and state their own needs, and interests, can the general interests of a great people be compounded into a policy suitable to all.

—*Woodrow Wilson*

Freedom is the coin of the realm, in the kingdom of human worth and dignity, and the coin has two sides. On one side are inscribed the rights and privileges of free men. On the other side are the responsibilities. Unless both sides are genuine and deeply cut, the coin is counterfeit.

—*P. E. Kay*

Liberty, when it begins to take root, is a plant of rapid growth.

—*George Washington*

The will of the people is the best law.

—*Ulysses S. Grant*

Democracy is something we must always be working at. It is a process never finished, never ending. And each new height gained opens broader vistas for the future.

—*Edmund de S. Brunner*

. . .Applied science and invention have influenced the life of the individual, the development of industry, the evolution of political societies and the course of history.

—*Glenn T. Seaborg*

Chapter X.
Sources of Advice

Leaders in new democracies will discover that there are many people in the older democracies willing to offer them advice. Although many of these potential advisors do provide sound counsel, careful evaluation of their experience and their motives is necessary to ensure that sound, workable solutions are offered by them. Academic type advisors should be used with considerable caution because university faculty, particularly in the United States, operate in a subsidized and protected environment foreign to private enterprise. Although boards of trustees and presidents of universities have authority over them and technically could fire them for gross malfeasance, in fact, senior faculty who have acquired life tenure no longer really have to be accountable to anyone, and this is not a good example of how democracies function.

Marxism still has a large number of adherents among educators in older democracies. For example, more than 2,000 of them participated in an extensive conference at the University of Massachusetts in the United States in the fall of 1992. Represented were a number of professions, but most of them were economists, philosophers and other specialists from universities. The collapse of the Soviet Union's Marxist economy and the triumph of capitalism in the western world seems to have strengthened the determination of these educators to spread their discredited Marxist ideology. Leaders in democracies must make sure Marxists like these are not invited to provide advice to their governments or to teach in their educational institutions even though they may be faculty members of major universities in the older democracies.

Some individuals and organizations consider countries where governments are undergoing change, as an opportunity to further their own objectives by offering advice and training. If they sincerely desire to foster democracy and understand the people and the situation in the country they hope to assist, they can be helpful. Unfortunately, however, there are organizations and individuals in the older democracies whose goal is to further world socialism rather than democracies based on capitalistic principles. Their advice and training may lead to the preparation of people to resist private enterprise and to rebel against democratic governments. Frequently, such people carry credentials indicating connections to, or positions in, organizations such as government agencies, labor unions, political parties, foundations or universities. If these types of people establish branches of their organizations and train and guide citizens in new countries, undesirable and tragic consequences for the governments may be the result.

Another type of advisor may seem especially attractive to leaders in the developing democracies because they do not cost anything and because they are government employees in the older democracies. Logically, it might seem that because they represent successful democracies their advice would be very useful. Unfortunately, this may not be true because most government employees have had little or no experience in the private sector, and they are likely to be participants in an inefficient and ineffective bureaucracy.

Also, government employees tend to be socialistically inclined and like to spend extensive time drawing up master plans for running a nation. This is the type of advice and assistance developing democracies cannot afford because it contradicts the fundamental objectives of a democracy. ***New democracies must maximize private enterprise and should be wary of advice from people who have not had experience in business.*** Similarly, government employees should be avoided because they tend to offer armchair guidance and come up with extensive plans which usually only duplicate their own large, expensive and ineffectual bureaucracies.

Advisors should be individuals whose experiences

are closely related to the conditions in the country that is using them. For example, a banker from a rural area of an older democracy was sent to a country to assist in developing credit for farmers. The response he received from the rural people was very positive. They said they had never known any banker who actually came out to their farms and talked with them about their farming operations and credit needs. After he left, however, the advisors who replaced him stayed in the central office of the bank and made recommendations based on the extensive training in banking they had without knowing or considering the practical aspects of farming.

Owners of urban businesses as well as farms and other agricultural businesses in new democracies have a serious need for banking institutions. Financial institutions must recognize the special needs of these owners and must provide amounts of credit and arrange repayment requirements that suit the situation rather than to rely on guidelines found in conventional banking textbooks.

Citizens expect their new democratic government and free enterprise capitalistic system to solve their social and economic problems quickly. Unfortunately, even sound government policy and programs that fail to improve the level of living and quality of life in the short term can be very discouraging to citizens. Therefore, it is imperative that the best possible guidance be obtained. Attention to the information presented in the rest of this book may help leaders in the developing democracies choose consultants with experience and training directly related to their needs. The publisher of this book, the College of Democracy, a private, independent and non-governmental institution, may be contacted for suggestions of individuals and organizations that may provide valuable counsel.

****

One eye-witness is of more weight than ten hearsays.

—Titus Maccius Plautus

While democracy must have its organization and controls, its vital breath is individual liberty.
—*Charles Evans Hughes*

The constitution preserves our liberty by providing that all of those given authority to make policy are directly accountable to the people through regular elections. —*John Marshall*

Most of us don't understand that we will get just as bad government as we are willing to stand for and just as good government as we are willing to fight for.
—*Luther Youngdahl*

The liberty of the press is essential to the security of the state. —*John Adams*

Advert, sir, to the duties of a judge he has to pass between the government and the man whom that government is prosecuting; between the most powerful individual in the community, and the poorest and most unpopular....The Judicial Department comes home in its effect to every man's fireside; it passes on his property, his reputation, his life, his all. Is it not, to the last degree important, that he should be rendered perfectly and completely independent, with nothing to influence or control him but God and his conscience?
—*John Marshall*

Chapter XI.
Issues In the Establishment and Maintenance of Democratic Governments

A. Initial Elections and Constitutions

The first thing that usually happens when people in a country decide that they should change their government to a democracy, is to have an election. Sometimes, however, they first design a constitution which is a written document describing the objectives of the government and how the government will be organized. Both of these actions are necessary but insufficient by themselves to establish a democratic representative form of government. Plans described in a carefully worded constitution may not be followed and an election may be a method of manipulating the people by dictatorial leaders to justify their authority. Nevertheless, ***an election may be the only first practical step toward democracy.***

Earlier chapters have made the point that democracy, or any other type of government, is not a natural phenomenon. The men and women who take leadership roles in promoting democracy in countries that have not enjoyed that type of government very seldom have sufficient knowledge or understanding of what a democracy is or what must accompany it to make it successful. Practical participation in democratic processes can help new leaders acquire these skills. However, because of this serious deficiency, many such leaders may not be willing to accept the changes that must come with an effective, representative democracy.

Therefore, a first step forward in a potential democracy is for those taking leadership roles to learn what is involved in having a democracy and to adjust their systems of value so that they really can support it. Unless this learning takes place, either the democratic efforts will be destroyed or replaced with leaders who can accept the democratic way and/or by the citizens who no longer want to be subjects, or by the rule of a dictator, or a committee of dictators.

A democratic government is a government of laws derived from the Constitution of the nation. Therefore, legal scholars in a country should be stimulated to develop Common Law for their nation based on their new Constitution and not in isolation from it. Current members of the judicial branch of the government should be oriented or retrained to replace old common law concepts with decisions based on their Constitution. Faculty of law schools should immediately begin to educate future members of the judiciary to derive their decisions from a modern constitutionally sound Common Law rather than to rely on their society's former nondemocratic customs and conventions that had made up the previous fundamental law of the land. For example, if the Constitution of the country guarantees to citizens the right to have their own religion, laws prohibiting this cannot be invoked. Whereas Common Law before the Constitution might have justified such laws, Common Law after the Constitution cannot.

When formulating the new Common Law, it should be recognized that there is no such thing as "natural law" for humans. There are authors who claim there is a prehistoric "natural law" derived from, or imposed by, nature or a divine entity. The sources and manifestations of their "natural law," however, vary in accordance with their cultural background, particularly their religious beliefs. Thus, what they consider "natural law" has been constructed by humans and differs from one authority to another and one society to another. Actually, when "natural law" is considered the law of nature, its stipulations would range from survival of the fittest to the symbiotic relationships among many plants and animals who survive through essential inherent cooperative functioning.

For animals, then, "natural law" varies from one species to another. For humans the type of "natural law" from which common law is derived, according to some authors, is dependent on the learned beliefs and patterns of behavior people developed as various societies evolved their cultures.

The formation of Common Law from the Constitution in a new democracy will be a cumulative process by which legal decisions become precedents for legal decisions that follow. These early decisions, as well as those that follow must adhere to stipulations of the Constitution. The judiciary should discuss these openly as should legal scholars, particularly during the training of lawyers.

Democratic constitutions must require that law enforcement officers and the courts consider the accused to be innocent until proven guilty or found not guilty through due process of law, as all such constitutions should. Those former common law practices that stipulated that the accused be banished to prison or executed without trial must be changed. What happened to a soldier who was accused by South Korean officers during the Korean War of stealing a pair of boots, illustrates the conflict between two systems of justice.

Although South Korean officers agreed with officers of other countries composing the United Nations Armed Forces that a court martial proceeding against the accused prisoner would take place, the soldier was summarily shot after being forced to dig his own grave. When asked about the court martial procedure they had just agreed to and the execution that had already taken place, the officers exclaimed, "Of course we are going to conduct it as soon as we get time." The usual procedure of assuming guilt and rendering punishment, in this case, executing the assumed guilty individual, had not yet replaced the judicial procedure of determining whether or not the accused was actually guilty.

Without adequate and timely training, old ways will prevail and the words in the Constitution expressing the rights of citizens and the functions of government, no matter how noble, will not become the foundation for the law of any democracy.

When the Constitution is written, it should be constructed by representatives of all segments of the nation's population. Its authors should keep in mind that if designed carefully, it is an instrument that stipulates how the government is to function. In reality, it creates, organizes and defines the functions of government — the judicial, legislative and executive branches — and how they relate to one another. In addition, it must ensure that the judicial can act in a completely independent manner. If the Constitution guarantees control by leaders of the government, as with a one-party political system, and restricts or prohibits the influence of the rest of the citizens, the nation for which it is written can never become a democracy until it is revised to guarantee citizen control of the government.

Along with a blueprint for operating the government, the Constitution must include procedures by which the branches of the government — legislative, executive and judicial, will work together and share the power of governing. Each must be able to carry on its legitimate functions and at the same time be empowered to resist encroachment of the others into areas not stipulated in the Constitution. Known in democracies as the "Checks and Balances," such rules prevent one branch from becoming more powerful than was intended in the Constitution.

A democracy is a government by the people and for the people. Therefore, the Constitution must contain a clearly written, definite statement about the rights of citizens and how they are to be protected from their government. Protected from their government means that people are free to speak, assemble, vote, write and publish their opinions and appeal government actions in the courts. These essential rights of the people, called a "Bill of Rights," should be written into the Constitution rather than added to it as amendments.

To design a Constitution is not easy if there are large cultural variations among the citizens. As has been suggested, all segments of the population must be included if their Constitution is to reflect the desires of the citizens. When invited to discuss the constitution, representatives of each cultural subgroup in the nation should be informed that the Constitution will be the basis for their democracy, that ***in a democracy it is essential for people to compromise — to adjust their demands out of respect for the demands of others.***

People will come to a meeting on the Constitution with different ideas as to what a democracy is. A first step in writing a constitution would be for each one willing to speak to describe their concept of democracy and for these to be made available for everyone to read and discuss. A second step would be to have participants describe the dangers to democracy they want to avoid. From these two activities should come a consensus about democracy that will be a major contribution to progress in writing the Constitution.

The constitutions of the older democracies as well as the younger ones should be made available to everyone participating in designing the Constitution for the new democracy. Being able to criticize sections of other constitutions will tend to release some of the hostility participants may have for other participants whose ideas differ widely from theirs and thus lead to a more constructive approach for arriving at decisions for the new Constitution. It should be remembered that democratic governments are functioning under the constitutions being reviewed. Therefore, becoming familiar with their provisions can be very useful to those writing a new Constitution.

It is important to emphasize again that the key to designing an effective Constitution for a democracy is the involvement of citizens representing the varied cultures of the country. The actual drafting of the Constitution, however, must be done by a committee of concerned individuals large enough in number to ensure that minority interests are represented, but small enough to make it possible for its members to reach agreement on the words that appear in it. Between five and ten members for the committee is suggested.

The Committee should be made up of members dedicated to democracy sufficiently to respect the varied desires of the citizens in their nation. They should be statespersons who appreciate the necessity of preparing a document that will become a permanent set of rules for their nation, yet provide a means for adjusting its provisions in accordance with needs of the citizens in the future. The words and phrases in constitutions being designed should be simple and understandable and not composed to impress academicians with their complexity. A democracy is "of the people." So too, should be the Constitution.

A constitution cannot be a means of justifying

majority control at the expense of minorities. Therefore, the provisions of the Constitution must be decided by a majority such as by a two-thirds or three-fourths vote of the representatives or delegates to the conference where the Constitution is designed. Also, all amendments to the Constitution after it has been approved, whether they change its provisions or add new ones, must be decided by a similar vote. If this is done, members of the minorities who comprise the necessary one-third or one-fourth of the population and of the representatives in the nation's legislature, can be confident that their interests will be protected.

Leaders of small minorities (less than one-third or one-fourth), may need to join others as well as to induce repre-sentatives of the majority to support their interests. Otherwise, they will not have much influence in the government. For example, if there are several minorities that by joining together comprise 40 percent of the country's population, the 60 percent majority would not be able to decide stipulations of the Constitution under a two-thirds or three-fourths requirement. Nor could they change the Constitution later in a manner that would favor their interests to the detriment of minority interests.

A technique that has been successful in a number of countries is to have minority interests represented by an individual or individuals already internationally recognized for their integrity. Such highly respected people usually are religious leaders or are widely known as authors or performing artists. When they support a cause, well known celebrities will be listened to and may influence many people to join them in supporting it. This can change the number of legislators or citizens in favor of the cause from a minority to a majority.

B. Ameliorating Critical Differences Among the Citizens of a Nation

In many countries there are segments of the population whose members feel very strongly that their beliefs should not be dominated by those differing from them and that the land they occupy or their section of a country should not come under control of others. They can be very hostile to a central government that they feel they do not control. These ideological differences can result in serious problems if members of the groups that do not share the same views are not willing to adjust some of their ideas to allow those differing from them to meet some of their special needs. Unfortunately, cultural variations among citizens in a country who are not willing to cooperate with others in solving their problems can lead to armed conflicts.

The United States was very fortunate during its early years because it operated as a confederacy of 13 states beginning in 1781 as is indicated on pages 122-125 of *The Evolution of a Democracy* referred to on page iii of this book. While a confederacy, the central or national government was very weak. Ethnocentric strong-minded people in the states operated their own governments without feeling dominated by their federal government. This type of independence lasted long enough for leaders of the states to appreciate the necessity to have a strong national government.

Thus, when the United States Constitution was written six years later as a substitute for the Articles of Confederation, and put into effect, people were ready to accept a federal government. Conflicts among the states would have made it almost impossible for all 13 to unite under a powerful central government immediately after leaders of the confederacy declared the independence of their new country from England. It is recognized, however, that cultural differences among people in some of the new democracies today are greater than those among the states during the early years of the United States. The majority of people in that part of North America from which this new country was formed more than 200 years ago had the advantage of having originated in countries that were semi-democracies with similar common law.

In the light of the United States experience, it is not surprising that issues of cultural diversity lead to bloodshed in some new democracies where previously totalitarians controlled the ethnic, religious, or nationality subgroups before democratic government was initiated. After the totalitarian authority is desolved, the freedom provided by democratic processes may encourage resistance to a centralized government, perhaps because of the fear that such a government might also become totalitarian. If the numbers of people in subgroups are sufficiently large, and their members are not willing to compromise their beliefs to the extent necessary for them to cooperate with their neighbors in a common government, devastating civil wars can erupt.

The objective of citizens in democracies should be to design their government in a manner so that significant groups of citizens may continue to maintain their ethnocentric beliefs in such a way that this does not endanger existence of their nation. For example, after a devastating civil war, Nigerian leaders divided their country into 19 states, with the hope that this would give the various ethnic peoples a feeling that they had a fair share of power in the national government. This division did not prevent leaders in some of the Nigerian states with similar values from joining together to control the government at the expense of other people in the nation. Instead of sharing power with representatives of all 19 states, this ethnocentrism tended to undermine the purposes of the division. Following a second division into 20 states they found their ability to govern was still difficult. Nigerian leaders then made a further division of their country into 30 states. They now hope that this will be a workable solution and the issue of cultural variations will gradually become unimportant as representatives of the citizens of each of the 30 states gain experience working together on national problems.

This ethnocentric problem has to be considered at the very beginning of a new democracy by all the parties together because cultural diversity can destroy the country. A majority group must not attempt to subdue other groups with a national government they control. Instead, a plan must be followed that stipulates how each can function with considerable independence. It may be necessary for each to be a separate country, a course followed when the Soviet Union collapsed. Because China has such a large geographical area, huge population and great diversity in agriculture and industry, its citizens might be served better by a confederation of independent provinces, each with its own government, than by today's distant centralized government.

The Soviet Union, however, had been created from independent states. Therefore, the return to their original independence for the 12 countries resulted in internal conflicts in only a few of them. When it becomes necessary for a country to be divided, the preferred arrangement for each is to constitute a government for its own geographical area that is somewhat independent but still remains a significant part of a whole nation. This confederation type of cooperation can work if each functions as a democracy, but not if one decides to be a theocracy or dictatorship. An advantage of a confederation may be that each may have resources the others need, such as industrial capacity, agricultural lands, or natural resources like water, ores and oil.

Unfortunately, it is difficult for some geographical areas of countries to be economically independent. Therefore, if all parts are to be prosperous, their economies must be integrated. In fact, the economies of some countries are so specialized that their citizens cannot be prosperous unless their economic enterprises are linked with those in nearby countries. One may have the natural resources and another may have the facilities to process them. Some countries must receive products they need and send products they produce through other countries because of their locations. A confederation or community of independent nations can help improve the economic conditions of all of them.

It is difficult to use the separate country method of solving ethnic conflicts when people claiming strong ethnocentric differences live among each other. A representative quota type of approach may be followed when this situation exists. In this, it is recognized that cultural variables among the people are serious enough to justify allocating the number of representatives each can elect as legislators in accordance with the number of people in each group. At the same time, the education of children and continuing education of adults must emphasize that ***in a democracy power is***

shared and issues are settled by concessions made by the parties involved.

In summary, if it becomes necessary for people in a nation to divide their land into more than one country, they should form a permanent bond with each other through which they can assist one another, particularly in the economic sphere. This action is important because people in sections of countries that want to become, or already have been made independent, frequently do not have the range of resources necessary for their citizens to be prosperous.

C. Conflict Resolution

The objective of this section is to explore some of the underlying causes of conflicts among humans. To begin with, ***there is less conflict between individuals and between groups of people in the world now than there has been in centuries.*** This conclusion may not seem to be true because knowledge of conflicts almost anywhere in the world is widely circulated through modern communication technology. We quickly learn about fighting that occurs as communist guerrillas attempt to overthrow governments by subjecting villages to their control in countries like Peru and the Philippines, for example. We have day to day reports of ethnic and religious factions attacking one another in some new democracies. This constant flow of news about unhappy events, may lead us to conclude erroneously that the majority of the peoples on our globe are constantly involved in catastrophic conflicts.

Until recent times, the history of human beings is a history of conflicts among them. Almost everywhere in the world in pre-modern times, people were fighting each other in an organized manner. The conflicts involved leadership, territorial and property disputes and/or religious beliefs; that is, one group trying to take land from another or property such as scarce minerals, or even wives, or people trying to capture other people for slavery or to annihilate others because their religious beliefs conflicted. Disagreements were not just between nations but also between families, small bands of people, tribes, villages and cities. Fighting, either for defense or as an aggressor, was a regular activity and part of the values people passed on from generation to generation for thousands of years.

The primary occupation for males in many societies was fighting, while leisure time was devoted to telling war stories and preparing arms and battle plans. Status as a male was obtained best through military exploits. Violence, including torturing and murdering men, women and children, was a gratifying activity for which individuals were praised.

Why has there been a reduction in this type of behavior and a change in the amount of conflict in the world and what does it take to stop conflicts from occurring? These are questions best answered through an understanding of the causes of conflicts as well as how adjustments among peoples have actually taken place. One example of conflict reduction that has happened over a period of about 200 years, involves the Western Arctic and Subarctic Region of North America.

The Arctic area, almost barren of trees, was the home to Inuit people commonly known as Eskimos. Just south of them lived various tribes of Indians. These two groups, although they did some trading, were enemies who fought numerous battles over use of hunting and fishing territories. The last major battle occurred during the early part of this 20th century. The victors stood the frozen bodies of the vanquished in a row on the snow and ice of the frozen mighty MacKenzie River forming a line across which the other was never to cross without further deadly violence.

Today, representatives of these groups, some old enough to remember the former violence, live together in villages without any organized fighting between them. Both Eskimos and Indians have gone through an acculturation process. The author described this at an international congress of ethnological and anthropological sciences at Moscow State University in 1964 during an unusual, but short, peaceful interval in the Cold War. A typical pattern of acculturation — one society adopting the technology, ways of meeting needs and beliefs of another more powerful society — begins when explorers enter an area. Explorers are soon followed by traders who buy and sell to the people. Right behind the traders go the missionaries to convert the population to the missionaries' religions. Then, to protect the missionaries, police posts are established. The indigenous people then find themselves under pressure from the traders and missionaries to substitute the new technology and beliefs for their own. If they resist, the police are there to subdue them.

This same sequence of events has occurred in many areas of the world including the Western Arctic and Subarctic region of Canada. The explorer, Sir Alexander MacKenzie, traveled west in northern North America, that later became Canada, and then north up a large river to the Arctic. The MacKenzie River, named after the explorer, became a means by which traders moved into the area to obtain fur from the Indians and Eskimos. Catholic missionaries followed to save the "heathen" Indians from their native religions that were in harmony with their physical environment. When Catholic priests met resistance from the people, police moved in to protect them. Later, Protestant missionaries traveled to the Arctic to compete with the Catholics in converting Eskimos to their faith. Soon the national government established offices to administer the area and impose its justice system.

As representatives of the two Christian religions destroyed the Indian and Eskimo religion by substituting their own, church leaders became accustomed to existing side by side and soon stopped openly competing with each other for converts. With their conversion to Christian beliefs, the native peoples no longer physically fought one another although they tended to live in different parts of settlements. Indians primarily were Catholics and most Eskimos tended to be Protestants. The two groups had separate churches, schools, hospitals and cemeteries.

The effect of the church leaders' policies, backed by police power and national government programs of welfare, has destroyed, in addition to their religions, the former roles of men, women and children who had functioned together while obtaining a living from the environment. This process has essentially eliminated the organized conflict between two peoples and has resulted in individuals, particularly men and youth, having to seek new ways to occupy their time and compensate for loss of status in their society. This was caused by the society becoming largely dependent on a distant government for the livelihood of the people rather than on the resources of the local environment as was previously true.

In the case of the Arctic Eskimos and the Subarctic Indians, organized conflict was resolved, but their culture, that is, the original way of life of both Eskimos and Indians, was destroyed. This example of what happened in the Western Arctic of Canada was given because it is the method that has reduced or eliminated conflicts between indigenous groups of people in many parts of the world. That is, a nation or group of people with a superior military technology conquers all the independent nations or groups of people living in an area. When it is completed, this action makes the world more peaceful, but in doing so it destroys hundreds of small societies.

One way to stop local conflicts therefore, is for a national government to apply sufficient control, usually with a police force, to keep the adversaries from fighting each other. This method also is being used on an international basis by countries under sponsorship of the United Nations, as when Iraq invaded Kuwait and was repulsed by a military force from many countries. Another example involved United Nations approved military action in Somalia designed to prevent War Lords from interfering with the provision of food for starving people.

Although it is being tried on conflicts between factions of citizens within countries, such action poses serious disadvantages because it involves interfering in the internal affairs of countries. The disadvantage of interfering in a country's domestic affairs has to be weighed against the advantages of stopping people from killing and torturing one another. It is expected, however, that the reduction or elimination of armed conflict within countries, when it occurs, will be accomplished by United Nations' sanctioned actions more in the future than it has been in the past. Such military intervention will be instigated more frequently as the number of democracies increases in the world. This will be true because of the positive value placed on human life by people in the democratic countries in the United Nations. They will insist that efforts be increased to reduce violations of human rights.

External military action can be especially important when there are internal conflicts during the early stages of democratic government formation. ***If members of ethnic groups in new democracies vying with each other for control can be kept from killing each other and destroying each other's property long enough, the chances of settling their differences without violence increases substantially.*** People then can get along with each other better because reasoning begins to take the place of emotional reactions. Irrational behavior is changed to rational behavior through acquisition of knowledge about and experience with adversaries. ***Action as the result of the use of the brain must replace action based on emotions if conflicts are to be resolved without violence.*** When individuals or groups of people bitterly oppose one another, it takes time for them to reduce their emotional excitement to the point where they can understand and appreciate the position of their opponents.

In beginning to understand why some conflicts may occur between two or more people, interactional patterns should be examined. For people to get along well with each other, an interactional equilibrium between them has to be established that is satisfactory to both. This process can be diagrammed by recording conversations of individuals to learn whether or not they are synchronized or in conflict with one another.

The interactional equilibrium diagram shown in Part 1 of Figure 5 on the next page records a conversational pattern between Individual A and Individual B who meet each other and begin a conversation. During the early stages of their discussion their talking conflicts; that is each tries to talk at the same time. If one of them is talking and the other one interrupts by also talking, the first one soon is likely to become angry. Similarly, if the second is talking and the first one tries to talk at the same time, the second one may become angry. In the diagram an X is used to indicate each time the two individuals' conversations conflict.

Part 2 of Figure 5 is a diagram of the interaction of two people who have synchronized their talking so that they share the time about equally and do not conflict. Of course, it is possible, as Part 3 shows, for one person to accept the dominance of another while interacting without becoming angry, but this is not what usually happens. Individual A in Part 3 is likely to be egocentric. Such

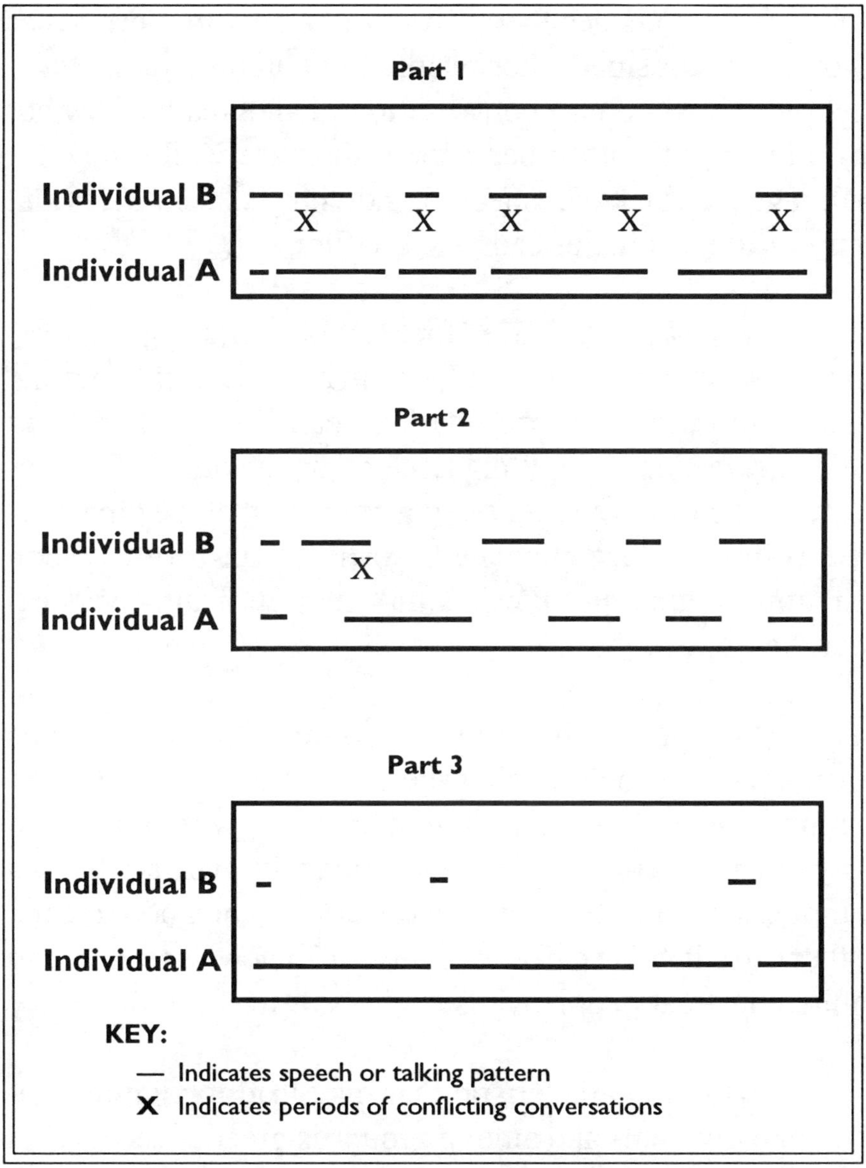

Figure 5. Interactional Equilibrium Diagrams

individuals consider themselves to be very important, or worse yet, consider other people to be unimportant. Most people who dominate conversations do not realize how out of adjustment with other people they are while they are talking. This lack of respect for individuals, their ideas and way of life is a major cause of conflict.

When a person's need for recognition during a conversation is not met by those with whom he or she is interacting, the person prevented from talking can become frustrated and may respond by talking louder than the others. Frustration can be followed by a feeling of distrust of the others. If the distrust is not alleviated, hostility can result. Soon shouting erupts and the hostility may turn into physical conflict.

A second cause of conflict is ethnocentrism. Groups of people who believe that their rights to land and other property as well as their religion or ideology is superior to any other, are ethnocentric. Unfortunately, even a religious empire in which followers are exhorted to be good to each other can still be an evil empire in light of how its leaders and adherents treat people whose beliefs differ from theirs.

A third characteristic that may lead to fighting between individuals and among groups is greed. One attacks the other to acquire the territory or possessions of the other.

Any of these reasons can lead to vicious behavior on the part of one person or group toward others. When egoism, ethnocentrism and greed are combined in the beliefs and actions of one person or group of persons, the treatment of people by them can be inhuman. Widespread torturing, killing and devestation, without regard to age, gender or guilt, may be rendered on those thought to be enemies.

Humans being devastated by other humans may be considered so inferior by those doing the torturing and killing that they are relegated to non- human status. As such, they pose no moral problems to aggressors. Instead, those considering themselves superior believe they are improving the human specie by eradicating inferior beings. When seen as a duty to their god or ideology to rid the world of nonbelievers, infidels to them, they believe they will be rewarded on earth for their behavior as well as in their after-life. During the last two hundred years, people who still were using stone tools have been slaughtered like animals to enable immigrants to acquire their lands. Men were proud of their killing, as in Tasmania where European intruders would pile up bodies of natives they had killed during a Saturday hunt.

Combined in the brains of men like Hitler, Mussolini, Lenin, Stalin and Hirohito was the unfortunate combination of egoism, ethnocentrism and greed. Each wanted to conquer most of the world or all of it and use resources of the controlled lands for their own purposes. In addition to considering themselves superior, they believed their ethnic type of people and their ideology should dominate all others regardless of how many people would have to be killed to achieve that objective.

In discussing how to resolve conflicts or prevent them, it is easy to suggest that: 1) people will get along better if they get to know one another better; 2) children and adults should learn to be tolerant of one another; 3) people should improve their negotiating skills; 4) individuals must adjust their goals in respect for those of others; 5) people should be cognizant of results of their bitterness toward others and amend their ways to reduce conflict; and 6) those who tend to dominate while conversing or in their actions need to realize the negative affect it has on most people and stop doing it. These adjustments have and are being made by some people, and conflicts have been and are being reduced because of them.

The type of conflicts that may be ameliorated by the changes in human behavior just suggested, although common, however, are of a minor nature in terms of loss of life and suffering that result from inter-ethnic or inter-ideological disagreements. For example, a person can learn to get along with those with whom he or she differs without fighting if their basic beliefs are similar. Likewise, by applying negotiating skills, labor union leaders and management representatives can reach agreement on issues of concern to them without shutting down factories. Education also can lead to less conflict because there seems to be a direct relationship between the amount of secular schooling of individuals and their tolerance for others, as well as their willingness to resolve differences with people without resorting to violence.

The intensity of hatred between people who differ in their fundamental ideologies and have not had the education and experiences that would have increased their tolerance and understanding of each other is not easy to overcome. For instance, in South Africa members of the communist-backed, socialistic African National Congress (ANC) believe so strongly in their cause that they are unwilling to accept equal participation in government of other segments of the population in their country. To counter the inhumanity of ANC actions against individuals whom they believe oppose them, members of Inkatha, another major segment that is not backed by communists, retaliate with similar actions. Killing and torturing representatives of each of these organizations by the other would have been much more extensive if the "white" government had not attempted to stop it. Instead of cooperating with the existing government officials, the ANC has resisted the formation of a democracy in which all ethnic groups in the population would be represented.

Leaders of the ANC have not been willing to work with the leaders of the other groups because they do not believe the proposed new government would be as socialistic as they want it to be. Furthermore, they would have to share control. Other leaders, including the Inkatha have been more willing to participate with their neighbors in planning a new democracy. Only when the ANC and Inkatha, whites and others finally come to realize that a representative democracy is more important to them than their own ethnocentric goals will South Africa achieve a government of all the people.

The South African situation in the 1990s is similar to what has been happening in a number of countries where, for example, fundamental religious beliefs are adhered to so strongly that any opposition to them, and in some instances, just the existence of nonbelievers, is met with vicious attacks designed to eliminate the "enemies" by killing them or forcing them to move away. There is little concern for human life; rather, the religious beliefs are used to justify eradicating nonbelievers, frequently, the more gruesome the slaughter the more rewarding its undertaking seems to be to the true adherents.

The question of concern in this section is how can such awful treatment of one group of people by another be prevented? If conflicts are occurring within a nation and are not caused by the people who operate the government, the local police forces may be used to prevent the antagonists from attempting to destroy one another. When the problem is between leaders of nations, joint military action to separate the two by a number of countries under auspices of the United Nations has been demonstrated to be effective. As has been suggested, such United Nations action is expected to be used, when necessary, much more frequently in the future. This united peace-keeping military action can be undertaken quickly and effectively as long as there is a benevolent superpower in the world and/or major countries remain friendly and support one another in reasonable cooperative peace-keeping endeavors.

The real problem in resolving conflicts within a country concerns two factions opposing one another without a common strong central government to control them. If the United Nations, or any nation, intervenes, it can be charged with interfering in the internal affairs of the troubled country. Such interference has long been considered unlawful unless it is invited by the country involved. Although all the methods available to stop international and intranational fighting involve serious questions about relations among countries, the trend is toward resolving such conflicts with external force.

With a larger and larger proportion of the people in the world learning to respect individual freedom and to value human life, including their own, it is expected that humans will not stand by doing nothing while horrible

atrocities are taking place in other countries. There will be intervention in relatively small countries and strenuous objections and economic sanctions against large countries for this type of behavior.

The optimistic aspect of the advancement of civilization is that the amount of objective knowledge acquired by people in many parts of the world is increasing. By objective, what is meant is observable knowledge, that is, knowledge that comes from studying phenomena. This view contrasts with information that is derived from reading scriptures or quotations attributed to someone who spoke on the basis of what they thought was true rather than what was found to be demonstratively true. The replacement of this scholastic method, of deriving knowledge by thinking without observing, with the scientific method leads to less reliance on an abstract force guiding behavior and more attention to reality. When this happens, underlying ethnocentric beliefs dependent for their existence on limited knowledge, are weakened. Taking their place is an understanding and appreciation of other people and the world around them. It is this broadening knowledge that reduces friction among people by increasing tolerance for diverse behavior.

With sound knowledge, the process of reasoning replaces emotions as the determinant of attitudes toward others. With reasoning comes problem-solving on a give

and take negotiation basis rather than by using force to injure and kill one's opponents. To accomplish this goal, a formal educational system for children and young adults is necessary that is not under control of leaders with ideologies that limit individual freedom. Although it takes time to produce generations with the essential flexible mentality, it is occurring now and thus will continue to transform conflict resolutions from armed conflicts to friendly discussions.

D. The Election Process

Citizens choosing people they want to represent them in government is the foundation of democratic government. For a government to function as a democracy, this selection must be done in a manner that provides complete freedom of choice for the citizen. Each individual's voting by secret ballot has served as the technique by which this has been accomplished in the older democracies. An election with secret ballots tends to legitimize those elected. Therefore, it is highly desirable for leaders to be selected by citizens in this way.

The secret ballot that protects people from abuse from those who would not agree with them if they knew how the individuals actually voted, is a critical method by which the people control their democratic governments. The secret ballot method, however, can be subject to abuse that would destroy its function and make a mockery of democracy. Therefore, careful attention must be given to each stage during the voting process to safeguard this essential democratic process. There are at least five parts of the process where fraud can occur.

The first possibility of fraud involves the person who is to vote. Restrictions may be placed on who is allowed to vote by those desiring to influence the outcome of elections. For example, people with certain characteristics may not be allowed to vote such as: 1) women; 2) people who do not own property; 3) individuals who have not lived in the community for an exceedingly long period of time; 4) those who have not paid a voting tax; 5) individuals who are not members of a specific religion; or 6) people who have not joined a certain political party or parties. Such restrictions must be prohibited in democracies.

To force people to vote the way someone wants them to, pressure may be put on them in several ways. Their lives and families may be threatened. They may be promised jobs or other benefits if specified officials are elected. They may be paid for their vote. Also they may be given a ballot already marked to put in the ballot box. Groups of people who are paid for each vote cast may be taken from one location where voting is underway to another location to vote using names of people who have not voted, are deceased but their names are still on the list of voters, or even for fictitious people listed as being qualified to vote. Dictorial leaders, or their representatives, may be present at the voting locations to tell citizens how to vote and to see that they mark their ballots in favor of the leader. Under this type of pressure, voters know that disobeying the leader will result in punishment for them.

A second type of voting fraud involves the ballot itself. People in control may keep the people they do not want elected from becoming candidates. They can do this by establishing requirements for candidacy they know certain potential candidates do not have. Another way is to allow only individuals selected by the ruling government to be candidates, as has been true in communist controlled countries. This ensures that the citizens would vote only for the people already selected for them. In democracies, individuals have the right to be on the ballot for an election if a political party nominates them or when a specified number of citizens sign a petition to have them listed on the ballot even though they have not been nominated by a political party.

Fraud may also occur when names of candidates qualified by such petitions, are left off the ballot, or placed on it in such a way by those in control so as to make it difficult for people to vote for them. Of course, both of these deceptions are illegal in democracies.

The ballot box or voting machine itself is another place where voting fraud can occur. The box may be delivered to the voting location with ballots already in it or the vote tabulating machine may be wired to record multiple votes when a citizen selects certain candidates. After the voting is completed, ballots may be added to the box or recorded on the machine. Ballot boxes with ballots already marked also may be added to those from legitimate voting locations when they are delivered to where they are to be counted. Then, if the people counting the votes are controlled by someone who wants the results to come out in a certain way, their count may reflect this rather than how the citizens actually voted.

Finally, the report of the election may not reflect the actual results. By ruling invalid the votes from certain areas or not allowing the results to be public information, elections may be controlled by people in power. An entire election that does not suit a dictator or ruling group, may be ruled invalid.

In summary, the stress points in voting are:

1. The Citizen — who is allowed to vote.

2. The Ballots — how the ballot is written or arranged in the voting machine.

3. The Ballot Box or Voting Machine — how they are safeguarded to prevent fraud.

4. Counting — how the ballots are counted.

5. Reporting of Results — how results of the voting are reported.

Voting fraud is a serious problem. Leaders who want to control a country know that an election where the peoples' ballots are supposed to be secret, legitimizes those elected. This is especially true in the minds of people who do not know that an election is fraudulent. To have this legitimization is highly desirable, especially for national offices. Therefore, power seeking individuals and groups may resort to fraud to win while proclaiming to the world that they were elected in free elections.

Leaders in democracies must continually strive to prevent voting fraud and not allow unfair elections to be a front for dictator-type leaders. Citizens must be confident that their votes are secret and that their votes will be counted and reported accurately. Therefore, an Election Commission consisting of citizen members is needed that has the responsibility to investigate any type of fraud and declare elections invalid when necessary.

A procedure to reduce election fraud that has proven

effective in many countries has been to have officials from foreign countries present during the elections. By allowing individuals from other countries to observe the election process, particularly the actual voting by citizens as well as the counting of ballots, manipulation of the election by unethical leaders can be significantly reduced. When observers include imminent world leaders such as former President of the United States Jimmy Carter, the positive effect on the honesty of election officials and thus the validity of the results of the voting are greatly enhanced.

Citizens in democracies are very thankful that distinguished individuals like President Jimmy Carter have been willing to devote their time and prestige to serve as observers of elections in troubled areas of the world. Requests for election observers can be made to The Carter Center in Atlanta, Georgia, United States of America and to the United Nations as well as to organizations established for that purpose in a number of other countries.

E. Political Parties

In totalitarian countries people who want to discuss how their government functions are not allowed to meet with each other to discuss their feelings. Nor are they permitted to express their feelings in speech or writing. When they do, they are punished severely. In democracies quite the contrary is true for it is the joining together of people to criticize their government and to suggest how it can be changed to conform with their desires that epitomizes democratic processes.

A political party consists of an organized group of people involved in the election process for government offices. They are united by common interests, similar beliefs and past experiences, and they agree as to what should be the goals of their government. When citizens of a country form an organization to promote their interests in how their government should be operated and who should be responsible for running it, they have invented a political party.

A political party serves to satisfy the egos of its members because they feel that by joining the party they will have an influential role in their communities and nation. At the same time that membership in a political party is egocentric, that is, centered on the individual, the members develop a feeling that together they are different from nonmembers. This ethnocentricism, or group centered activity, unites them in their efforts to obtain political objectives. The egocentric and ethnocentric feelings are advantageous because the first induces individuals to join others in political activities and the second tends to cause them to adjust their personal beliefs sufficiently to produce the cooperative efforts necessary for a political party to be effective.

On the other hand, both egocentricism and ethnocentrism have disadvantageous aspects in a democracy. Egocentric individuals may exert extraordinary pressure within a political party to further their own personal interests when they acquire leadership positions. The political party then becomes their means for achieving their own ends rather than a democratic process involving all its members.

Ethnocentric pressures also can endanger democratic processes if the political party is operated by professional administrators who ignore the desires of its members. Instead of being representatives of the members — their servants — administrators and party leaders may become independent and use the political party as a means of obtaining their own financial and ideological goals. That is, they present themselves as having the backing of all the party members, and, thus, use the threat of their potential votes to induce legislators, officials in the executive branch of government and the judicial to meet their demands.

Because of the ethnocentric characteristic of groups, members of political parties may become so loyal to the party that they neglect to insert their own independent thinking into its deliberations. For example, a member who strongly advocates family values in his or her daily activities, may support a political party and its candidates who openly violates what he or she stands for. Another person may condemn government interference in private business, yet support his party's candidates who publicly denounce private business and advocate increasing government control of the private sphere. They do this because they cannot vote for members of the other party about whom they have strong negative feelings. Actually, they may have campaigned for years against its candidates.

The most serious threat of a political party to democratic processes is that it may become so powerful that it is a deterent to the formation of other political parties. In a democracy that protects individual's rights of written and spoken expression and of meeting with others who agree with them, it is difficult for one party to prevent the formation of others. When there are two or three major parties, however, their combined control of governmental processes may make it extremely difficult for leaders of another party to increase its membership to the extent necessary for it to become a significant force in influencing government.

Major parties tend to undermine minor parties by adopting the positions of the minor parties programs that have popular appeal to voters. In other words, a small party may have as their objective the reduction of property taxes. If large numbers of citizens begin to support the small party, a major party also will include in its objectives the reduction of property taxes and thus induce those voters who had become interested in the small party to support the major party.

In newer democracies where people have not had extensive experience in freely associating with each other to the point where they can trust those with whom they have not interacted on a face to face basis, they will form numerous political parties. For example, Czechoslovakia at one time had about 40 political parties. When there are a large number of political parties, each with a different agenda for the government, it is very difficult for elected leaders to coordinate their legislative efforts. Most of their time has to be spent in fostering their own objectives and in maneuvering to gain support for their interests from a sufficient proportion of the other legislators. This process of debating and soliciting support, however, is desirable in democracies because it strengthens them. Eventually, these cooperative relationships among political party leaders result in the combining of several parties into one or two.

Political parties, feared by all types of dictatorial rulers, are essential in democracies because they make it possible for individuals to participate in the selection of candidates for elected offices. Political parties are a means by which the interests and concerns of the citizens are made known to the government. This process is accomplished by means of the publicity given to them and by the election of their candidates to governmental offices. Government officials should never do anything to prevent political party formation nor interfere in their functioning. Similarly, government funds or facilities and services should not be used to support political parties. They must receive their support from their members and be independent of the government but still not violate laws of their nation.

In selecting candidates for elected offices, political parties tend to favor individuals trained in law. Because of their knowledge of law, their experience in the practice of law and in articulating issues and their skills of persuasion, attorneys tend to become candidates more than individuals with any other training or background. Because issues legislators must consider are much broader in scope than just law, others, such as business persons, scientists, farmers and medical professionals, should be encouraged to seek office.

Multiple political parties are necessary in democracies because they allow citizens to participate in government where they live while at the same time give members the satisfaction that their participation counts all the way to the national level. Political parties help people learn about critical issues and possible solutions. Also they provide opportunities for people to gain knowledge about their government as well as experience in evaluating solutions to problems. Because of participation in political parties, many individuals are willing to become candidates for office. The widespread involvement of people in political parties deters autocratic and dictatorial leaders from replacing democratic governments.

F. Corruption Controls

Corruption among humans is one of the most widespread maladies. It occurs in all societies and in all nations. It also is extremely difficult to control because it is frequently considered "normal" human behavior both by those benefiting from it and by those suffering from it. Although the variety and degree of corruption varies, every act reflects unsound ethics on the part of the individuals involved and is a danger to the establishment and maintenance of human relations based on respect of one person for another as well as being an unnecessary cost to the society and nation. Although corruption was discussed in Part H of Chapter VII, its importance warrants the additional attention given it here.

Taking or paying bribes is a common form of corruption throughout the world. To comprehend corruption and devise methods of eliminating bribes requires the recognition that there are two types of people in every corrupt act. One of these is the individual who is seeking to personally gain something through the action to which he or she is not entitled. The second type is the individual who is seeking to obtain something through the action that he or she cannot obtain any other way.

In other words, bribery involves a market in which someone has something to sell and someone wants to buy it. It is not a fair market, however, because the briber has to pay more than would be necessary in a free market system or that is stipulated in rules governing the transaction. For example, if an individual or organization needs a permit from the government before a business may be launched or a building constructed, it is very important to that person or organization that the permit be granted in a timely manner and at a cost that is stipulated by the government agency. It costs the permit applicant a considerable amount of money to have to wait for the permit. If it is necessary, therefore, to pay the individual, or individuals, who grant the permit extra money that they personally keep, the briber is likely to pay what is understood to be necessary unless it exceeds the amount that can be afforded. To make the permit more attractive, the bribee may restrict the operations of competitors who want to establish a similar enterprise, thus, creating a monopoly for the one who is willing to pay the bribe.

Unfortunately, this type of bribery corruption frequently does not stop with extra payments. If an individual's values are such that he or she participates in either receiving or paying a bribe, other dishonest practices can follow. For those not willing to pay bribes or who complain, more serious action may be taken against them even though it also is illegal. Property of the person seeking a permit, product or other service may be damaged or destroyed and their lives threatened or taken.

There can be an association between the genuine desire of individuals to improve their economic conditions and corruption because corruption can be accepted by them as a means of meeting their goal. In a free enterprise economy and one where progress is desirable, it is necessary to have individuals who are striving to achieve, and thus to better themselves. If they believe being honest is important, people will not chose unethical ways to meet their achievement goals.

Bribes are not always paid in money. They may be services or favors that are granted by the briber, including sexual activities. For example, to remain in business in one city in which the government was controlled by criminals, small businessmen had to provide their teenage daughters for the pleasure of the men running their city. There are many other types of bribes such as when bribers arrange for bribees to have their pictures taken with high ranking officials, or bribers arrange for roads and utilities to be provided for private property owners, or for criminal offenses to be ignored.

After an election, office holders sometimes reward people who helped them get elected by appointing them to their staffs or helping them to get government jobs. Other supporters may be retained for some purpose, like writing a report, even though the report they prepare may not be needed. The rewards given by elected officials to supporters, known as "payoff," can be legal as well as acceptable ways of carrying out government tasks that need to be done, or they may waste taxpayers funds. To prevent misuse of government monies, legislators cannot be allocated funds for which they are not held accountable. Expenditures of all such funds must be known to the public and carefully audited.

Corruption, whether it be payoffs, bribery, the embezzlement of funds from government or private enterprises, or stealing of property, is done by people with morals, that is values, that are detrimental to the community and nation. Good morals — those that prevent people from taking actions that are unfair to others, and bad morals — those that result in people becoming corrupt, are learned when children are young. This learning, for which the family is the most important source, continues in schools and in neighborhood and community activities. To instill the type of ethics that will keep individuals from being seduced by corruption, parents in families have to be very ethical themselves. In addition, the informal and formal organizations in which children become involved, such as schools, religious institutions and youth groups should reinforce positive ethical values.

Because many parents do not impart honest morals to their children, and schools and other organizations fail their responsibilities, children can come to believe that corruption is a normal activity. Prevention of corruption must be emphasized in democracies, but because prevention frequently is unsuccessful, efforts to detect corruption and punish offenders also must be unrelenting. To accomplish this goal requires continuous monitoring and auditing government activities as well as those in private enterprises. A well-trained and well-paid police force as well as a courageous and dedicated judicial staff are essential. At the same time, citizens must feel free to report bribes and know to whom they can present such evidence as well as be confident that appropriate action will be taken against the offender by the authorities. Direct participation by elected representatives of the people in setting performance standards of the law enforcement and judicial sections of their government is necessary to curb corruption by bribery.

Unfortunately for good government at the local as well as federal levels, corruption in some countries or parts of countries is so rampart that many individuals of high integrity decline to run for public offices. Others who do become elected, leave office in disgust after a few years.

G. Democracy From the Grass Roots to the National Level

To an outsider, older democracies may be viewed as a system of government where citizens only elect national legislators to make laws for the country and perhaps a president to administer them. How these national level officials become elected and how they behave in office is newsworthy on an international basis because of the effect of their actions on world wide affairs. This attention to the top levels in a democratic country may prevent the recognition that elections are occurring for officials at every level right down to the very smallest neighborhoods.

The democratic philosophy is that local problems are best solved by the people who know the most about them and not by a distant government. Therefore, citizens, and there may be only a dozen or so families living in some of the smallest jurisdictions, elect local representatives to decide issues that concern them such as road construction and schools, along with the amount of taxes to pay for them.

A democratic country like the United States contains hundreds of thousands of democracies each having its own operating rules and elected officers. Also a significant part of concerned citizens' time is devoted to participating in organizations run democratically. New democracies need to develop such a pattern from the national level to political subdivisions at the very local "grass roots" of the country. "Grass roots" is a name given to rural settlements distant from the urban center where a national, or major political subdivision of the government has its headquarters.

To illustrate political organizations from the grassroots to the national level, the structure of the jurisdictions in the United States is presented here. Government in the United States has at the national level the Supreme Court, the Legislative Branch with a Senate and a House of Representatives, and an Executive Branch with the President as its top executive. Below those are the 50 state governments, one for each state, the government of the territories and the District of Columbia that are part of the United States.

The next level below the states is the counties, sometimes called parishes, in each state. Townships, smaller in geographical areas, are next. Within the townships are districts. There also are cities within the counties and villages within the townships, although some cities are independent of counties. Within cities there are divisions frequently called wards and in those, precincts.

All of these political entities, except for the wards and precincts, have governments organized and operated by people who live in them. Citizens have responsibilities for electing representatives all the way from their neighborhoods to their nation. People who value their citizenship expect to become involved, at least to the extent of voting, in the neighborhood organization where their residence is located as well as in all other political jurisdictions that apply to them because of where they live. Therefore, they will attend neighborhood meetings, most of which are concerned with the quality of life in their area. They also will vote for neighbors they want to represent them as well as pay the fees assessed by their organizations.

For example, in one geographical area houses were built on rural land that was forested. Soon after the first few families purchased and occupied their homes, the men and women in the neighborhood met in one of their homes to discuss common interests. They decided to obtain a large receptacle into which they all could put their trash and to contract with a trash collecting business to empty it twice a week. Each was assessed their share of the cost. This saved them considerable money that they would have had to spend having the trash collected at their individual homes.

To legitimize their actions and to restrict their personal liability in case their activities harmed someone, such as a child being injured in some way by the trash receptacle, they incorporated their citizens' association as a not for profit organization. As a corporation, they could enter into contracts for services they desired and hire employees if they needed them. To be incorporated they had to describe their purpose, list their officers, and register this with the appropriate government office. To keep their corporation current they must submit a brief report to the government at the end of each year that includes receipts and expenditures of their activities.

Another important issue these homeowners discussed was how they might have natural gas piped to their homes. They discovered that they all wanted it and that together they would pay the cost of the pipe to transport the gas from the end of the existing pipe to their neighborhood. Similarly, they decided that families keeping cats and/or dogs would be required to restrict them to their own property and not allow them to range around the neighborhood.

These decisions, and others, did not all come easily or quickly. Rather, most were discussed many times before it was decided what should be done. Because issues about which decisions were made were considered during many monthly meetings, almost all the neighbors were in complete agreement by the time they voted. Also, by that time, data relating to costs in neighbors' time and money as well as a time schedule to complete the proposed action were obtained and presented by a committee of the organization. This required many discussions both during and between their meetings. To keep themselves from spending all their time visiting about their children or their jobs when they met, and to have members designated to sign contracts, they elected a president and other officers. One of these was a treasurer who had the responsibility of receiving the assessments and paying contractors. The treasurer's accounts were reviewed by members of an audit committee.

In reviewing the process these families followed in establishing rules of behavior and cooperative endeavors, it can be understood why each of the families as well as new people moving into their neighborhood have to give up some of their independence. With assistance from people already residing in the area, members of new families quickly learn who their neighbors are and how to live in peace with them. In communities like this, sometimes there is a conflict that leads to a family being isolated from the rest or to such a family leaving the neighborhood, but most of the time neighbors find a way to work together by each giving up some of their freedom to satisfy the needs of others, who also give up some of theirs. People participate in the meetings because they enjoy being with their neighbors and because they want to have their interests represented when issues are discussed. They realize that with the freedom they enjoy in a democracy, they must assume some responsibilities for maintaining their democracy and thus cooperate with each other.

Neighborhood associations like the one just described are formed voluntarily by the people. Geographically larger organizations are districts within townships. Districts, in contrast to the voluntary neighborhood groups, are jurisdictions mandated by some state constitutions. That is, citizens living within the district's specified geographical boundaries are required to form a local government that has a number of responsibilities. An important one during the first 150 years of United States history concerned the establishment and maintenance of a public school, usually for grades one through six which generally was for children from seven years of age to thirteen. After completing the sixth grade, those children who continued their formal education attended village or city schools.

To establish a school, neighbors met to elect a board of three to five members every year to make decisions for them. Board members use funds from taxes to pay for supplies needed for the school, including fuel for heating it in winter, and they interviewed and employed teachers. In doing this, they drew up a budget and determined how much tax would be needed to be paid by the land owners to meet the costs of their programs. Those residents not owning land paid the tax indirectly because they paid rent to owners of the land on which they resided and the owners then paid a tax reflecting the income from the rents.

Frequently local residents built their own school, or enlarged it, dug the well for water, did the landscaping or did maintenance chores on the property with each contributing their time and equipment. I remember the great occasion when all the men came with their horses and wagons and picks and shovels to build a playground at a one-room school I attended in rural New York State. They moved a lot of soil with their picks, shovels and wagons, spread it out for the playground, planted trees and built a concrete platform under the hand operated drinking water pump. The women brought them their lunch. They had a good time, saved money they would have had to pay in taxes to have the work done and became better acquainted as they worked.

These township school districts contained from about five to 50 families. With the professionalization of education and the bureaucratization of government that has taken place, most of the township districts and their self governments in the United States have been eliminated along with their schools. Public education was centralized in large schools to improve the quality and efficiency of the education. In most states, citizens still elect members of school boards that control the schools but they do this in general elections rather than on a township basis.

Although there are few districts within townships left, the townships have remained. Citizens living in all the township districts, or former districts, elect members of a Town Board, usually no more than five people, every few years depending on the town rules. Also elected is a Supervisor to manage the town's programs, a Town Clerk who collects the taxes and keeps the records and several Assessors who determine the value of property on which taxes are to be paid. Frequently, local judges of minor law infractions, such as traffic violations, called Justices of the Peace, also are elected. The picture on the next page shows members of one Town Board who serve as legislators for the citizens who elected them.

The Town Board members, who may be called councilpersons, determine the amount of taxes to be paid by the people in relation to the type and amount of services they decide should be provided. One of the most essential functions of town boards is to provide for the maintenance of streets and roads in a condition that makes travel possible on them throughout the year regardless of the weather. The Board Members' most important responsibility is to design a budget which is their plan of action for the year. Their second most important responsibility is to ensure that the programs they approve are carried out well. The budget usually is drafted by the Town Supervisor or Manager based on past experience and needs for the next year. The Board members discuss the expenditures and receipts and decide whether or not each program should be done.

This is a list of some of the services that town board members must consider:

1. street lighting in the villages
2. protection from fires

This is a picture of four Town Board Members and a Town Supervisor. It is around the table at which these elected officials are sitting that decisions concerning government programs that may be conducted each year are made by them for the 2044 people living in their Town. Their Town consists of 133.13 square kilometers and has two villages, one with about 150 citizens and the other with about 200.

Clockwise around the table starting at the left front, are Mr. Millard E. Boek, a retired Rural Letter Carrier for the United States Post Office, Mr. Lawrence Mierek, a computer specialist, Mr. Francis Uhl, the Town Supervisor, Mr. Albert Kiffer, a farmer, and Mr. William Lux, Sr. a Sales and Marketing official in a manufacturing corporation. The Town Clerk and the Town Attorney usually also are present at these meetings. Citizens living in the Town can attend and ask questions of the Town Board members as well as comment on Town affairs.

3. road building and maintenance
    a. road repairs and construction
    b. weeds and brush control along roads
    c. snow removal
    d. bridge repair and construction
4. a clerk for collecting taxes and maintaining records
5. justices of the peace
6. external auditing of financial records
7. land and property assessing
8. legal services for the board
9. organizing elections
10. control of dogs
11. traffic control
12. upkeep of town owned buildings
13. inspections for safety and fire
14. registration of vital statistics (births and deaths)
15. insurance, including fire and liability
16. employee benefits
17. social services such as family home relief
18. veterans services
19. programs for
    a. children and youth
    b. adult recreation
    c. senior citizens
20. maintenance of cemeteries
21. collection of refuse and garbage
22. operation of public libraries

Before the programs they support and the amount of taxes they need to pay for them become the law of the town for that year, however, they must have a "public hearing" to which citizens can come to give their opinions for or against the board's plan. Following the hearing, members of the board may adjust their program. They may increase or reduce some services as well as taxes in response to the citizens. If a citizen or citizens still object to the taxes and/or the programs, they can file a complaint in court.

In the United States, public roads for vehicles are classified as town roads, county roads, state roads and federal highways. Federal highways cross two or more states, thus providing a means of transportation for vehicles that make those types of trips. State roads cross one or more counties together, whereas county roads are built across one or more townships. The building and maintenance of the remaining roads are the responsibility of the towns, villages or cities.

Townships used to provide welfare to families needing such assistance but now this is done by counties or cities. Townships gave some direct grants of funds to needy families but, more importantly, they provided jobs doing road building and maintenance if there was a healthy man in the family. Many such families were helped through a critical period in their lives without having their work ethic values weakened. Similarly, during the great depression of the 1930s, national government agencies were formed in the United States to provide employment for unemployed youth and adults. One was the Civilian Conservation Corp (CCC) and another the Works Progress Administration (WPA). Part of the wages of the young people working on reforestation and other environmental projects in the CCC was sent to their parents' homes, whereas employees of the WPA, who built schools, post offices and roads, were paid all their wages directly.

New democracies should avoid the professionalization of public education as well as of welfare and other services to the extent that it prevents direct citizen control of them. Research has shown that large centralized schools are less efficient and more costly than smaller ones and that they do not provide a significant increase in the quality of education. Similarly, welfare and social services that are provided by staffs of large government agencies with headquarters distant from people needing their programs tend to provide impersonal assistance that endangers the independence of their "clients." The township welfare system never had clients. Instead, they helped fellow citizens in need on a temporary basis. Welfare was not a way of life passed on from one generation to another as it is for some people today.

Families were given financial assistance by their local government when they did not have sufficient income to live due to circumstances such as the death, injury or sickness of members who otherwise would be working. When this happened, those receiving such help usually were very appreciative, but also somewhat ashamed. The objective of most individuals receiving aid was to overcome the obstacles preventing them from supporting themselves as soon as possible. Their neighbors respected them for this, praised them and helped them become independent. Unfortunately, today, most welfare is provided by professional social welfare employees in government agencies who tend to consider individuals in families needing assistance as being entitled to it. These professionals insist that their "clients" should never feel ashamed about being supported by the government.

The welfare check becomes the accepted income for many families from one generation to another as they match the professionalism of the providers with their own professionalism acquired by learning what they need to say about their needs and what to do to continue receiving welfare. Thus, some teenage girls deliberately have a baby even though they do not have a husband, so "I can get that check" as their mothers and friends have done. Social workers in government welfare agencies know how to legitimize the dependency of people but not how to induce them to become productive members of society. Some attempts are being made to assist people to support themselves but what is needed is for the mission of welfare agencies to be changed from providing welfare to altering the values of recipients from being happy with their dependency status to being determined to leave it.

Similar to township governments are village jurisdictions with a few hundred people up to a few thousand in size. That is, citizens vote for members of a village board and for a mayor to make decisions for them regarding services they need. They must have budgets and collect taxes to pay for services they provide such as fire protection, street repairs and street lighting. Also they must present their plans for public debate before they make a final decision about them.

Larger than most villages in geographical area are cities. Cities range from a thousand to hundreds of thousands of people. They usually have geographical subdivisions called wards. Each member of their governing boards generally represents a single ward and is elected by the citizens living within it. A mayor may be elected by all the people to administer the government and to construct a budget and program plans that the board members can approve or disapprove. Most city charters that are given by the states require a public hearing on the annual budget.

Most cities are within counties that also have elected legislators and administrators. County judges also may be elected to serve terms of as many as eight years. Members of the governing boards frequently are called county supervisors or county council members. Counties that have townships may have a member elected in each town. The process and the responsibilities are the same as those in cities, villages and townships. Issues are discussed by the board of supervisors and decisions reached. On those that are of serious concern to people, meetings are arranged during which people give their opinions about whether the subject is a problem and, if so, how it may best be solved.

At each jurisdictional level, citizens can petition for a referendum during which all citizens are given an opportunity to participate in the decision-making process on an issue by voting for or against it. Usually, a required number of citizens' signatures on petitions have to be obtained in order for a referendum on the issue to be placed on the ballot.

States, next to the national government, are the largest jurisdiction. Nearly all states have legislatures with two legislative bodies, a judicial system and an executive or administrative branch. One house of the legislature is usually called the state senate with one senator being elected in each county. The other may be called the state assembly with members elected in districts whose borders are arranged to have an approximate equal number of citizens. The boundaries of districts may overlap cities and counties depending on population density of the area. Governors elected by all the people head the executive branch. The state courts are organized into district courts with geographical boundaries and courts that focus on types of issues such as appeals from lower court decisions. The higher court is a state supreme court that considers the decisions of lower courts that are contested, or appealed from, or the judges themselves feel may not be in accordance with the state constitution.

Including the geographical area of all of the states, the territories and the District of Columbia, is the national government. This federal government has a Legislative Branch composed of a Senate and House of Representatives, an Executive Branch headed by an elected President and a Judicial Branch with the Supreme Court of the nation. The Constitution of the nation limits the powers of the federal government so its officials cannot interfere in state and local affairs, except as stipulated in the Constitution.

This detailed description of the many levels of government in an older democracy, illustrated in Figure 6 on the following page, was presented to emphasize the importance of citizens of a country participating in democratic decision-making about issues that affect them from the narrow scope of neighborhoods in which they live to the broad scope of their nation. In new democracies governmental jurisdictions should be organized at several levels if they do not already exist. The smallest jurisdiction could be the village with larger ones being districts composed of more than one village and the geographical areas around them. Each city could be another jurisdiction. At each of the levels, the

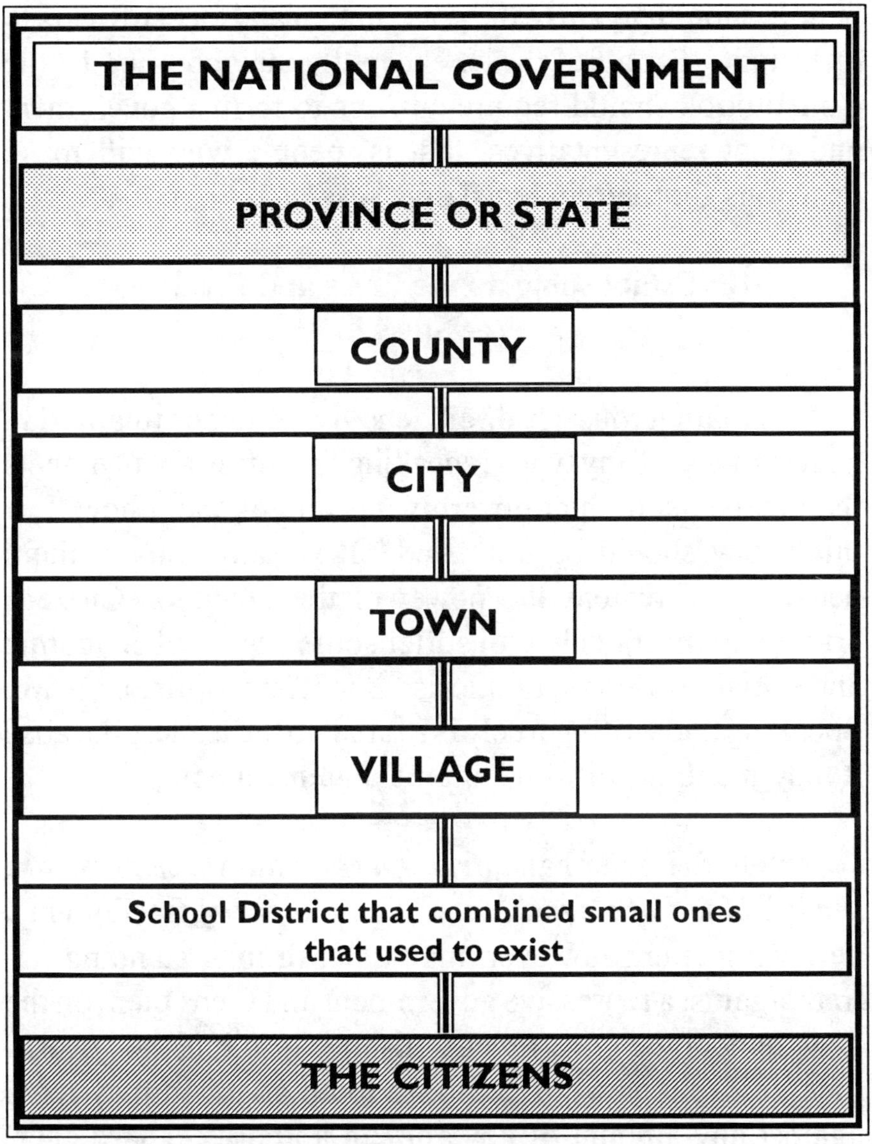

Figure 6. Government Jurisdictions from the Local Towns and Villages to the National.

people should organize the government and elect officers to operate it. For all of these, except the neighborhoods, the Constitution should require citizens to form a government and elect representatives, that is, people who will make decisions for them in legislative sessions.

H. Establishing a Free Press and Ensuring Free Speech.

A dangerous act of citizens living under totalitarian governments of any type is speaking or writing about defects they feel exist in their governments and/or about how they think they should be improved. It is dangerous to them because it threatens the power of the dictators. Citizens criticizing most likely will suffer some degree of economic and social restriction, or imprisonment and torture or death. Speaking and writing freely is a threat to the leaders because it may incite the citizens to rebel against them.

On the other hand, ***free speech and a free press are the life blood of a democracy***. These types of freedom in a new democracy, however, may unleash long standing hatreds against a repressive government and focus them on the new democratic government. Just because it is the government, citizens newly freed from totalitarianism may rebel against any amount of government authority. These cherished freedoms of democracies, however, must be granted immediately in new democracies and guaranteed by the constitution as soon as it is written and adopted. Free speech and a free press, however, cannot be used to justify some acts of individuals, such as death threats against others, or the advocation of a violent overthrow of the government.

There may be some other restrictions on free speech and a free press that it may be necessary to impose, such as the prohibition of oral or written presentations that adversely affect the morals of children or conflict with some basic religious or moral beliefs of the people. An example of this might be the false depiction of a national religious leader as a criminal or an evil person by someone who does not agree with the doctrines of his or her religion. Citizens and organizations about whom incorrect information is printed, particularly if this is deliberate, must be permitted to seek retribution against the offenders in the courts.

The policy of democratic governments should be to let the speeches and discussions take place and let the printing presses produce newspapers, pamphlets and books on any subject within the confines of reasonable restrictions like those just mentioned.

I. Citizen Voluntary Activities

One of the striking differences between the activities of citizens in some democracies, particularly the United States, and other types of government is the tremendous number of groups and organizations in which United States citizens participate on a voluntary basis. These voluntary associations vary from very informal cliques formed by friends of all ages — from young children to people 90 to 100 or more years of age — to formal organizations with written purposes, rules of behavior and rituals.

An individual may belong to many organizations, perhaps one for each type of interest he or she has. In a city of ten thousand people, there will be over a thousand organizations, with many being identifiable only by information obtained from the members themselves. In size, these groups vary from two member cliques to chapters of national or international organizations in which total membership is in the millions. Each group has a leadership structure, no matter how small or informal.

In a democracy where the importance of the individual is one of the strong principles, this practice of joining groups and/or forming groups may seem to be in conflict with individualism. To remain psychologically healthy, however, each person must have security-giving relationships with others. In modern societies with a vast variety of activities in which people are involved, it is necessary for individuals to feel they are supported, needed or respected by those in each major field of activity in which they become seriously involved.

For example, they need such relationships in their families, neighborhoods, communities, occupations and recreational activities. When they have complete freedom to associate with others, they will form and participate in many such groups on a voluntary basis. In doing this they actually will be reinforcing their individualism because they join only those organizations that support their own beliefs. People tend to avoid personal emotional stress by associating with others who think and act as they do.

Although becoming part of a group is an egotistical action, in that it is done for personal fulfillment, usually it also is ethnocentric, because the specific characteristics of the members of a group are reinforced. At the same time, the group may be very altruistic in that its members join to be able to carry out activities that contribute to the well-being of people in need or to improve their communities or nation.

Voluntary organizations serve as very significant integrating forces in a nation. For example, by participating in organizations already existing in communities, whose members share some common interests with them, immigrants can become assimilated into their new society as well as contribute ideas from their own culture to the group and thus broaden the knowledge and understanding of its members.

Because the American way of living provides constant participation in small groups, individuals have considerable experience with leader/follower roles in groups. This tended to frustrate North Korean communist efforts to break up American prisoner of war cliques by removing the leaders. As soon as they took a leader away from a group of prisoners, another soldier in the clique replaced him and the group continued to function as a morale booster for its members. This communist technique of depriving groups of their leaders, however, tended to destroy the group produced security of soldiers from some other nations who without their group's support no longer had the reinforcement from each other to help them resist torturing by their communist captors. This was because a new leader did not emerge from those left behind who had been followers.

Under a capitalistic economy, individuals strive to better themselves. They seek to improve their skills, to enlarge their enterprises and to advance in their professions. Joining the appropriate organization is an important way to accomplish such objectives. This association also provides the social recognition of one's achievements. Being successful is not important to most individuals unless it is acknowledged by others, especially those people whom the individual respects.

Still another reason for taking part in groups, is to control those variables that affect the members. People who desire to influence what and how their children are taught and how teachers grade them, become active in parent organizations at schools. This type of expression of interest and concern can affect, to some degree, what is taught as well as the instructional methods, and it can result in special treatment of children of parents who exert leadership in the parent organizations. Because they want special attention and better grades for their own children, some parents tend to accept and praise educators for what is being done in schools even though they may really think improvement is needed.

Laborers who work in industries also form organizations, usually called labor unions, because they want to receive more for their efforts than they are being paid and protect the benefits they already enjoy. Similarly, the owners of industry and the managers of their businesses organize to promote their interests. Professionals in the health, educational and scientific fields do the same thing, as do government workers. All these organizations benefit their members. The labor unions have made significant contributions to improving the level of living of workers while the professional organizations have improved the knowledge and skills of members in their fields of interest. The business organizations have been important in improving production and distribution technology.

Another very significant type of voluntary action involves people contributing their time and funds to help others. Some of this type of voluntarism occurs when a neighbor or someone else has a tragedy such as having their home destroyed by fire or wind. Neighbors of people in trouble will invite them to stay with them until they find another place to live and people who do not even know them will contribute clothes for members of the family to wear. Also volunteers provide a significant part of nonmedical help for many nonprofit organizations providing medical care.

It is interesting to note that many of the individuals contributing their time to community programs consider this activity as a job even though they do not receive pay for it. Many people have worked in libraries and hospitals or organized and managed activities for youth for 15 or 20 years on a regular basis after they retired from their vocations. The work ethic is part of their values. To be happy and healthy they must keep busy.

Freedom to participate in a wide variety of voluntary activities in a democracy, along with leisure time people have because of the capitalistic economic system, benefits both the volunteers and those receiving the assistance. Millions of children and youth participate in eductional and sports activities because volunteer adults lead them. Elderly citizens and sick people have their lives enriched by teenage youth who assist them as volunteers.

Participation in political affairs as volunteers is an important activity of citizens wherever this is allowed. With the freedom to organize and operate political parties in democracies, it is possible for citizens of all ages to become directly involved in their government by helping to select candidates for office. Political parties and the subsequent voting, provides a primary means by which citizens participate in their government. Many devote all of their spare time and others work full time as unpaid volunteers to carry out all of the tasks of campaigning for office. These include addressing envelopes in which information is sent to voters, writing campaign literature, giving speeches to convince people that the person they support is the best qualified, and telephoning citizens to encourage them to vote.

This discussion of citizen participation in a variey of organizations, because they have the freedom to associate with each other in democracies, pointed out the extensiveness and importance of this activity in democracies. Therefore, older democracies must continue to encourage such interaction while newer ones must make sure that their Constitution guarantees the right of people to associate with one another in both informal groups and formal organizations they form. In addition, there should be no government policy or action that inhibits such activities on the part of citizens. Instead, the government should enhance participation of citizens in organizations by making it easy for people to obtain charters for the formal organizations they want to establish. Charters are necessary for many groups because with a charter, usually achieved through forming a corporation and registering it with a government agency, the organization becomes a legal entity and can own property and enter into legal contracts.

J. Judicial System

The importance of the judicial function of governments is indicated by the fact that it is strictly controlled by all totalitarian leaders. They cannot allow any judge to make a decision that is not in their favor. It is the judges they control who provide the justification for them to rule. To allow citizens who disagree with a dictator, or who do things the dictator does not like, to have their guilt or innocence determined by a judge not completely dominated by the dictator or by a jury of citizens from their communities, is not permitted by dictators.

In democracies, the ultimate authority over human behavior is the law, and their constitutions must be the basis for the law rather than any former "common law." The law is carried out through a system of courts presided over by judges. The judges must base their decisions on stipulations in the Constitution rather than on their own biases. They must provide the same treatment to everyone who comes before the court and yet be sufficiently flexible to consider each person's particular act in relation to the situation in which it occurred. To be objective, judges have to act aloof from the beliefs of the people, yet they are part of the society and carry the values of its culture. Although prestigious, judges' roles can be lonely and stressful because their socializing has to be restricted so that they are not emotionally involved with, nor socially or economically dependent on, people or organizations about which they might have to make a decision in court. Their roles are stressful, because they must hear about the terrible things that happen to people and the unhappy situations in which they become involved with and yet remain objective about the problems of people.

Why then are some people willing to become judges? The relatively high salaries and job security are two reasons. Another is the prestige of the position that satisfies their need to feel important. Still another reason that may be the most important one, is altruism, a desire to help people with their problems and to play a significant role in making a better society.

Judges qualify for their positions in several ways. First, they must have a knowledge of law and the constitution along with the respect of other lawyers and citizens. Secondly, they are supposed to be unbiased without any opinions about issues that come up in the court until the evidence is presented. Political connections of judges, however, play an important role in their selection or election. This is indeed unfortunate when the judge accepts control by political or criminal leaders because the judge has such an important role in the community and nation. For example, when jurors in a court were asked why they did not indite, that is accuse, members of the Mafia of many crimes that citizens considered them to have committed, they said "The judge ruled out all the evidence and we did not have anything we could use to indict them." These citizen jurors remarked to their friends after their Grand Jury duty was concluded that they believed the judge was controlled by the Mafia.

The answers to these three questions indicate the objectivity of judges: To whom do judges answer? From whom do they receive praise? And, whom do judges want to please? If they have a criminal or political boss to whom they respond and strive to please, and if they are rewarded at special celebrations arranged by them, judges likely are not carrying out their responsibilities as objective presiders over the courts.

Two other important qualifications for judgeships are a strong belief in democracy and sufficient experience with the court system to have maturity of judgment. These qualifications enhance the judge's ability to be independent.

In democracies, judges may be appointed by elected officials or they may be elected by the citizens. When they are appointed, it is usually by the elected head of the executive branch of the government with approval of the legislators. Some judges however, are appointed by superior or senior judges, that is, judges at a higher level in the court system or by those already in the court. The appointment process for judges can be influenced by political interests in that elected officials may strive to please their supporters by selecting individuals whom they want as judges even though such judges may not be honest. When judges are elected by the people, they also may be influenced in their decisions because they desire to be reelected. Judges, however, should serve long terms and this would tend to protect them from some political pressures.

When a justice system for a country is being considered, it should be recognized that there are several reasons given by people for seeking justice. One is for revenge. Individuals or groups want to get even with someone whom they believe has harmed them. Another is to right a wrong that they believe has occurred. A third is to prevent crime by penalizing the person who is guilty so that they will not commit further crimes. A fourth is to set an example of what will happen to someone who commits a similar antisocial act. It is the responsibility of judges, however, to make decisions on the basis of evidence of wrongdoing and not on the basis of what the offended person or community desires.

What a crime is may be defined by the mores of a subcultural group in a society or by the total society.

Similarly, there may be considerable variation between the sacred rules of behavior and the secular. Although beliefs and behavior that are acceptable to one segment of a society and not to others can be considered by judges, the objective has to be to provide one general set of judicial standards and practice for the whole society.

Leaders in democracies must remember that the balance that keeps the legislative and the executive branches of government from exceeding the limits of their functions as stipulated in the Constitution is the Judicial Branch of government. Because they make the final decision about the legitimacy of laws, members of the Judicial Branch have the power to subvert stipulations of the Constitution. Judges, at every level in the judicial system of a democracy, need to accept the fact that citizens are sovereign because they elect the legislators and it is the Constitution of the people that must be kept sacred.

Fortunately, usually there are lawyers in the jurisdictions where judges hold court with just as much, or more, knowledge of law and the Constitution as well as experience practicing law than the judges. It is the well-trained lawyers in the nation that are the means for preventing members of the judicial system from perverting the Constitution with their decisions. One way lawyers do this is by writing about decisions in relation to the Constitution in law journals and by presenting talks at meetings of lawyers. Citizens in democracies, whether or not they are lawyers, must pay attention to decisions of judges to make sure they do not violate the Constitution or laws of their countries. Because citizens are free to speak and write about decisions they believe are incorrect, judges who make them can be influenced to carefully consider the constitutionality of the issues before they give their decisions.

K. Maintaining Law and Order

Citizens in a democracy live together under laws formulated by them through legislators they elect to represent them. Because a few people may not agree with the laws or their interpretations, or are not informed about them, they will break some of the laws. Behavior of other citizens may violate the laws because of their inadequate enculturation into the mainstream of society while they were children and youth. Anti-social and criminal acts also may occur when people are emotionally disturbed or when they value personal goals more than the rights of their neighbors.

Totalitarian leaders use their military forces to suppress citizens who violate their strict rules. Democratic leaders can not do this, nor should they. In democracies, the military exists to defend the country against aggressor nations. Therefore, reliance must be placed on local police officers to keep order when necessary. Elected legislators in each jurisdictional level of government may, with laws they pass, establish a police force that would function under their authority. The geographical area policed by such law enforcement agencies is limited to the boundaries of the jurisdiction in which they serve. Thus, village, city or county police must limit their responsibility and authority to their village, city or county. In democracies, governmental jurisdictions of provinces or states may have a police force for enforcing laws of the province or state. Such a police force, however, must not have authority over village or city laws and must defer to the local police when local laws are broken.

Just as there is a specialization by criminals, there needs to be police trained and equipped to provide special services. For example, illegal drug use and distribution may require specialized attention. Similarly, it may be necessary to have laboratories to analyze evidence relating to criminal activities that is gathered by regular police. These may be provided by the national government when requested by the local police authorities or may be organized on a cooperative basis by police in several jurisdictions.

The principle that must be adhered to is that the police are under the authority and supervision of the civilian government as stipulated in laws passed by legislators. Police operations must be limited to law enforcement, which is the prevention of illegal acts and arresting and temporarily imprisoning alleged criminals until they can appear before a judicial official. Police can never be allowed to adjudicate the accused, that is determine whether or not they are guilty or decide what their penalty will be if they are found guilty. Police must be held responsible if they act illegally while involved in carrying out their law enforcement responsibilities. If they violate rights of individuals or make illegal arrests, they must face arrest themselves and subsequent judicial action.

L. The Tax System

Every government costs money to operate. Money to support the government must be obtained from one or more sources. The amount of money a government spends may be determined by the programs its legislators initiate or the extent of government services may be determined by the government's income. ***Unfortunately, government officials, especially at the national level, launch new programs and expand current ones with little regard to where the money will come from to pay for them.*** Too often the government borrows money to pay the costs of new programs. When this is done year after year, paying interest on the deficit may become the largest expenditure of government. Citizens need to make sure their legislators prevent existing programs from increasing in size beyond what is needed and that they do not initiate new programs that require tax increases beyond the level acceptable to people.

Taxes imposed on citizens are by far the greatest source of government funds. There are a great variety of taxes instigated by government officials to make it possible for them to carry out programs. For example there are property taxes, income taxes, business taxes, sales taxes, fuel taxes, road use taxes, franchise taxes, luxury taxes and many more. Some taxes are designed to control citizen activities by reducing what they have to spend or by making the price so high on an item that they will not buy it. Current examples of this are the taxes on halogen gases used in cooling systems and refrigerators. These gasses are considered dangerous additions to the environment by some people. The objective of the government that imposes these product control or elimination taxes is to make the price of the gases so high that manufacturers will develop substitutes and consumers will stop using them to recharge their refrigerators and other cooling equipment. The contribution of gases to the atmosphere by these artificial sources, however, is trivial compared to similar gases emitted each year by volcanoes.

Another tax that may do more harm than the income it produces justifies, is a fee imposed on products imported and exported in countries. These taxes called "tariffs" or "customs duties" increase the cost to citizens of what is purchased and reduce the amount they receive for what they sell. To impose this tax requires a large number of officials to enforce it against all vehicles and individuals entering and leaving a country. Tariffs and customs taxes on imports inhibit international trade and reduce the variety of goods available to consumers; therefore, such taxes are resisted by citizens. The imposition of such a tax was a critical factor influencing people who had moved to North America from Europe and/or their descendents to declare independence from England. Although the amount of taxes obtained this way at the time was significant for England, today tariffs and custom duties may cost more to collect than is obtained from them.

Fees for various services provided by the government are another source of income, but government officials are reluctant to charge fees sufficient to meet costs of services, such as recreation areas and medical care because they want the services to be used by many people. They also want to have large numbers of participants to justify having these programs, otherwise, there would not be much of a need for the positions they fill.

All taxes restrict economic development because taxes use money that otherwise could be used to expand production. When taxes do not produce enough income to pay the cost of operating a government, the government may borrow money from other countries or from its own citizens. If it cannot borrow funds, it may just print more money without having it backed by any assets.

When a country has an operating deficit each year, the cost of maintaining the debt in interest and fees may make it impossible to pay the interest or to repay the debt and still meet the cost of government operations out of current governmental income. Many countries currently are in this condition. In recognition of this situation, governments of the industrialized nations that provided funds to developing countries, as well as private banks in them that also made such loans, have cancelled billions of dollars of debt in a number of countries where they knew they could not collect it.

The primary focus of attention of government leaders should be on reducing the cost of government rather than on imposing taxes. The privatization of most formerly government owned businesses and the sale of most government property along with major reductions in the number of government employees, including the military, will reduce government expenditures in many countries. Before any tax is levied, its effect on the economy should be carefully estimated. This evaluation of the effect of the tax should be carried out by members of a commission consisting of citizens who are not government employees.

M. Controlling Bureaucracies

One of the most perplexing issues for older democracies is the vice-grip of bureaucracies on governing processes.

A bureaucracy which is operated by socialistically inclined government employees who feel that they should answer to no one but themselves and their bureaucratic colleagues, is in direct conflict with democratic principles. Yet it is absolutely necessary for the government to have employees who are trained and organized in an effective manner to carry out governmental responsibilities. The usual way to organize responsibilities of employees is to have one person supervise a number of people who, in large organizations, supervise others who then supervise the employees who do the work. For example, a government health care agency may have a national director who has staff under him or her. Each of these staff supervise several regional office directors. Regional directors are in charge of district offices. The district office directors supervise the medical care professionals who provide the service to people.

In such a pyramid structure, each director's or supervisor's authority is limited by the rules of the level at which he or she functions. Orders are received from above and relayed to those below. This type of structure, as diagramed in Section B of Chapter VI, whether in government, education, or industry, is a bureaucracy. A bureaucracy is an expensive manner of carrying out responsibilities of a program because there are many well-paid employees at the supervisory levels who do not directly provide the actual services for which the bureaucracy was established. Most bureaucracies can be reduced from 10 to 50 percent and still meet program objectives. In fact, one major retail business with thousands of stores, kept its national and regional administrative staff small, because they found that local managers were more successful when they received little supervision from superiors.

In new democracies, the bureaucrats pose a serious threat to development of a democratic government. For example, a country progressing from communism to democracy is burdened with a communist bureaucracy. Under those circumstances, what can a newly elected leader and legislators do? The possible alternatives to be discussed next leave much to be desired, but can be effective if properly administered.

One alternative would be to dismiss all communistically inclined government employees. This radical procedure, however, most likely would result in a shutdown of services essential to keep the government and the economy functioning if a sufficient number of noncommunists experienced in handling the governmental responsibilities were difficult to find. On the other hand, if left in their positions of control in the bureaucracies, communists can slow down or stop progress toward representative government and a free-market/free-enterprise economy. If they want to sabotage democratic processes, it would be difficult to prevent them from doing it.

An effective way out of this dilemma is to:

1. Eliminate all non-essential government agencies like the national security police, who had been empowered to control the people, national planning and enforcement agencies for business and agriculture, and citizen registration and control bureaus.

   This selective reduction in services can be a very positive step forward because there will be a very large number of such government functions that will no longer be needed in a democracy and should be terminated quickly. Remember, it is the bureaucrats in the government agencies that have enforced the repressive policies of the former type of government.

   Some services that may be eliminated quickly are the security police with their extensive records on citizens and the border patrols and the police bureaucracy that prevented the free movement of citizens in the country. Additionally, agencies controlling the currency and those keeping people from carrying out free enterprise endeavors will not be needed.

2. Appoint democratically inclined citizens who are appropriately qualified to head the government agencies along with their major divisions.

3. Develop a program of training in democratic procedures for all government employees quickly. Do not assume that the employees will change their way of reasoning and acting from the old to the new by themselves or that they will know what democracy is, or accept it if they do understand it.

4. Set up an open and highly visible system of monitoring government operations to identify inefficient and malfunctioning programs. Although government employees can obtain the data, the authority to determine what should be done with their findings must rest in a commission. Commission members would be non-government employed leaders appointed by elected legislators. They would serve as unpaid volunteers with travel and other necessary expenses paid while attending meetings.

One activity that may require monitoring involves control of imports and exports at borders of countries. If goods are held at the borders many hours or days in order to be cleared by inefficient customs procedures, badly needed increases in commerce are slowed down and may be stopped. This was happening at the Polish-German border crossings in 1992 where trucks on their way into Poland were forced to wait in a single line, kilometers long, as shown in the pictures on the next page, while the records of each truck, one at a time, were processed. Several uniformed customs officials were standing talking instead of opening several more gates for multiple processing of trucks.

In a country encouraging free enterprise, the products these trucks were carrying, some of which were perishable, were badly needed. The waste of fuel and drivers' time, the inefficient use of the capital invested in the trucks, as well as in the machinery and facilities where the products were to be utilized, and the increase in pollution from the wasteful burning of fuel by the waiting trucks is a very serious impediment to economic progress. Even though trade restrictions on products that could be mixed with the main cargo of the trucks might have required special searches, and thus be one reason for the lengthy delays, a change in policy that would provide for additional customs officials at the borders to open several lanes for inspecting trucks could have solved this serious problem.

At the same time that there was a long line of trucks waiting to enter Poland, there were no trucks waiting to enter Germany from Poland at the same crossings, yet about the same number of trucks were traveling in each direction. This

A view toward the border crossing

A view away from the border crossing

Trucks Lined up at the Border of a Newer Democracy Waiting for Customs Officials to Process Their Papers.

Polish problem could be solved quickly if there was a simple system of monitoring the customs clearance process to make sure the movement of trucks was expedited.

There are many other operations of the government that require monitoring by concerned officials. For example, it may sound wonderful that a large number of individual dwellings are to be constructed according to a national plan, but when it takes months or years for builders to obtain building permits, the national plan does not result in the building of many residences.

A system of monitoring government operations should focus on everyday activities. Answers to questions such as these should be sought by the elected leaders of the country: How long does it take for a truck to be processed at a border, or a shipment at an airport or waterport? What is involved in an individual starting a business? How well is the communication system functioning, such as telephones, mail and package deliveries? Are farmers able to obtain the machinery, seeds, fertilizers, and animal foodstuffs in a timely manner? What proportion of agricultural products arrive in the markets where they can be obtained by citizens and what is their quality when they do arrive? Are sufficient capital funds available to meet the needs of businesspersons, including farmers? Answers to questions such as these indicate how the economy is operating as well as what may be done to improve the weaknesses. Data to answer these questions must be obtained directly from the sources and can be acquired by legislators and other elected officials.

N. Controlling Government Regulations

Chapter VI contains a discussion of the negative influence on democracies of excessive government regulations. In this section, the focus will be on furthering an understanding of such regulations and on emphasizing the necessity for citizens and legislators to prevent democratic governments from imposing unnecessary regulations.

The purposes of government attempts to regulate human behavior are many. As is noted in Section N of this chapter, regulations are sometimes imposed to secure income for the government as in the case of many tariffs. Although tariffs or customs duties may help the governments control or keep tract of international commerce, they also inhibit trade.

Totalitarian governments regulate individuals by requiring them to carry identity cards. When everyone has to carry an identity card, report to authorities their activities, obtain permission to change jobs and residences, as well as obtain permission to travel, the government officials know where they are and what they are doing. Such a requirement severely limits the freedom of individuals and is not permitted in a democracy.

A type of regulation that is acceptable if administered fairly is imposed to protect individuals from others or from themselves such as the restriction of a person with a contagious disease or mental illness to their homes or to an institution. Another type of regulation has to do with the profit motive that is a necessary driving force in free enterprise. Because the desire to accumulate money may lead to practices by people that restrict the rights of others, regulations may be necessary to prevent such practices. For example, some businesspeople may have to be prevented from gaining control of all supplies of an essential product for the purpose of creating a monopoly so they can charge high prices. Similarly, labor union leaders who try to prevent anyone who does not join their union and pay them fees from working in their industry, may need to be controlled.

A much more pervasive purpose of government regulations, however, is to further the special interests of groups of people. Their special interest may be to preserve old buildings and sections of urban areas with their original narrow, crooked roads and streets. The purpose of some other regulations relate to environmental facets such as the preservation of specified plants and animals, of wetlands, rivers, deserts and mountains or the reduction of air, water and soil pollution.

The extension of government regulations beyond the scope intended by legislative policy-makers is a serious

problem. This extension is due to the objective of regulation agencies' staffs to preserve and expand their responsibilities and their administrative powers. They feel the need to justify the budget and staff of the programs they are running. They are thereby functioning like regular bureaucrats whose rewards come from the number of staff they supervise and the amount of money they spend.

To ascertain whether or not a regulation is required, an analysis must be done of benefits and damage from it for the nation. This analysis should be conducted objectively by individuals knowledgeable about the subject of the regulation who are not emotionally involved in the issue. Along with it, alternatives to government control should be considered. Unfortunately, much reasoning about whether or not a regulation is needed is based on emotions rather than fact. When emotions determine the action to be taken, faulty research methods can be followed to secure data on the issue and biased information accepted. This nonscientific approach occurs because those promoting the regulation usually are not scientists in the field of concern and are not interested in considering the reliability of study methods or the validity of data presented to justify the regulation. Legislators in general, are not interested in scientific evaluations either, because the education they received did not provide them with an understanding and appreciation of the scientific method.

A blatant example in which invalid data were welcomed by a regulatory board occurred when the chairperson of one regulatory board, a lawyer, opened a hearing on a regulation by stating that hearsay evidence would be accepted. She meant that opinions that were not backed by valid data along with results from any type of analyses speakers wanted to present would be welcomed regardless of how untruthful they might be. Although her statement shocked scientists who were to participate, she conducted the hearing in that fashion and allowed unsound information to affect the decision regarding the regulation.

Frequently it takes years before views of qualified scientists who have done research on an issue are accepted. Such a delay occurred for example, when it was concluded by one researcher, who became widely known and praised, that small amounts of lead to which children were exposed caused them to be mentally retarded. It took more than a decade before conclusions of the original researcher were shown to be questionable.

In considering alternatives to government regulations, attention must be given to self-regulation, that is, voluntary regulation by citizens and their businesses and organizations. This private type of regulation is extensive in most societies. Many individuals voluntarily refrain from activities that are harmful to the environment or offensive to others. Materials that adversely affect the environment or are harmful to people, animals or plants, are not used or produced by most people because by doing so their own beliefs would be contradicted. At the same time, there can be a serious conflict between the desire of citizens to maximize profits from their enterprises or to receive special pleasure from activities and the need to protect both the short-term and long-term rights of others.

If current government regulations were in effect during the early years of the older democracies, the economic success of those countries today would not have reached its current high level. Many scientific and technological developments could not have been used as quickly as they have been. One example is plastic. The production of this difficult to decompose product, that contaminates so much of our land and water, probably would not be permitted if it were developed today. Large numbers of people would lobby their legislators to pass regulatory laws to prevent its use. The positive contribution of plastic to the welfare and prosperity of people that has taken place, however, reinforces the conclusion that advantages of a product have to be considered as well as disadvantages from not having it when regulations to restrict its use are being considered.

Another technological advancement that might have been prevented from being developed is atomic energy. In arriving at decisions as to whether or not nuclear powered plants that produce electricity should be prohibited, many factors must be considered. One of these is their potential health hazards compared with those of feasible alternatives. Opponents who oppose the generation of electricity atomically and support coal fired generators usually neglect consideration of the number of people killed, maimed and condemned to years of suffering and early death from subsurface coal mining. Although large surface coal mining operations utilizing modern machinery with strict safety and health practices have a low rate of mortality and morbidity for their employees, much of the mining is still below ground where the risk is greater, especially in small mining operations.

Regulations by the government should be limited to those absolutely essential to the preservation of democracy and free enterprise. Before any regulation is imposed, it should be evaluated to determine its negative and positive effects on the nation. Then, the legislators who impose regulations must oversee their implementation rather than just to pass regulatory legislation leaving enforcement to a bureaucratic staff.

O. Controlling the Military

In most countries that have just become democracies or are about to change to democratic governments, the military issue is very serious. For those that have been military dictatorships, the question as to how the military is to be brought under control of the civilian governmental leaders in a subservient role, must be answered quickly. Similarly, citizens in those countries in which the military has been the means by which leaders maintained a totalitarian repressive rule, must solve the problem of how to control the military when their governments become democractic.

Although the military issue is discussed in Chapter III, some of the information in it will be summarized in this section along with suggestions as to how the military issue may be handled.

The first question that must be considered, however, is whether or not a military force is necessary at all in newer democracies. With the need no longer existing to subjugate citizens of their own country or to have a military force to protect the nation from other countries, the principal reason for a military force, presumably, must be to conquer other countries. If leaders of a democracy want an army to conquer another country, when they start to invade it they will discover that much of the rest of the world will come to the assistance of the nation they are attacking. Therefore, they should decide against having a national military force because it is unnecessary as well as a possible threat to civilian control of the government.

The willingness to interceed in conflicts between countries and between factions within countries on the part of democratic nations with sponsorship of the United Nations will continue to increase as the number of democracies in the world increases. People who are free and who value human life become concerned when they learn about attrocities inflicted on fellow humans during armed conflicts. Because of their deep conviction that individuals, no matter where they live, should not have their basic rights violated, citizens of democracies will demand that their nation become involved in attempts to stop such agression. This is especially true because civilians suffer death, injury, hunger, disease and property loss in the fighting.

Countries becoming democracies already having large numbers of people in their armies must make use of the capabilities of the men and women in beneficial civilian employment. If large numbers of personnel are released from military service, however, there may be no way for most of them to be employed until private enterprise expands to where they are needed. In addition, their attitude derived from being superior to civilians while members of the military, needs to be changed. This may be difficult if they have served the function for their former non-democratic government of arresting, imprisoning, torturing, and killing civilians who wanted freedom and independence. The people they had controlled are the same ones who will be the entrepreneurs, and their possible employers, under the new democratic government.

Therefore, an intensive training program in democracy and private enterprise capitalism should be instigated for the military personnel. At the same time, a program should be designed to direct the energy of the military to community and national service projects such as the construction and/or improvement of transportation and communication facilities. Actually, many of the skills learned in the military can be applied to jobs in the civilian sphere. For example, truck and other motor vehicle mechanics can become automotive mechanics while truck and heavy equipment operators will be needed in the private enterprise economy. Those in the medical fields can fill an unmet need in the civilian medical care field.

The military should organize a program to train soldiers for civilian careers and help them find employment in the free enterprise economy. Many of the officers may have leadership qualities. If they are trained to accept the advantages of private ownership and learn the techniques of private ownership, they can become successful businessmen and women. They should be assisted in such endeavors by being allowed to purchase surplus government owned military machines and equipment that can be used in civilian endeavors, at prices and with interest charges that the businesses they establish can pay. Similarly, civilians who want to start private businesses should be given the same opportunity to acquire such equipment.

For example, a person who was in charge of a motor pool in the army should be able to operate a garage for repairing automotive vehicles. A truck driver should be able to operate a truck in the private sector if fundamental bookkeeping skills were learned before the change was made from military service to civilian life. The infrastructure of transportation usually is one of the serious deficiencies in new democracies that may be reduced by having military trucks and busses operating in the private sector.

****

I place economy among the first and important virtues, and public debt as the greatest of dangers.... We must make our choice between economy and liberty, or profusion and servitude. If we can prevent the government from wasting the labors of the people under the pretense of caring for them, they will be happy.

—*Thomas Jefferson*

[The projection of government into business] would impair the very basis of liberty and freedom not only for those left outside the fold of expanded bureaucracy but for those embraced within it.

—*Herbert C. Hoover*

I believe in democracy because it releases the energies of every human being.

—*Woodrow Wilson*

Smart and lively people make the economy go, whether they are running companies or working for them. It is men and women, not machines, that compete.

—*John B. Anderson*

Chapter XII.
Economic Factors In Democracies

A. Property Ownership

One of the most important rights in a democracy is individual ownership of property. Private ownership also is absolutely essential in a capitalistic society. In many monarchies the land and its improvements, including the homes of citizens, belong to the monarch. In most communist countries, property belongs to the government and extreme measures are taken to prevent citizens from owning any property or business, especially if it has the potential of producing income.

For example, in the early 1930s Joseph Stalin, while head of the Soviet Union, invited farm workers who wanted to own and operate their own farms, to apply for permission. With this technique, he was able to identify those workers who did not completely believe in his communist government ownership system. He then eliminated these nonbelievers by having them killed. Also people in countries that came under control of communists, such as the former East Germany, were deprived of their homes with little or no compensation. The widow of a man whose business had been constructing homes, for example, was given 2,000 East German Marks for their home worth more than 100,000 Marks and then forced to move to a small apartment in the city with her children. This was because she was not supposed to own property or be able to use the amount of space she had in her private residence.

Under socialism of the Soviet communists, children were indoctrinated to believe that private ownership of property was wrong. Seven year old children living in an institution apart from their parents or who did not have parents, were interviewed by researchers at the time the Soviet Union collapsed in order to produce a videotape about children kept in orphanages. Not one of the children believed that people should own property or businesses. When asked if they owned anything themselves, one boy said the pen he wrote with was his. Some of these seven year olds expressed their opinions about capitalism in which people owned the businesses. They knew that people under the capitalistic system had more than those under the socialistic system but they said that the communists would soon catch up.

After the videotaped interviews were completed, the children were taken back to their families and the institution was closed. When they are 14 and 21 years of age the researchers plan to interview them again after they have lived under the democratic, free market, capitalistic system that is being established in the countries of the former Soviet empire.

Although the institutionalized children may have been indoctrinated by communists to believe that private property ownership is not right, strong desires to own property on the part of many people living under socialism remained throughout the time they were dominated by a socialistic government. As a result, many were able to maintain ownership of their homes, or, at least they acted as if they owned them even though the government may have considered the people only as occupants rather than owners. Similarly, many urban people had very small parcels of land outside of the cities and villages where they maintained gardens and had a small building they could stay in during the summer weekends as shown in the picture on page 306. Even though they did not own the land which provided vegetables and fruits that made it possible for families to survive food shortages, they could keep renting it year after year.

Because private property ownership, including businesses, is such a critical right of people in a democracy and a necessary principle of capitalism, citizens must be protected from the possibility of government confiscation of their property. Similarly, they must have complete freedom to buy and sell property without interference by the government and to keep the return from any sale. This right and how it is to be protected must be clearly stated in the constitution of the country.

Carefully taken care of gardens with small weekend houses in a former socialist country.

In new democracies that are changing from socialistic governments, it is necessary to encourage citizens to become owners of homes, farms and other businesses. Private ownership entails taking on management as well as financial responsibilities. This responsibility may be considered by some people to be too difficult and economically too risky for them to become involved. They also may be worried that the government might revert to communist controlled socialism with them once again subject to imprisonment as well as loss of the property and all the improvements they would have made on it.

People who are ready for independence and the challenge and pleasure that can come with the ownership of homes, farms, businesses and equipment, should be assisted in achieving this goal by the government. This assistance can be rendered in ways that will not only result in less government ownership, but also reduced government involvement in business.

The first step the government should take is to ensure that those citizens already owning property legitimately have clear title to it. Not only must their ownership be secure but they must have the right to sell their property and keep the returns for themselves.

The second step should be to restore ownership to citizens from whom property had been confiscated, even though this may have occurred many years before and only the children or grandchildren of the original owners remain. This means that those who were assigned property taken from others by the socialist government, perhaps because they were willing to cooperate with government officials, would have to relinquish their ownership rights or compensate the original, rightful owners.

The third step is to sell to citizens government owned businesses including farmland along with business facilities, equipment, buildings, machinery, and motor vehicles. The terms of the sale should be lenient, especially for small businesses. That is, the length of time the purchaser has to pay should be as long as possible and the interest on the debt very low. Of course, the time allowed for paying for the property has to be related to the nature of the property. The time allowed for paying for equipment, for example, has to be less than the expected life of the equipment. Consideration has to be given to providing for the necessary costs of maintaining the property and for replacing equipment and facilities as they become worn out or outdated. The new owner will need to budget funds for maintenance and replacement each year and place them in a reserve account restricted to that use until they are needed.

It would be more advantageous in democracies formed in formerly socialistic countries to give economically viable tracts of free land to farmers and then tax them in relation to their ability to pay rather than to sell it to them. This procedure would increase production of agricultural products quickly and provide a sound basis for taxation that will stand the test of time.

In selling government property to citizens the government officials should consider these advantages:

1. The government will no longer have to meet the costs of maintaining and operating it;

2. Private property ownership will generate commerce which will produce profits for the owner and increase the income of all those involved;

3. Private ownership produces much of the income that pays for the operation of the government because it is on private property that taxes can be assessed;

4. Private ownership of businesses increases the flow of money in the economy because individuals tend to invest their income in all aspects of their businesses instead of hoarding it or using it for nonproductive purposes;

5. When property and businesses belong to people they will be stimulated to increase their efficiency and thus produce more than under government ownership;

6. Private ownership results in less waste and a greater return for the capital invested;

7. Private owners of businesses will seek to influence consumers to purchase more thus providing a steady increase in the level of income and quality of life of families and the extent of commerce in the nation.

B. Free Market/Free Enterprise Capitalism

In Chapter II it was poined out that there is a direct relationship between capitalism and democracy. ***Capitalism requires the freedom provided by democracies and democracies need the economic foundation of capitalism.*** In the older democracies, the issue is how to preserve freedom from government controls to safeguard the free enterprise system. In newer democracies the issue is how to transform the economy into a free market/free enterprise capitalistic system and maintain it that way.

The greatest danger to capitalism in the older democracies is the expansion of government bureaucracies and government regulations that strangle free enterprise, as noted in Chapters VI and VII. Associated with these harmful effects on democracies is the negative attitude of government employees about private enterprise. There is a tendency for some government employees to believe that the government can provide services and manufacture products of better quality and at lower costs than private businesses. This tendency is destructive to free enterprise capitalism and needs to be overcome by government officials who support the private sector. Therefore, the director of each government agency must be appointed or elected from outside the government rather than being one of the members of the existing bureaucracy.

One of the greatest problems faced by new democracies is how to achieve a balance between the supply of products and the demand for them. This balance is especially needed in countries where private ownership has replaced government ownership of the means of production and strict government control of all commerce. Usually during the first year demand will exceed available supplies, particularly for food and other necessary consumer goods and equipment. Also, there may be a surplus of supplies in part of the country and a lack of them in other areas.

One way supply and demand may become balanced is for the suppliers to increase their prices so that fewer people can purchase the goods. When this happens and prices go up, government officials usually want to place controls on the prices. Although these methods for equalizing supply and demand may be used, neither is fully desirable. Letting those that have goods to sell charge as much as the purchasers will pay, however, is the normal process in a free market economy.

Government control is not natural and should be

avoided unless the seller has a monopoly on the product. A monopoly occurs when the only source of the product is the one person or organization selling it. A monopoly may occur in new democracies after people are allowed to buy and sell freely but before private enterprises are producing enough to meet the needs of people. Thus, the government may have to impose temporary price controls on the item if it is a product that people must have to survive.

Similarly, the currency of the nation should be freed from government control and allowed to float on the domestic and world money markets. When this is done, business persons, both within the country and outside of it, know the actual value of the currency. Thus, they can base their decisions about the prices for which they sell or buy products on a realistic value. Also, they will be better able to judge levels of return possible for the money, time and effort they might invest in business ventures in that country.

The value of the floating currency, however, may vary considerably because of the degree of confidence people have in the stability of the government and its economic policy. This variability may cause some misgivings on the part of people in a formerly communist country who have been accustomed to a stable value for their money. Although there may be large fluctuations in the value of the money at the beginning, allowing the value of currency to vary in the marketplace is a principal way to stimulate private commerce, including agricultural and industrial production. Any artificially controlled value of currency leads to reluctance on the part of individuals interested in exporting or importing products. Similarly, it raises concerns on the part of citizens who can grow, process or manufacture products because they do not know when the government might change the values or what the values placed on the money really mean in the marketplace.

For example, government leaders may discover that prices of goods, property and services are so high that business people in other nations no longer are trading or investing in their country. To counteract this, they proclaim that the currency is worth only one-half of what it had been. Consequently, the manufacturer who has spent money at the first value to produce a product discovers that he now receives one-half of what he expected because of the devalued currency. Because he has lost money he might have to go out of business. Certainly, he will not want to manufacture anything else unless he knows that the currency will have a stable value.

As soon as people are free to sell and buy goods on their own in a country where they had not been permitted to do this before, some of them will have products to sell. An example is an automobile sales business in one of the new east European democracies pictured on the next page. In

A new automobile dealership in a new democracy

fact, many people may have been selling goods secretly before on the "black market," that is, without letting the government know about the transactions. Therefore, the first thing that a new democratic government should do is to lift government restrictions on the selling and buying of products. Then it should encourage its citizens to produce goods by transfering from the government to the people businesses, land and other property that they can use to produce products.

Property ownership as well as the initiation and operation of all types of businesses require legitimizing laws. Citizens must have title to their property and their right to have businesses must be backed by courts in the government. Thus, there have to be procedures for registering deeds to property, corporation charters and transfers of property. These registration procedures can be simple with just essential data needed to be supplied to the government by registrants. Registration must be administered fairly to enable all citizens to have their property rights legitimized quickly.

In newer democracies where government ownership had predominated, the writing and adoption of contract laws and property and business ownership authorization laws must be undertaken quickly. Otherwise, free enterprise capitalism, and thus economic development, will be seriously hampered.

Another act the government can take is to eliminate or reduce government regulations that affect growing, processing, manufacturing, transporting and marketing products, except those proven to be harmful in terms of the health and safety of users. At the same time, taxes that impose a handicap on the production and flow of products to consumers should be eliminated or reduced. Similarly, any government processing of essential permits, such as those for building facilities, storing supplies and processing or manufacturing products whether for health, safety or environmental reasons, should be sped up so that enterprising individuals will not be hampered by delays. The objective should be to make sure that the energy, inventiveness and management skills of people driven by the profit motive are not hampered by government rules and processes. Under private enterprise, people work harder and tend to place work before pleasure in the tradition of Protestantism (discussed in Chapter IV, Part H.)

Matching supply with demand sometimes becomes difficult even in the older democracies. For example, World War II came to an end suddenly following the dropping of the atomic bombs on Japan. The United States industrial complex had been operating for years to supply the military. Suddenly, there was no longer a need for many of its military products and most of the manufacturing that was conducted during this period was to support the war effort. With the shutdown of much of its wartime industry, the United States had a problem of unemployment. At the same time there was a large demand for consumer products that resulted from shortages of these items during the war.

Congressional representatives and senators from states where unemployment was high pressured President Harry S. Truman to do something about it. They wanted federal funds to be spent in their states for government programs. Dr. John R. Steelman, in the role of Chief of Staff to President Truman, knew that it would be much better to have this serious problem solved by private enterprise. Dr. Steelman, therefore, met with the legislators to ensure them that their requests were under consideration. He had to affirm repeatedly that attention was being given to their demands because the legislators were very worried that they would not be reelected if the unemployment and inflation problems were not solved.

At the same time Dr. Steelman was meeting with legislative leaders, he was also contacting industrialists across the country. His objective was to find out what the industrialists needed to begin manufacturing the scarce consumer products. In some instances it was fuel that previously had been allocated for the military. In others, it was steel or another metal. In still others, chemicals. He then found out who had some of the material that were needed and arranged for a supply of them to be shipped to the manufacturers. Therefore, in the face of the mounting pressure from legislators on the President to initiate government programs, the private production of scarce products began to increase in the country and people began going back to work to produce, ship, store, and market them. Economic recovery was accomplished by private enterprise under the capitalistic system and not by socialistic government programs. President Truman and Dr. Steelman are pictured on the next page.

President Harry S. Truman of the United States and Dr. John R. Steelman Conferring in the President's Automobile.

The end of the "Cold War"with the collapse of the Soviet Union and the communist controlled eastern European countries resulted in a somewhat similar situation to what happened in the United States after World War II. These two momentous events led to a drastic reduction in the production of war materials with the result that defense businesses sharply reduced the number of their employees. Many workers remained unemployed until the companies were able to convert their businesses to peacetime products and services. A by-product of the unemployment was the loss of the United States Presidential election by the main hero of a short war between the United Nations forces and

Iraq that occurred in 1991-1992, President George W. Bush of the United States. He was Vice President while Ronald Reagan was President from 1981-1989, after which he was elected President. Both of these Presidents were Republicans.

It was President Reagan's administration policies, with some support of a Democratic Congress, that played a significant role in the ending of the Cold War and the final collapse of the Soviet Union. These included the strengthening of United States defense against the possibility of communist aggression, the development of the Strategic Defense Initiative, commonly referred to as the Star Wars Concept, the increase of support to people fighting communist dictators in other countries and the intensification of radio and television programs about the free world beamed to Soviet Union citizens.

Another government program following World War II in the United States also helped to stimulate private enterprise. In this program, American war equipment and supplies that could be used in the civilian sector were sold to war veterans. Veterans purchased trucks, tractors, trailers, heavy earthmoving equipment, buildings and all sorts of supplies at a minor fraction of their actual cost. This equipment was put right to work in communities all over the country by veterans who obtained it, resulting in increased economic activity. As a result, people no longer in the military or employed in defense industries found employment.

A more serious unemployment problem exists in new democracies where war industries were owned and operated by the governments. In those countries, however, there is a tremendous need for products to help the people increase their level of living. They need all types of household equipment, transportation vehicles and home improvements as well as food products. To meet these needs, the government owned manufacturing plants, agricultural lands and food processing facilities must be transferred to private owners. When this is done, the private ownership that results will stimulate independent businesspersons to respond to the demands of the market by producing what is needed and can be paid for by consumers. Although these entrepreneurs will face competition from producers in more developed countries, they will have several advantages including better knowledge of customer's requirements, lower transportation costs for their finished products and lower labor costs.

In socialist countries that have become democracies, the sale of government property to individuals and businesses should be done as quickly as possible. The government should sell the property at a price and with terms that purchasers can pay or repay. These transactions should be considered as an important means of stimulating production, rather than a means of supporting the government with funds that are obtained from these transfers of property. The importance of this privatization may be better understood when the example given in the next paragraph is analyzed.

Suppose that government owned equipment for making shoes is worth $100,000. If the government sells it to a business for a fraction of that, let us say $10,000, it may soon begin producing shoes. To do this, owners of the business must employ skilled and unskilled workers, they must purchase leather, rubber, plastic, cardboard and other packaging supplies. Other businesses will benefit from the orders for those supplies and also employ citizens and purchase supplies. In addition, the shoe company must engage an advertising and sales staff and pay for shipping the shoes to where they are to be sold. All these activities will require money in the form of credit at banks as well as deposits in the banks and an increase in general banking activities. Thus, the $10,000 may in a few years generate many times more in economic activity than the $100,000 the equipment originally cost the government. In addition, all the businesses and individuals involved will help support the government with taxes they are able to pay because of the private shoe manufacturing induced increase in associated business.

Leaders in new democracies sometimes believe that their economic development problems can be solved with money borrowed from sources outside their borders, such as from the International Monetary Fund, World Bank or banks in countries that obtain their funds directly or indirectly from capitalistic enterprises. Frequently, when such funds are obtained, they are used for consumption items instead of being invested in the means of production. Of course, some borrowed money may need to be used for food and/or fuel to enable the population to survive until enough necessities can be produced in their country. If most of the funds are used for that purpose, however, the productive capacity of the borrowing country will not be increased.

The result of borrowing for consumer items is to worsen the economic condition of the country because of the debt on which interest is due at the same time that the country has had little or no increase in its gross national product. Borrowing money to pay for food and other consumer items above those necessary for survival also tends to reduce the desire to produce on the part of citizens when they learn that the items they need will come to them without much personal effort.

It is recognized that some emergency funds may have to be borrowed from external organizations established for that purpose to purchase food if the food shortage is critical. The principle objective of borrowing should be to increase the agricultural and industrial production of the country to meet its internal needs and to produce for export. Increasing productivity will also lead to other benefits such as improvements in transportion of raw materials from the farms and mines to processors and manufacturers. These developments also benefit consumers.

C. Training for Successful Businesses

Because a significant proportion of small businesses fail — even in countries like the United States where the failure rate by the end of the second year is about 24 percent — small businesspersons must be given assistance by new democratic governments. The greatest unmet need is for training in all aspects of business. Training should include management decision-making, acquisition and analysis of critical supply and demand market information, and, perhaps most importantly of all, appropriate, complete, and timely accounting procedures.

Small businesses can be successful if:

1. They make products or provide services consumers need rather than those the small business owners would prefer to provide. Therefore, owners must study the market for the products they want to produce before they launch their businesses and then keep themselves informed about supply and demand and market trends;

2. They use their resources, labor, equipment and facilities efficiently and wisely. Many small businesses that fail purchase unneeded equipment and/or hire too much or inappropriate labor. Others fail because their owners attempt to operate their businesses without adequate equipment;

3. They do not invest their own personal funds in their businesses, or obtain credit, beyond the future ability of their enterprise to recover any money they advanced or repay the loans and interest on money borrowed;

4. They make management decisions on the basis of fact and not on religious or pseudo-scientific beliefs. For example, some farmers have produced poor quality products because they delay planting crops until the "moon is right" thus losing the advantage of excellent growing weather that occurred before the moon was in the right position, according to their beliefs;

5. They keep careful accounting records, and pay attention to their receipts and expenditure records that indicate whether or not their efforts are financially sound; and

6. They do cost analyses of each part of their business operations and base their decisions on valid cost data in comparison with realistic expectations of receipts. That is, they must list all of their expected costs such as: rent or construction of facilities, equipment, supplies, labor, management personnel, taxes, travel, communication costs, packing and shipping, interest on their capital investment and borrowed money, insurance and maintenance. They must evaluate and compare these costs in light of their expected income. For example, modern dairy farmers vary the amount and type of feed for each cow in accordance with the amount of milk and its butterfat content from that cow. Individual cows are replaced when the return from the milk they produce, in relation to cost of their food and care, does not meet the standards set by the dairy farmer. A cow may be replaced even though producing more income than expenses because another cow would produce an even larger return.

To be successful businesspersons must also learn how to prepare a careful business plan that takes into account all of the factors just listed and then learn how to determine whether or not their proposed enterprise can be successful and productive and what the financial risks are if they do undertake it. To evaluate the financial risk, potential businesspersons have to determine:

1. the amount of capital that will be required, including personal funds, loans or lines of credit;

2. the income they would receive during the same period of time from other work if they did not launch the business; and

3. the possibilities of success and failure.

By evaluating factors such as these, they can arrive at an estimate of the chances of making money or of losing all or part of their investment in the venture. They also can compare this with what they would have made by not doing it. These types of analyses provide a measure of the financial risk involved.

One principle involved in successful businesses is the necessity for the businessperson to know and understand thoroughly all aspects of production and marketing for the product or service he or she offers. In technologically advanced societies, acquiring the needed understanding may require formal training as well as practical experience. Some businesses begin as a hobby or small activity and later increase to large undertakings when the entrepreneur learns what customers want and how to supply it.

When businesspersons recognize the importance of training for themselves and their personnel, they will develop ways of obtaining it. Their own staff can conduct some of the essential training aided by experienced people in their industry within or outside their own countries. Other training can be obtained from organizations specializing in providing what they need. In new democracies, training organizations may have to be imported from other countries at first, but soon internal ones will be formed to meet training needs.

D. Supervised Credit for Small Businesses

Most small businesspersons need credit to initiate their businesses and/or to keep them operating. Because they know that a high proportion of small businesses fail, (some studies indicate that about one-fourth fail), the risk for lending money usually is more than most banks are willing to accept. To make a loan to people who intend to start a small business or are operating one, banks require that the owners already have a majority of the needed funds themselves. Banks do not help most small businesses because owners lack sufficient capital to meet their guidelines.

Since regulatory requirements generally do not permit banks to make high risk loans by themselves, governments need to establish programs that insure loans to citizens who want to start or expand their own small businesses. To provide these loans, an insurance system may be established by the government that is financed by a small charge on every loan, such as one percent. The government should establish a reserve of funds to reimburse banks in the event that a businessperson is unable to pay back the loan to the bank. Along with credit, governments in the newer democracies should provide business management training for small businesspersons in order to increase their rate of success, as suggested in Section C of this Chapter.

Such a program for small farmers was started during the depression of the 1930s in the United States. Credit, in the form of loans secured by farmers' land, buildings and machinery was granted only after each had developed a detailed plan of operations covering several years. After the farmers had a practical plan that indicated that they could pay the interest and principle on a timely basis, and it was approved by a committee of successful farmers living in the area, a supervised loan was made to them.

The loan included sufficient funds to pay all past debts of the farmer. With the loan, the farmers paid off prior mortgages on their land and other debts and purchased equipment, animals, animal food, fertilizers and household goods in accordance with their approved plan. The key to the success of this government program was supervision provided by experienced, successful farmers. These supervisors would visit the farm before the loan was made and then frequently during the year to ensure that the plan was being carried out. Adjustments were made whenever the farmer faced unusual problems such as illness or weather damage to crops or buildings. The cost of supervision came from the interest paid by farmers on their loans.

A weakness in this type of program is its eventual bureaucratization. That is, after following the initial design for a number of years, it becomes controlled by people who emphasize formal education on the part of its administrators and loan supervisors more than practical farm experience. This type of supervised loan for farm, or other businesses, does not have to be initiated and run by government. The government, however, is usually the only organization with sufficient resources to insure the large number of loans that are necessary.

In essence, many rural banks in the United States and Canada have a type of supervised credit for farmers, agricultural product processors, manufacturers and retailers because the bank owners, members of the banks' governing boards and administrators are, or have been, successful farmers or small businesspersons themselves. Thus, they know acceptable farm and other business practices and provide essential counseling to people borrowing money from their banks.

Governments in developing democracies should consider supervised credit for small businesses such as farming, processing, manufacturing, transportation, distribution and marketing. The credit should be supplied by private banks and the supervision by people with practical experience. Otherwise, there is a great possibility that the small businesses will be ruined, by being required to add unneeded administrative staffs or to maintain expensive and complicated accounting systems. For example, a Spanish speaking consultant with extensive experience in growing sugar cane and in the production of sugar and other by-products, assisted managers of a large Bolivian sugar production operation. By following his advice, owners of the business improved its operations. Instead of losing money it was beginning to be profitable. Not only were sugar cane yields improved and cane processing greatly increased, but a beef cattle enterprise was launched in which processed cane was used for part of the food for the cattle. To increase cane processing, new machinery was purchased overseas and shipped to the coast of South America.

Because this project was subsidized by the United States Agency for International Development, administrators decided that they should have representatives of one of the large auditing firms take over the management consulting service provided the owners. In less than a year, these inexperienced non-Spanish-speaking graduates of one of the highly-rated law schools, spent nearly two million dollars, but, because of their incompetence, caused the firm to go bankrupt. These well-paid advisors had no idea how to solve simple problems of sugar production such as transporting the already purchased machinery from ocean ports to the factory nor would they allow local managers to arrange this transportation. Their Spanish deficiency made it difficult for them to communicate with local authorities or to have effective rapport with them. As a result, the machinery was left to deteriorate where it was unloaded from ships and the factory was never enlarged and modernized.

The substitution of theory for practical experience by the new consultants produced an economic tragedy for the region of Bolivia in which the sugar mill was located, a financial loss to people in several countries who had invested in the operation, a waste of United States taxpayers' money, a dietary deficiency for the people who needed the protein that would have been produced by the beef cattle farms, and a loss to the environment that was beginning to have a diversified agriculture. The sugar production business became bankrupt but the consultants had a fine source of income while it lasted.

The recommendation made here is that a type of supervised credit for businesses be developed with assistance from the government but that the officials operating it be people with practical experience who know the local situation. Those receiving such credit must qualify for loans by preparing careful business plans that include management procedures, all costs and a market survey that determines the demand for the product or service. The increased success of the businesses will make it possible for loans to be repaid with interest, and also pay for the use of the money and for the management and supervision required.

E. The Limitations of Cooperatives

Many idealists have an unrealistic belief about cooperatives and try to have this type of economic organization established in developing democracies. To them, the word "cooperative" suggests that this type of business organization will solve the economic problems of the people. A cooperative is an organization owned and managed by the people who use its services. A cooperative grocery store is one in which the customers who buy the groceries for their personal use are members of and own it. A farm cooperative may be one in which the farm equipment, fertilizer, seeds and animal feedstuffs are purchased by farmers who are members of the cooperative that is managed by representatives they elect. As members, they share ownership with all other members.

Some cooperatives serve the purpose of their members well, but many of them are inadequate business organizations. Members frequently make the mistake of not realizing that every cooperative, if it is to be successful, must be operated like a regular business with strict accounting methods and management techniques that result in receipts matching or exceeding the expenditures. In addition, because the returns from cooperatives are divided among all the members, the incentive for cooperative employees to work hard is not as real to them as it is for employees of regular businesses. In some cooperatives people are considered to have joined just by doing business with the cooperative. Thus, many do not even know they are members or care about membership. As a result of factors such as these, many cooperatives fail. It would have been much more valuable to have had a regular profit-making business from the beginning instead of the cooperative.

In socialist countries where farming is being changed from state ownership of land and businesses to private ownership, each newly independent farmer can be allocated sufficient land for an economically viable enterprise. The pictures on the next page were taken in a East European newer democracy where some of the large government owned and operated farms are being divided into privately owned family farms.

Dividing state owned machinery among farmers, however, can become a problem. If they intend to grow crops such as grain, for example, every farmer must have the use of a grain combine. A combine, however, is expensive equipment for a farmer with limited capital. It also is used

Family farming in a former communist controlled country with the use of horses for power or small tractors and family labor.

for only a short time each year. The same situation is true for other major farm machinery such as a large tractor with gang plows or a corn harvester. The cost of the required capital to buy and maintain such equipment is a heavy burden for individual farmers when related to the limited use of the equipment.

There are several ways expensive farm machinery may be made available to small farmers. For example, one farmer may own a grain combine, another a corn harvester and a third a large tractor and gang plows. Then the farmers could work out an arrangement to share their machines among themselves. From a practical standpoint, this type of cooperatively used equipment is subject to problems because the equipment has to be kept in working condition due to wear and breakage and the work has to be done on each farm at about the same time. Who is responsible for the maintenance and who has priority for using it may be difficult to answer and lead to conflicts.

A second possible solution is for a group of farmers to own the machinery together. This is possible if each accepts his or her share of responsibility for maintaining the machinery and each member ofthe group agrees when to use it. A third solution to this problem of ownership and use of major farm equipment is for one person to own it, who then charges farmers for combining their grain, harvesting their corn or plowing their land. In this case problems of maintaining the equipment and determining priorities for its use are taken care of. It is the owner who has to keep the equipment operating and contract with each farmer to do his or her work.

The ownership of major equipment by nonfarmers, unfortunately, can lead to their ownership of other parts of farm operations such as the livestock, land and buildings. When this happens, the farm family loses much of its control of farming because they become contract employees of the corporations. The personal attention, dedicated work and innovation of farm families that made American agriculture so productive would be changed drastically by corporate ownership.

When the privately owned farms in the developing democracies become sufficiently productive, consideration can be given to allocating tasks requiring larger machines and their repairs to specialists. Large expensive, luxurious, and computer programmed machines are out of place in agriculture where land has just been divided into family farms. What really is needed, of course, are small tractors as well as the other machinery that can be maintained and overhauled by the farmers themselves. Having small machines they could pay for and then keep in repair themselves made possible the transformation of subsistence farming to the economically successful modern American and Canadian family farms.

F. International Trade

The importance of international trade should not be overlooked in developing democracies. In a nation where the economy operated under strict government controls, that is, what was produced and made available to consumers was determined by central planners, changing to free markets usually results in price increases. When prices increase, it is because the goods available are not sufficient to meet the demands of the consumers. Along with the new freedom to buy and sell in an open market, will be the freedom to establish businesses, including farming, manufacturing and processing enterprises that produce products to meet the demands. It will take new, private businesses some time to meet demands for products, however, because among other factors, they will be hampered by insufficient capital, and difficulties in obtaining production machinery and supplies of raw materials. Thus, prices would be expected to rise until the supply increases in response to the demand.

Temporary importation of the needed products should be enhanced by the government as a means of reducing inflation of product costs. Similarly, importing equipment required by businesses to produce goods may be essential. At the same time, exports may be necessary to produce income to pay for imports as well as for development of processing and manufacturing that can be done in the country.

The main methods the government should use to enhance international trading — importing and exporting — should be to allow it to occur without the barriers of tariffs and customs duties and to permit the country's currency to float in the world market. With a stable currency and free trade, businesspersons in other countries may be induced to buy and sell to trading partners in newer democracies.

Also needed is an efficient and quick system of moving goods across the country's borders. The export and import permits and any necessary inspections to determine whether or not actual contents of shipments match the list of contents indicated as being transported, must not delay trucks at the borders or keep goods on ships or in airports unreasonable lengths of time.

As noted in Section M of Chapter X, a very serious deterrent to importing in Poland in 1992 has been the length of time it took to process shipments by truck. Because of inefficiency involved in handling the paper work, lines of trucks waiting for clearance at the borders were kilometers long. In addition to the waste of fuel and time of drivers, it was an extreme under-utilization of capital invested in equipment. By increasing the number of customs officials working at the borders, much of this problem would be solved.

The possibility of unrestricted international trade, raises other questions that should be considered. An important one is: What products should be produced for export? Countries with natural resources such as ore and oil, although they may need to export natural resources to obtain capital for development, should have a long-range strategy for their management. Exporting natural resources in the raw state produces a much lower return than is realized from the sale of products processed or manufactured from them. Therefore, if it is necessary for some unprocessed natural resources to be exported, the return from them should be used primarily to improve the processing and fabricating industries and not to purchase consumer goods.

Government policy should make it possible for private businesspersons to own and develop natural resources and stimulate added value to them by processing and fabricating the raw material. ***Natural resources, no matter how much a country may have, should always be considered scarce — not unlimited.*** A method of continual evaluation of the extent and quality of natural resources should be devised in each country.

One error in international trading that has been made is the devotion of so much effort to producing products for export that the production of necessities is ignored. For example, when Europeans started trading for furs in North America, Native Peoples neglected their hunting, fishing and agriculture to obtain furs, eventually causing them to become impoverished. Under the "Five Year Plans" in the 1930's, Joseph Stalin emphasized production of grain in the Soviet Union, which the government exported in exchange for machinery. By taking the grain from peasants who raised it, and shipping it out of the country, millions of rural and urban people starved. Although considered barbaric by much of the rest of the world, this loss of life was justified by the communist leaders because the imported machinery strengthened the state and made it possible to build a large mechanized army.

Under a socialistic system where the industry is owned and operated by the government, rules imposed by central planners hinder meeting citizen needs. For example, factories in China were required to sell a sufficient amount of their production on the export market to pay for the supplies they needed to produce the products. An example of this was when special steel had to be imported to make razor blades. The problem the plant faced was to sell enough razor blades outside of China to pay for the steel, or shut the factory down. Because they were unable to export a sufficient quantity of razor blades, they had to limit their production even though the demand for their product within China was such that they would have had to operate 24 hours a day to meet it. With free enterprise in an uncontrolled economy, private owners of manufacturing firms would keep on producing to meet the need. The need for special steel also would stimulate steel manufacturers in their own country to produce the type of steel required.

Chinese communist leaders who set policy for their

centrally controlled economy were seeking to keep their socialistic businesses from spending Chinese funds outside of their country so that they could use the funds themselves to purchase what they wanted for the government — primarily armaments.

The balance of trade, that is the value of exports compared with the value of imports, has to be a concern of leaders in all nations. Rather than restricting imports, emphasis should be on increasing exports. Exporting and importing has to be understood as activities in a world market. Therefore, by decreasing the amount allowed to be spent on imports, a nation also may be decreasing the purchasing power of the country from which the imports come. Therefore, the nation restricting imports may be preventing its own businesses from exporting because they cannot sell their products.

Because international trade is so strategically important in the economy of most democracies, methods of increasing it should be emphasized. In addition to lifting restrictions on importing and exporting, means should be developed to ensure that market information is available to all possible foreign and domestic traders.

G. Improving and Maintaining the Country's Economic Infrastructure

One of the most serious problems facing developing democracies is an inadequate economic infrastructure to support a free market/free enterprise, capitalistic system. This problem includes inadequate communication, transportation, banking and credit. For a free enterprise capitalistic economic system to function adequately, the consumers, manufacturers, processors, farmers and sellers require complete information about the demand for products and the supply of products. To produce, transport, store and display products, each businessperson involved must use a standard currency and have sufficient financial resources to initiate and complete his or her part of the process, including the cost of producing the products on farms or in factories.

Thus, a banking system is necessary that allows for sound currency to flow among manufacturers and processors of products, providers of services and consumers. The banks must have sufficient funds in order for their officers to make loans so that 1) the producers can purchase the means of production including labor, 2) the distributors can build storage facilities, 3) the transporters can purchase and maintain equipment to move the goods and 4) the merchants can receive, maintain an inventory and sell the products.

In most new democracies, transportation and communication facilities usually need major improvement. There is a direct causative relationship between the success of the economic system and the ability of people to transport products, machinery and equipment to where they are needed and to communicate rapidly over long distances. These needs were recognized in countries like the United States where "farm to market" all weather roads were constructed with federal and state funds allocated to local governments. These roads were built from the villages to the farms, most with a gravel or crushed stone foundation topped by an asphalt mixture. It is these types of roads that need to be constructed in many countries.

Later, in the United States, a national network of major highways across states was built by the federal government to make possible rapid movement of products by large trucks as well as transportation of people in personal vehicles and buses. Most of these roads were built by private road building businesses who were given contracts by the government. A tax on gasoline and diesel fuel was used to pay the cost of much of this road construction. The cost of a few major highways in some states was obtained by selling bonds to the public on the basis that a charge would be made for each vehicle traveling on the highways. Most of these "toll" roads have been very successful both from a financial and a transportation standpoint.

One of these, built in 1940, that crossed the whole state of Pennsylvania is still operating. Truckers and automobile drivers were willing to pay the tolls on this 581 kilometer road because it saved them time and cost them less to drive on it than on other roads. It is straighter and smoother than other roads and the drivers do not have to slow down and stop in villages along the way.

The extent of the transportation and communication problem in democracies needs to be determined as accurately and as quickly as possible. One method might be to plot on a map of the country where the resources are, including the people who supply the labor as well as serve as consumers. Then determine what means of transportation between the critical areas are necessary and which should have priority. The role of national and local governments in building transportation facilities should be determined as well as the means of paying for them. Included in every plan must be a method of maintaining the facilities when they need repairs and replacing them when they become worn out or outmoded. If such a long term plan is not followed and funds are not provided on a regular basis, the country will be faced with unsafe bridges, worn out road surfaces and overcrowded highways. Road construction and improvement must be emphasized and not delayed as was the building of a replacement bridge in a country under communist control. This is indicated by rusting steel girders on a bridge shown in the picture on the next page.

Rusted steel girders beside a bridge that cannot be used until it is rebuilt.

Governments have important functions to perform, especially in newer democracies, if free enterprise is to become successful. Every possible action, however, should be evaluated to determine whether it enhances development of free enterprise or whether it provides government substitutes for private endeavors. Governments should undertake only those tasks that cannot be done by individuals or private organizations, such as building roads between pro-ducers and consumers. Even building and operating some roads for motor vehicles, might be done privately. For example, a number of important roads in the early history of the United

States that made it possible to move people and goods, were built and maintained with private funds as profit-making businesses. Ferries across rivers, canals between cities, and railroads also were privately owned and operated. When people demanded higher quality and larger transportation facilities, yet were reluctant to personally pay businesspersons enough for using them, sufficient capital was no longer available to construct and operarte such facilities. Thus, the government had to provide the facilities and pay for them with taxes.

Almost all essential services such as communication systems whether they be telephone, radio, television or computerized information gathering, storage, retrieval and transmission must be privately owned and operated. The owners and operators should be citizens of the country they serve. Businesses supplying electricity to residences as well as natural gas, where it is available, also should be privately owned and operated. The government's role should be to determine the best way to enhance development of such services by private businesspeople through minimizing government restrictions and bureaucratic controls and stimulating private businesses with credit guarantees, temporary subsidies and tax limitations. The government should make providing utilities needed by all sections of the economy attractive to entrepreneurs. The importance of privatizing utilities can be best understood if these four principles are kept in mind:

1. Most utility services have been found to cost less in other countries when provided by private means rather than by the government;

2. After the government starts providing utility services, it will be very difficult for the citizens to get them privatized;

3. The government will never receive any taxes from its own operations;

4. Government run services tend to be less responsive to actual needs of those people, businesses and other organizations for which they are provided. If a citizen does not like the service provided by a private business, he or she may be able to obtain it from another private business. If the service is provided by the government, however, it is much more difficult for people to influence the administrators because, even when they are contacted directly, their response is that they are furnishing the service as it is supposed to be done, or in accordance with the law, and they cannot change it; and

5. When a service such as electricity, gas or telephone is from the private sphere, the

privilege of providing it is granted by the government in the form of a monopoly. Thus, setting the amount of charges for the service becomes a government responsibility. The rate charged has to be fair to the consumers but high enough to make it possible for the providers to maintain and modernize the equipment and still receive a profit from the enterprise that compares with returns from other business ventures. To make rate decisions, a commission, consisting of a group of citizen leaders appointed by elected government officials, usually is established.

Modern technology has made communication services easier to install and less expensive. For example, to have telephones in every home and business no longer requires numerous wires across the countryside. Instead, relays at strategic locations can be utilized at a much lower cost. Businesses should be encouraged and assisted in building communication facilities that are essential in a modern free market economy, rather than having this done by the government.

****

Chapter XIII.
Social and Educational Aspects of Democracies

A. Religion and Freedom

When people come together in groups they can have the feeling that collectively they have special power, and that it is a power greater than that of all of them together. This feeling can result in individuals becoming part of a destructive mob that they never would have thought they could be part of, or it can be constructive and religious in nature. This feeling of a power stronger than their own individuality helps bind people together and reinforce their beliefs.

A religion is a set of values that guides the behavior of adherents and provides them with an understanding of their existence as humans. Some people are participants in an organized religion while others are not. An organized religion has leaders and a doctrine that spells out the beliefs of its adherents and the rituals by which the beliefs are maintained. It is the rituals that necessitate religious organizations with professional leaders. It must be stated clearly in constitutions of democratic countries that citizens will be free from government interference in the practice of their religions as long as it does not endanger the lives of others or violate health and safety rules in the society.

One problem with organized religions, as with other organizations, is the ethnocentrism that develops among members, that is members come to believe that they are better than nonmembers. In a democracy, citizens must be free to develop their own set of values, to determine their own morals, and to behave as they like, unless their actions are dangerous or very offensive to others. Neither the government or members of any religion can be allowed to restrict the rights of adherents of other religions.

Unfortunately, the leaders in some religious organizations exert such a strong influence on members that they are not free. The behavior of people is controlled by their morality, that is, the values they have learned in their families, neighborhood, religious or other organizations and formal schools. These values limit what people will do. There is a range of beliefs among people in most organizations from liberal to conservative, with some members adhering strictly to the group's doctrine and others who do not. Beliefs of members of organizations, including religions, and the rituals associated with the functioning of the group, do change from time to time and may vary from country to country.

The Judeo-Christian origins of democracy and capitalism were pointed out in Chapter IV. It was noted that when Protestantism developed out of Christianity, and religion no longer was all- encompassing, individualism became possible. This freedom to think, to worship and to better oneself through one's own effort led to the type of democracy that exists today. It also meant that people could insist that their government not establish a religion or interfere with people who practiced various religions. At the same time, religious leaders could be prevented from interfering with the government.

The constitution must protect the individual's right to practice his or her religion as well as to protect the right of people to choose not to belong to any organized religion. Religious leaders and their followers can be tyrannical against members of other religions and/or nonbelievers. On the other hand, lessons about being honest and helpful to others, provided to children by some religious teachers can cause them to be tolerant of people who differ from them and supportive of the freedoms that come with democracy.

B. Population Planning

The number of people in a nation becomes an issue when there are too few to utilize the resources or when there are so many people that the resources are not sufficient to meet their needs. Prevention of childhood deaths and the lengthening of the lifespan of the population of a country due to disease control and improved diets, has resulted in more people than can be supported above a minimal level of living in some countries.

A country has to have land and water from which its citizens can obtain sufficient food to feed themselves along with other natural resources such as forests and minerals from which they can produce clothing, housing and all the other items people require, or it has to have a way of obtaining them. If enough food cannot be grown in a country, the people must be able to exchange manufactured goods or natural resources such as oil, gas, or minerals in international markets for what they need. The exchange of natural resources for food and other goods needed is feasible for only a few nations, however, because many do not have resources others want, and those that do, face increasing costs of mining and extracting. Therefore, overpopulation problems in most countries will not be solved by exchanging minerals for family necessities.

The policy in countries where leaders deemed it desirable to increase the number of citizens has varied from encouraging people to come to the country as immigrants to glorifying large families and to giving awards to mothers who have many children. When Hitler ruled Germany, he wanted more children so that he could increase the number of youth in the military force when they reached their late teens. To encourage citizens to have large families, he honored women who had large numbers of children. To emphasize the role of husbands to sire and wives to bear children, a risque statue was cast and publicly displayed in Germany depicting a man pursuing a woman for that purpose.

For countries whose leaders feel that there are too many people to be supported by the resources, government policy varies from educational programs about preventing pregnancies to decrees prohibiting marriages until citizens are in their 20s or limiting the number of children they are allowed to have. Those disobeying the population control laws face loss of employment and/or compulsory abortions and fines.

Because overpopulation is a critical issue in some of the older democracies as well as in a number of newer ones, it must be given serious consideration. Before policy is made, however, the variables involved in population decline or growth should be understood. Therefore, some of them will be discussed in the next few paragraphs.

Perhaps, the most important question to consider in relation to the population is why people have children. Unfortunately, children frequently are by-products of sexual relations where the goal is sexual pleasure. Pregnancies resulting from such unions may be accepted as when married couples have one child after another for many years, or the possibility not even considered, as when couples, particularly teenagers, engage in casual sex. For certain ethnic groups, men believe that they must have children, particularly sons, to prove their masculinity. When the child is a boy, the male parent with those beliefs celebrates by telling everyone he sees about his parenthood and giving his friends small gifts. When the man is married to the mother, being proud of fathering a girl or boy is laudable. Unfortunately, however, teenage boys also may feel that they must father a child to prove their manhood. To them, marriage is not part of their thinking nor do they consider caring for the child their responsibility. Some girls also deliberately become pregnant to gain the approval of boys or prove that they are mature women.

In many societies, children are considered to have economic value as additions to the labor supply. The number of children of a farm couple has been a factor in determining whether or not a bank has been willing to lend money for the farm operation. Unskilled child labor is still a significant factor in the economies of some countries but, as the production and service segments of the economic systems become modernized, less unskilled labor is required and child labor becomes less important. The expectation then is that families will have fewer children who will be better educated to become part of the skilled or professional labor force. This reduction in family size occurs as countries become industrialized and people move from rural to urban environments.

Large numbers of children have been considered in some countries as being important because they are consumers of the products of the society. When there already is an excess of people in relation to the resources, however, the amount and type of consumption possible by the increased number of children is at a rudimentary level.

A strong desire to have large numbers of children exists in areas where parents want to ensure that they will have children to care for them in their old age. As indicated by the picture on the next page, infant health care combined with family planning programs are being operated in a number of countries. An important goal of these is to counteract the fear of parents that they may become old without children to care for them as well as their desire to have children to improve their family's economic situation. The message to parents and potential parents in these programs is that by having fewer, children can be better cared for and provided more formal education. Therefore, they would live to become more productive adults who would be of much more value to their parents as the parents aged than adult children hampered by illness and poor formal education because there were too many for the parents to feed, cloth and nurture.

A distinguished public health physician and behavioral scientist, Julius Prince, M.D., DPH, with mothers and children in an African Village. Dr. Prince spent many years teaching health workers how to prevent childhood illnesses and death while instructing parents about the merits of having fewer children who would live healthy long lives and thus be of great help to their parents as they aged.

Another significant factor in the number of children families have is a religious one. The doctrine of a number of religions is that married couples should play a significant role in populating the earth with children who will become members of the religion, thus extending its influence. The special consideration given to mothers and children in other religions, encourages mothers to have more.

The question of who has the most children in a country needs to be analyzed. Is it married couples who have a stable union and a prosperous level of living? Is it those families whose economic status is low or those dependent on government aid? Or is it the very young who are not married nor yet capable of handling responsibilities of children? Are most children being born into two-parent or one-parent families? Some of the data to answer these questions exists on records kept by most countries to register births of children. Most of the information, however, would have to be obtained directly from the people in scientfically designed samples of the population.

The number of people in many areas of the earth used to be controlled by environmental resources. Overpopulation would be reduced by food supply famines for two reasons: first, major famines caused by variables such as lack of adequate rainfall, would lead to the deaths of large numbers of people; and second, seasonal famines and a generally poor diet resulted in a low birth rate.

For a female to become pregnant, she cannot be extremely thin. For example, women in a dry African region had few children, and practically none when they were nursing babies because their body fat was very low. When these families were moved to small settlements to make room for the waters of a dam that was to flood their lands, they began to have children every year or sooner. Their diet had changed from the food they and their husbands gathered and hunted to grains and meat supplied by the government. Instead of undergoing semi-starvation during parts of the year during which they became thin, they gained weight and kept it the entire year. Another example, this one from the early years of industrialization in England, relates to "shop girls" — those working in factories — who did not become pregnant while they were young due to their inadequate diets and long hours of work, even when they were married.

The role of women in a society is a major factor in the number of children they produce. As women become emancipated from the control of men and religious leaders, they tend to limit the number of pregnancies they have as well as the number of children they bear. When their self-conception includes active participation in their society outside of their homes, whether or not to have children and how many becomes a decision derived from rational discussion rather than an accident of emotional conduct. Whether or not parents can provide adequate health care and education of their potential children becomes part of their equation regarding having or not having children. When women control their own destinies, the widespread practice of preventing child birth through abortions may be necessary only for medical reasons or when women are raped.

In determining whether or not population size of a democracy is a problem for which solutions should be sought, focus should be on the quality of the enculturation of children and youth and the level of living of the people. What does adequate enculturation entail? It is transfering the culture of a society from the adults to the young. This includes family values from both a father and mother, along with knowlege and skills required to become productive participants in a free market capitalistic economy. The level of living should be one in which people have adequate diets, preventive health and medical care, a safe environment and educational opportunities.

The number of unwanted babies should be reduced from the high levels occurring in some segments of societies. To accomplish this reduction, effective pregnancy prevention methods need to be available along with education to influence individuals not to engage in sexual intercourse without first seriously considering the possibility of a pregnancy and their responsibilities if they become parents.

If potential parents accept the concept that the objective of becoming pregnant is to produce a productive member of society rather than a baby, population control will become a reality. This has happened in industrialized democracies.

C. Social Stratification

The division of people into social strata is a normal human characteristic. There are no classless societies. When seen in terms of the products of a society, some people have more material goods such as larger residences, vehicles for personal transportation, and higher quality clothes than others. There are numerous other ways individuals and groups of people differ from one another and most individuals are in more than one stratum of their society. For example, they may be immigrant adults working in a bank who belong to a special church and to an athletic club. These characteristics indicate they are in four types of strata. Most of the social characteristics of people like those reflect normal human behavior as a result of type of formal education attained, family background and occupations.

Regardless of the stratum of a person, however, the capacity of his or her brain is equivalent to the brain capacity of everyone else, unless it has been damaged by disease, physical injury or chemicals, while in the womb or afterword. ***"All men are created equal" stands out in the United States Constitution as a real truth.*** Americans who do not know that healthy people start with the same brain capacity will describe with wonder the progress of a person, whose parents had very little formal education and brought their children up in an impoverished home, to a leadership position in industry, education or government.

They do not recognize that the learning that occurs during the enculturation process from the time the person is born, varies tremendously. It is the learning that takes place that produces the differences among people. The child from a poor family who rises to the top was stimulated to learn and to achieve in some way, usually by a relative or teacher, and was able to obtain the necessary learning materials for increasing his or her knowledge and skills.

Although social stratification is a normal part of human behavior, there are serious problems that can evolve from it that must be solved in a democracy. In a democracy people must be free to move horizontally and vertically in their society. They must not be restricted from preparing themselves to enter into professions or to engage in endeavors, occupations or business enterprises of their own choosing. They cannot be restricted by governmental laws or societal rules from intermarrying or from entering into contracts with people regardless of their status or stratum in their country. If they are, democratic ideals cannot be attained or maintained.

When relationships among people are restricted by custom or laws, the society becomes a closed caste system instead of being stratified by a diversity of classes that they can enter or leave in accordance with their accomplishments and interests. Democratic processes are in danger when people in one stratum assist only members of their own stratum. For example, when members of one ethnic strata control a money supply and make funds available on a favored basis only to other members of that same ethnic group, the freedom and equality of the nation's population is endangered. Because of the freedom that does exist in a democracy, there is always a danger that one strata will control significant segments of society such as the banks or the mass media, or parts of the government. In new democracies, this type of control by one part of the population can cause the nation to revert to a nondemocratic government.

The language of the nation's Constitution must be carefully crafted to safeguard the rights of the citizens to determine their own roles in the society. The public education program must be designed to help all people prepare for productive roles in the nation. The selection of government employees must be on the basis of relevant qualifications for the positions and not on family connections, ethnic background or any other personal or group characteristic. If families and schools teach children that they are equal and that they can get to the top through their own efforts, social strata barriers will be weakened to the extent they will no longer be important to new generations.

D. Social Welfare

People in all societies have to face fluctuations in resources available to them during their lives. The variations may be caused by a variety of conditions, some personal and some impersonal. For example, they may have illnesses or accidents that prevent them from supporting themselves and their families. Their endeavors or the businesses where they are employed may fail due to poor management or a depressed economy. There may be a fire or storm that destroys their means of making a living or there may be an extended drought that prevents them from farming.

For some, however, their misfortunes result from their own behavior. The enculturation through which they went may not have transferred to them the work ethic or the belief that they should save during prosperous times to enable them to survive during bad times. Similarly, they may use health damaging products such as alcohol, tobacco or drugs or participate in anti-social activities. Still others may not have acquired necessary training to obtain economically satisfactory employment. Then, there are children who have lost their parents, and women and children who do not have husbands or fathers because they have died, have abandoned their families or never acknowledged fathering the children.

Regardless of the type of government, there will be some citizens who need economic help. Such help can be in the form of a social welfare program. If assistance is not provided, starvation, sickness and abnormal development on the part of children will result. An inadequate diet for pregnant women and use of tobacco, alcohol and drugs produces babies with growth and health problems as well as some with severe brain damage. A poor diet for children influences ability to learn as well as growth. In countries where diets were improved after World War II, the average height of children has increased several inches over the height that was considered normal before and during the war. Adequate diets have resulted in children's improved performance in schools.

Also, people who have passed their most productive years tend to have greatly reduced income. In a society where freedom prevails, social controls and internal strength of families is weakened. Old people become separated from their children and grandchildren. Their help is not needed around the farm, business or home, and they are not given the task of helping raise grandchildren. In countries where it is traditional for people to retire at 60 years of age, those living beyond that age frequently are not employed and have little income. Due to improving health standards and living conditions in most countries, a larger proportion of the population each year will live beyond retirement ages.

Retirement pensions based on insurance principles have been a means of providing income after retirement for people who have been employed as well as their spouses. Income insurance for retirement requires that the insured pay specified amounts to an insurance company each month or year during the time they are employed. When they have their businesses contribute, or when employers also contribute to retirement income insurance of their workers, the amount they may receive each month or year upon retirement can help them live independently at a satisfactory level of living.

Because a proportion of those having insurance will die before they reach retirement age, the money they paid for the insurance will not be used by them. Instead, it will be used by those still living, thus providing them with more money than they would have received just from their own payments for the insurance. In addition, money they paid during their working years will also have earned the insurance company interest, part of which the company uses to pay its expenses while the rest is added to the return for those living beyond retirement.

The government of some countries either pays elderly people a living allowance each month directly from tax revenues or requires employees and employers to contribute a percentage of the employee's earnings each pay day into a government controlled insurance fund. In some countries, such as the United States, the amount required to be paid each payday to the "social security" program is more than 14 percent of the wages, one-half usually being paid by the employers and one-half by employees. The amount already paid into the United States social security fund to pay retirees is tremendous; in a few years it will total nearly a trillion dollars. The amount paid each year to retirees is also very large; it totals more than two hundred seventy billion dollars each year.

There are two reasons the proportion of wages necessary to keep this government insurance financially sound is as high as 14 percent. One reason is that employees are living longer than anticipated. The second reason, much more important than the first, is that many of those receiving retirement income were not enrolled in the program for many years and thus did not contribute much to the fund. In addition to substantial income each month until they die, recipients receive other benefits that they did not pay for while employed.

In reaching an understanding of the social and economic status of people in a country, how such status relates to their life cycle should be analyzed. As may be seen in Figure 7 on the next page, people who live long lives pass through phases from birth to death. From birth to adulthood the phases are helplessness, dependency, sustaining, contributing, and leadership. Then as they become old, they again go through contributing, sustaining, dependency and helplessness. The age at which the average

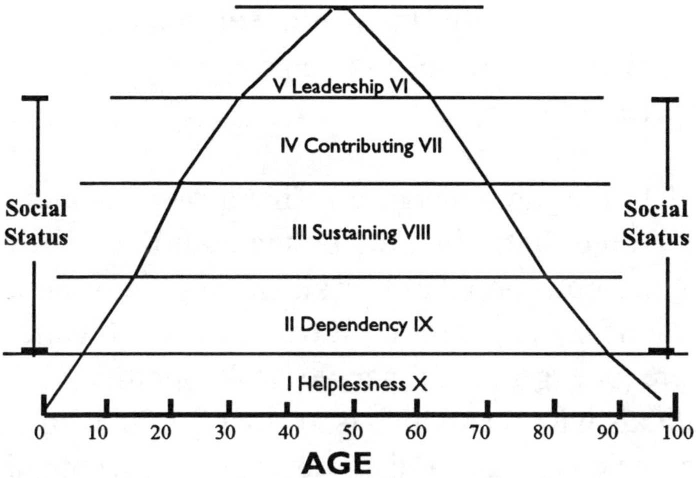

Figure 7 - Social Status and the Life Cycle

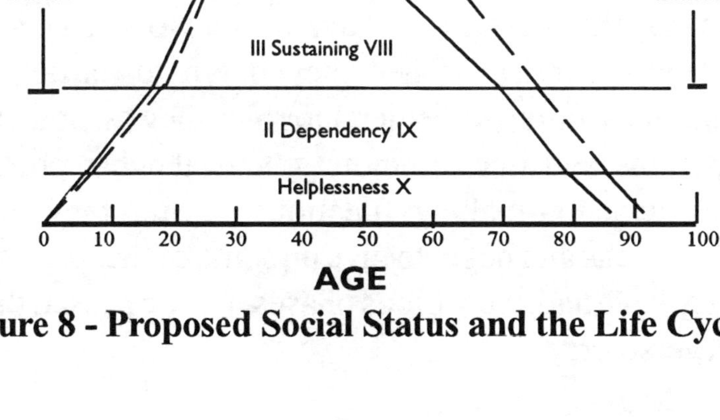

Figure 8 - Proposed Social Status and the Life Cycle

person enters and leaves these phases varies from society to society. Some individuals remain healthy and actively participate in their society until they are in their late eighties and nineties while others become unproductive in their thirties and forties.

The diagram in Figure 7, first developed and applied to the United States in 1961 by the author, can be used to depict a whole population's situation in any country or segment of the population. It can be a worthwhile way to compare one group of people with another as well as individuals with that which is normal for the whole group. Those making such a diagram must conceptualize the average situation for all people included in the group being analyzed.

Characteristics which together constitute the status of people at any age include: how long children remain with their parents, how much they help their parents around the home, when young people begin working in economic endeavors, the roles adults have in the workplace such as helper or supervisor, when they begin to participate in community affairs, the leadership roles they assume in their occupations and the community, and at what point they assume decision-making functions. After they become senior citizens and begin to give up some of the responsibilities they have had, the various phases may be passed through in a reverse order.

The chart also can be used to establish goals for the society. For example, if it is learned that the most productive period for most people is from 25 to 50 years of age, as the solid line in Figure 8 suggests, the goal could be to increase the productive period. This might be accomplished by providing more training for young people and better medical care and diets for adults. Under such improved conditions this period of high productivity would be lengthened so that the new high productive years are from 27 to 57 years as suggested by the dashed line in Figure 8.

Regardless of where they are in the life cycle, when citizens are not able to solve their food, housing and medical needs, the government has to provide assistance. The danger in having government programs, however, is that they may become a substitute for individual and family initiative. Moreover, when a social welfare program is launched, those administering it may come to believe that people receiving the aid are entitled to it on a permanent basis.

If the government assistance provided comes to be seen as an entitlement program, that is, money and services people are given that they consider they are entitled to for some reason, instead of temporary welfare, those receiving it may quickly become welfare professionals. Welfare professionals devote their energy to assuming the characteristics and learning the jargon that ensures that they will continue to qualify for the government food, housing, medical care and money.

Homeless adults — individuals who choose to live on streets, under bridges or in abandoned houses — have increased in number in many countries during the last few decades. Homelessness has also become professionalized for some people. That is, the homeless learn what they have to say and how they have to act to obtain free food, free clothes and free housing when they want them. Some also become professional beggers, using the money to support themselves at a minimal level or to purchase alcohol.

This welfare professionalization has a negative effect on the operation of a democratic capitalistic society for two reasons. First, it can be very expensive and a serious drain on government tax funds—taxes that individuals and businesses must pay, — thus taking from them funds they could reinvest in enterprises. Secondly, it keeps people from becoming productive members of the society as employees or owners of businesses. ***Unfortunately, prolonged welfare can change the values of receivers so that they no longer believe in being independent and lose the pride of supporting themselves.*** Worse yet, these values can be passed on from parents to children and then by the children to their children for generations.

Democratic governments have to provide welfare

assistance when it is needed, but at the same time beliefs about freedom from government control, independence, hard work, and self improvement must be preserved and strengthened. The best way to do this is to provide welfare assistance in exchange for work, if the individual or a member of the families receiving it is able to work. For example, people who were considered to be "down on their luck," that is, they had lost their jobs or incurred some misfortune, but were still able to work, were given employment by local governments building roads or some other task that had to be done during the 1920s, 1930s and 1940s in the United States. In this manner they received the assistance but contributed to the community and were not encouraged to give up work ethics. A program like this can be the best type of welfare for people who need it.

In older democracies, businesses and government agencies have cooperated in providing training for individuals on welfare who are paid while receiving the training. Although tremendous sums of money have been spent on such training, not many of the participants continued working after it was completed. The few successful training programs recognized that, not only did the welfare participant need to acquire knowledge and marketable skills, but they also had to accept work ethic values. The best results occurred when the trainees were integrated into the regular work force individually. When this happened, they formed friendships with other employees and adopted their work habits. To accomplish this change involved giving up some of their former friends and associates along with their old way of life.

E. Education

A democracy is a type of government in which citizens must be active participants if it is to be successful. They must be involved, not as slaves or robots or passive people, but as concerned individuals. Democratic citizens are participants in the decision-making process of their government — decisions that must be made on the basis of reason and respect for other people rather than on emotions and selfish interests.

The substitution of reason for uncontrolled emotional psychological reactions as the basis for judging issues requires special knowledge and tolerance. The knowledge must be based on objective observations of phenomena and not on information considered factual just because it has appeared in newspapers or magazines or is accepted as the truth by people who have not questioned its validity. Consideration of alternative solutions to issues offered by others, along with negotiation and persuasion necessary in a democracy, require a type of mental sophistication that can come from objective formal education. The responsibility of those planning democratic governments, or who are striving to improve those already in existence, is to design an educational system that will enhance citizens' understanding and appreciation of democratic processes and thus help them to become effective participants in the democracy.

Because every citizen in a democracy should be a participant, formal education that prepares them to become productive adults must be available to everyone regardless of their economic status. To function effectively in a democratic, free market, capitalistic society, people should:

1. be able to read, write and speak the language of their country;

2. understand and appreciate democracy and democratic principles;

3. be able to carry out mathematical calculations that are necessary for them to function in a free market economy;

4. know the history of their country;

5. know and appreciate how their government functions;

6. understand their duties and responsibilities in their democratic government and how they can carry them out;

7. have knowledge of science and the scientific method in these fields as a minimum — chemistry, physics, biology, geology and cultural anthropology;

8. understand the free market, free enterprise, capitalistic economic system and the fundamentals of how businesses, including banks, operate;

9. acquire knowledge of world geography including names, locations and resources of their neighboring countries and the major nations of the world;

10. have knowledge and appreciation of world affairs, that is, the interrelationships and interdependence of nations, especially as these affect their own country;

11. learn a second language that will be most useful to them as adults, such as the language of a neighboring country with which there is significant economic interchange. (With

English being widely used in the world, it should be considered as a second language in many countries where it is not the first language); and

12. appreciate the relationships between dietary and physical activity practices and healthy bodies.

Literature and the arts, considered so important by many educators, should not be overly emphasized. For example, coverage of literature deemed significant would enrich relevant sections of the curriculum rather than being isolated in separate courses. Similarly the arts, such as music and drama, should be integrated into the curriculum so they relate to the 12 critical areas rather than being isolated from them. Physical training should never be transformed into semi-professional athletics or sports.

The goal of formal education should be visualized as a method of ***preparing every child to be capable of becoming President or Prime Minister of his or her country.*** With that goal serving as the foundation of education, citizens will be produced who are productive members of their society and strong supporters of democratic principles. This will be true whether they become construction employees, members of the professions, scientists or businesspersons.

The 12 areas of knowledge advanced as being essential in an educational program for children can be achieved during 12 or 13 school years with an integrated curriculum. For children of all citizens to have this training, regardless of their economic situations, the government has to provide free schooling for all except those whose parents decide to pay for private schooling. For adults in the society who have not had the advantage of the newly organized school curriculum, the government should subsidize continuing adult education to help them acquire the knowledge and skills adults must have to participate in democratic processes and to function effectively in the free enterprise economy.

To develop the suggested curriculum, each of the 12 instructional areas should be reviewed to determine how the necessary knowledge and skills to be imparted can be fitted into an effective integrated curriculum. Some aspects of all the areas should be included at every level of instruction in the school career of children from the time they enter preschool programs at very young ages, or regular school at five or six years of age, until they complete the highest level. Except for a very small number of children handicapped by brain damage, every child has the same capability of learning. ***Success in learning is directly related to the quality and relevancy of the instructional methods and not to children's capacity to learn.***

The instructional team must include the support, participation and encouragement of parents, grandparents and other adults with whom children interact away from schools and from whom children receive security-giving relationships. Therefore, learning materials must be prepared in the schools for adults that will make it possible for them to help their children. For parents who have not had the advantage of formal schooling beyond an elementary level, these materials should be in the form of cartoons, pictures, illustrations and diagrams with a minimum of text. Such information, carried home by youngsters, should cover only attention stimulating aspects of the lessons rather than details or extensive information on the subject areas. The objective should be to catch the attention of the adults so they can be part of the instructional team by becoming interested in what children are learning and by helping them with their lessons. Thus, they also will benefit by learning with and from the children.

Extra curricular activities for children, such as science and engineering, journalism and drama clubs and sports activities, should be conducted by volunteer parents who have special interest and qualification in subjects that would enrich the lives of children. For adults, this opportunity to relay to children their own knowledge, skills and enthusiasm can be a most rewarding experience while for children it can have a lifelong positive effect.

Student involvement in their own learning should begin during the first days of school and continue throughout their school careers. Similarly, the 12 suggested areas of study for the first 12 years of schooling should be integrated in the lessons from the beginning. For example, students learning to read, write and speak can handle words like "democracy," "free enterprise," "respect" and "negotiation," if they are acted out in class. At an early age, children can practice forming and running organizations. In doing this they can learn to write constitutions and rules for operating their organizations. They can elect officers and conduct meetings in accordance with parliamentary procedures such as Roberts Rules of Order. By limiting their time in office to a short term, such as a week, children will learn to transfer control to new officers as well as how to be both an officer and a regular member.

F. Science and Technology

Science, which is a systematic method of analyzing problems and developing new concepts and relationships among concepts, evolved from the freedom to investigate questions by observing phenomena. The amount of freedom provided by democratic governments resulted in the rapid expansion of science in democracies and also tended to stimulate some nondemocratic governments to support scientific endeavors within their countries. Science that is fostered by totalitarian leaders of governments, whether they be socialistic, religious or military dictators, however, is directed science. That is, the scope of scientific inquiry is under the direction of government leaders who require scientists to focus on the problems of concern to the government officials. This narrows the scope of science and prevents scientists from investigating a wide variety of phenomena. Democratic government officials also support scientists to work on problems they select. The majority of grant funds, however, must be given to scientists who make proposals on subjects of their own choosing.

It is the individualism that democracies make possible that results in a vast variety of inquiries on the part of scientists. The scientific approach is a rational one in which findings and the methods followed to produce them are publicly described for other scientists to verify by their own experiments. At the same time that a scientist has an objective and rational outlook, and is a free thinker in that way, he or she may still be religious and/or be completely tolerant of the sacred aspect of life in the community and nation. This apparent dichotomy is possible because people tend to compartmentalize their interests in their minds as well as in their activities.

Science and free enterprise capitalism are dependent upon each other. Science needs capitalism for the funds required to carry on research and capitalism needs the results of scientific endeavors to produce the funds. Simi-

Hatten S. Yoder, Jr. PhD, Director Emeritus, Geophysical Laboratory, Carnegie Institution of Washington.

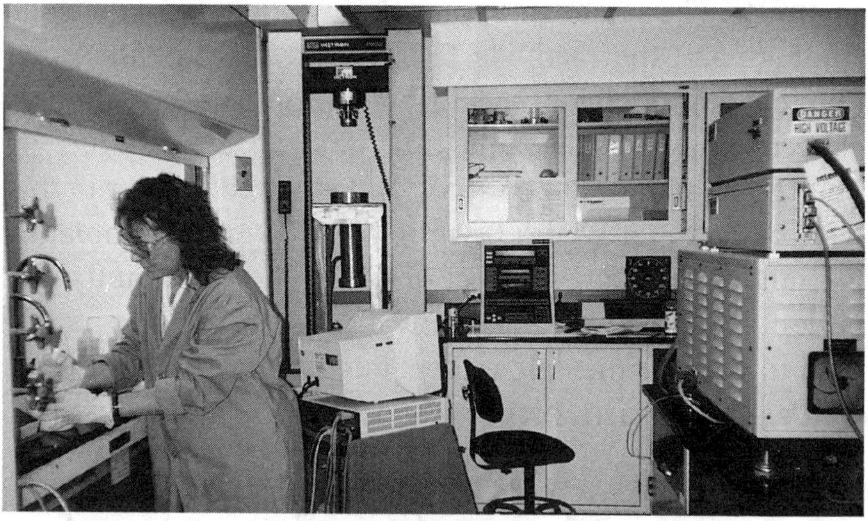

Heather D. Boek, PhD, Senior Research Scientist, Corning, Inc.

Scientists at Work

larly, capitalists need the techniques, equipment, processes and products developed from the concepts of scientists, that is, the technology. Without the inventions by scientists and engineers, the expansion of markets by businesspeople would be limited.

It is the ingenuity of scientists and engineers that produce the inventions and innovations necessary for an advancing technology. The ever increasing knowledge from scientists, who have the freedom to examine phenomena of interest to them, when applied to human needs improves the quality of life for everyone. To support the continual advancement of science, citizens and their elected representatives must have an understanding and appreciation of science and its contribution to their wellbeing and prosperity.

To stimulate inventions, the democratic government must have a "patent law" that protects the ownership rights of the inventor for a reasonable period of time. To provide such protection on an international basis, the government must cooperate with other nations. People and organizations will be willing to invest time, money, and effort in developing new products and technology when they know that they will be compensated for it.

A free press, free speech and the freedom to form organizations and meet with other people is essential for

the continual advancement of science. Ideas or hypotheses about problems in science as well as methods of solving problems originate and multiply during discussions of their work by scientists in oral sessions and in printed articles or documents. The printed word is a necessary method of storing knowledge and transferring it to the new generations as well as distributing it among people in the professions. Without printed journals and computer records, science and technology cannot advance rapidly. Nor can medical care personnel, educators, agriculturalists and all the other professionals in society improve their skills to any great extent and thus, increase the benefits of their service to the citizens without such exchanges of ideas and results.

In any country, scientific endeavors can be hindered by internal bureaucracy and external government regulations. The bureaucracy within universities and research organizations where scientists work increases the cost of scientific endeavors, reduces innovation, and lengthens the time required to solve problems. Bureaucracy causes scientists to devote a considerable amount of their time to paper work and less to their research. When decisions about methods of conducting research begin to be made by bureaucrats, scientists are required to follow standardized procedures and limit their efforts to problems selected for them. This results in more time being necessary to solve problems. Also government regulations may seriously limit the range of issues scientists are permitted to pursue as well as the materials and equipment they need for their experiments, thereby decreasing the possibilities for discoveries and inventions.

Leaders in democracies, especially new ones, should carefully examine government activities in relation to science to make sure scientists are encouraged rather than discouraged in their countries. ***Scientific analyses and experimentation and technology development can contribute more to make prosperity possible than any other factor in an economic system. If science is not expanding in a country, that country's freedom, education and productivity is likely to be limited.***

G. Democracy/Free Enterprise Study Groups

To assist people in understanding the principles of democratic processes and the free market/free enterprise, capitalistic economic system, study groups should be formed by citizens in newer democracies. These should be organized for all types of people. They should be for farm and village residents and for urban people in small and large cities. They should be for judges, lawyers, police personnel, businesspeople, legislators, government employees, scientists, engineers, employees of manufacturing industries and other businesses, youth and adults. The people already promoting democracy in their countries should initiate study groups among their members and promote this process by organizing other study groups in their communities. Also, there is a critical need for such study groups in schools and universities where both faculty and students separately or together can benefit.

The need for people to learn how to function under freedom is so great that the preparation of discussion outlines and well-illustrated informational materials should be made available free or at a very low cost. Each study session should concentrate on one facet of democracy or capitalism. For example, one topic could be simple procedures for conducting group meetings while another could be the production of individual wealth through private owner-

A Study Group

ship of businesses and how this process contributes to the improvement of the economic condition of everyone.

The study group participants would learn that because capitalists do not hoard their money but rather spend it to expand their businesses, the money flows to other people who are their employees or who supply them with the raw materials, machinery, office supplies, transportation and services they require to operate their businesses. In turn, the people they pay for the supplies use the money to buy the products they need and to employ people to produce the supplies they sell to the first businessperson. Of course, the employees spend their wages for the food and consumer goods they need.

A study guide should be prepared with case histories to illustrate the principles involved including statements by individuals already owning and operating businesses. Similarly, practice exercises for the group members to do individually and together would enhance the desired understanding. People who have lived under governments where their activities and thus their level of living were controlled, may be envious of a neighbor who, through hard work under free enterprise soon begins to live better than they. Those jealous of the new capitalists need to understand that the wealth the free enterprisers are acquiring is helping the whole community to prosper and that they have the right to own property and to start businesses themselves and thus improve their own living.

There are numerous principles and processes in free market capitalism that are not known and/or understood by those not having had the advantage of living in a capitalist society. Return on investment is one that is not understood by many people in formerly socialistic countries. After working on a potentially lucrative business proposition with individuals in a new democracy, capitalists are astounded when their new associates ask how they are to be paid. Their question indicates that they had not yet recognized that the return or profit on the investment of their time and money, would be their pay. This concept, as well as many others, can be learned in study groups where realistic case histories are used with members taking the role of entrepreneurs, employees, business partners and bankers.

The study guide for business people also has to emphasize the necessity of adequate accounting procedures and the use of market data. For law enforcement personnel, human rights and due process guaranteed by their Constitution must be emphasized. For each group, the focus has to be on issues of concern to them as well as on general principles of democracy. One session should be on the values held by members of older democracies as described on pages 109-110 of *The Evolution of A Democracy* published by the College of Democracy and referred to on Page iii of this book.

The promotion of study groups could be a voluntary project of spouses of elected leaders including legislators in the democracies. If this initiative is exercised at all levels of government, from the local jurisdictions to the national government, it would make participation in study sessions prestigious. The volunteer study leaders could form a nation-wide organization to provide encouragement, assistance and high status to study group leaders across their country.

****

The health of a democratic society may be measured by the quality of functions performed by private citizens.

—*Alexis de Tocqueville*

Effective government is honest government.

—*John B. Anderson*

Experience teaches us to be most on our guard to protect liberty when the government's purposes are beneficial.

—*Louis D. Brandeis*

Liberty is the only thing you cannot have unless you are willing to give it to someone else.

—*William Allen White*

All political power is a trust.

—*Charles James Fox*

The whole purpose of democracy is that we may hold counsel with one another, so as not to depend upon the understanding of one man, but to depend upon the counsel of all. For only as men are brought into counsel, and state their own needs, and interests, can the general interests of a great people be compounded into a policy suitable to all. —*Woodrow Wilson*

Chapter XIV.
Successful Democracies

This book began with optimistic predictions for the future of democratic representative governments around our planet and for improvement in the quality of life resulting from this superior type of government. Although numerous problems were discussed in the 13 succeeding chapters, the book ends with the same happy optimism.

There are many more democracies now than there ever have been and there will be more in the future. Although it does not label them democracies, Freedom House, an organization that evaluates civil and human rights, classifies countries into "Free States," "Partly Free States" and "Not Free States." Their evaluations from 1973 to 1993 indicate positive changes as shown here:

Number of Countries

Year	Free States	Partly Free States	Not Free States
1973	53	39	71
1983	52	56	59
1993	75	73	38

This increase in the number of Free States and corollary decrease in the number of Not Free States will reduce the killing of basically unarmed, nonresisting civilians who are arbitrarily put to death by their own governments. Of the 143 million people put to death in the 20th century, 115 million were by Not Free States such as Nazi Germany (20.9 million), Soviet Union (61.9 Million, Chinese Communist government (38.7 million), Chinese Nationalist government (10.2 million), Japan (5.9 million), Yogoslavia (2.6 million) and Armenia (1 million). The number murdered by the governments of Cambodia, Vietnam, Uganda, Iraq and a number of other Not Free countries are not yet compiled.

Governments of Partly Free States killed an additional 3.1 million while Free States put to death .8 million or about one- half of one percent of all those put to death from 1900 to 1993. These data were compiled by Professor Rudolph J. Rummel at the University of Hawaii. This information is another indication that democratic governments are by far the greater respecters of human life. Thus, a continual increase in the number of democracies, predicted in this book, would greatly reduce the number of citizens in the future who are murdered by their own government leaders wielding totalitarian control over them.

The evolution of democratic governments is in response to the progress most humans have made in getting along with each other. Instead of settling disputes with physical conflict as did their ancestors, people are relying on negotiation and concessions to solve territorial, economic and personal differences. For the modern human, reason controls emotions so that leaders in mature democracies do not use force to maintain peace with each other.

Unfortunately, however, some totalitarian ruthless governments still exist and will persist until the people being repressed by them can obtain sufficient influence to replace them. The process of gaining influence is very difficult because under repression people are prevented from acquiring essential characteristics needed, such as leadership skills and a favorable economic status that make it possible for them to resist totalitarianism. It is important, however, to recognize that although very unusual and surprising when it occurs, there have been a number of dictators such as the leader of Chile, who have voluntarily given up control of their countries in favor of democratic governments. Also, some monarchies are permitting and even encouraging establishment of elected councils whose members have limited powers of government. These councils can be positive movements toward eventual democratic governments.

The most important change instigated by a leader in the twentieth century was Mikhail Sergeyevich Gorbachev's policies in the Soviet Union. Under economic and military pressure from the Western World, and from people in countries under Soviet domination like Poland, as General

Secretary of the Communist Party and later President, he came to the conclusion that strict socialism could not compete as an economic system with capitalism and that change was essential. His "perestroika" doctrine, previously described by the Soviet sociologist Tatyana Zaslaluskaya combined with his "glasnost" policy of openness, resulted in freedom from the Soviet Union for countries like East Germany, Hungary, Poland, Romania, Czechoslovakia, and Yugoslavia.

This release of formerly independent countries from the strong Soviet military control was followed by the dissolution of the Soviet Union into its original republics. Gorbachev continued his policies, at great risk to his own life from conservative communist leaders in his country. Although he survived an attempted coup, another leader, Boris Yeltsin, became the hero during it by resisting the communist military with assistance of citizens who chose democracy over socialism. Because of his popular appeal, Mr. Yeltsin was elected President of Russia, the largest of the former socialist republics. He thus took the leadership of the new democratic government away from the man who made the changes possible.

It is emphasized that Mr. Gorbachev did not have to advance perestroika and glasnost. He could have operated as the head of a dictatorial regime as had his predecessors. Similarly, Boris Yeltsin could have become a dictator rather than an elected official subject to future elections with the necessity to cooperate with the elected legislators. These two men played key roles in changing the way of life for large segments of the world's population. This was especially true in the countries under domination by the Soviet Union as their governments were changed from totalitarian regimes to developing democracies. For people outside of the direct control of the Soviet Union, there was a general reduction in the fear of modern warfare between superpowers who suddenly began to cooperate with each other. Instead of remaining hostile they began the process of reducing the number of nuclear arms.

Significant participants also in this world shaking change, of course, were Presidents Ronald Reagan and George Bush of the United States and Prime Minister Margaret Thatcher of Great Britain. It was their administrations' policies that provided the economic and political pressure that President Gorbachev faced as well as encouragement for him to continue perestroika and glasnost.

The first step in the process of achieving liberty and the freedom to pursue happiness for citizens of a nation is the writing and adopting of a constitution that guarantees full rights for everyone. Constitutions of democracies evolve through much discussion and when adopted they legalize talk. Due to this freedom of expression, successful democracies may seem to outsiders to have chaotic governments.

This apparent confusion is because representatives of the people who make the laws spend a considerable amount of time talking about issues and advancing arguments in support of what they think is important and giving the reasons they intend to vote for or against a proposed law. Also, voters may seem to be frivolous in their political affairs because they may belong to one party yet vote for the candidate of another party. For example, although membership in the Republican Party in the United States is smaller than the Democratic Party, voters elected Republican Presidents in 1980, 1984 and 1988.

Legislators in older democracies may seem unpredictable in their reasoning and behavior by stating that they want to trim government spending yet demand large expenditures for projects in the districts they represent. They do this because they place the interest of the people who can vote for them over national interests.

The constant talking, criticizing of government leaders, and bickering among citizens about issues that concern them is evidence of an effective democracy. Further evidence is the tendency of citizens to exercise freedom in voting for individuals they want to elect, regardless of the political party affiliation of the candidates. Similarly, elected officials who seek benefits for their constituents are serving the functions of democratic government by representing citizens in their areas. At the same time, however, they should determine whether or not a program for their constituents is justified in the light of its possible effect on meeting national needs and thereby be statespersons.

When they live in a democracy, what people want from their government for themselves, their children and friends is important. They can value a paternalistic or maternalistic government that provides for them without their having responsibility for meeting their own needs or they can insist on one that encourages free/market capitalism, promotes science and technology, ensures religious freedom, requires law and order and justice for all, stimulates educational achievements and rewards hard work, self improvement, tolerance and cooperation. If their predominate vision of their government includes loyalty to the basic values of democracy including an acceptance of the fundamental dignity of humans and support of the principle of equality and brotherhood and they personally believe in honesty and fairness, their government will prevail. Such a vision will produce a secure future where men and women will have meaningful lives during which they will strive to improve their communities as well as the economic, intellectual and social status of their own families in a just and humane society.

Can democratic governments help people achieve their goals better than other types? The concepts in this book provide a positive answer to that question. An answer, however, may be meaningless if it does not come from the individual himself or herself. People must be stimulated to realize that it is their own beliefs — their own way of life — that either limits their obtaining a satisfactory level of living and having a government they can control, or makes these possible. Similarly, it is what they want, and their willingness to work for it, that offers the best possibility for a continual improvement in their quality of life as well as a democratic government that permits them to be free.

For those who have lived for years under totalitarian rule, the freedom of a democracy may make essential a change in their beliefs and behavior. They must overcome those values and ways of living learned from their previous experiences that are stored in their brains. Otherwise, the habits of the past will destine those unwilling to adjust, to a life of mediocrity and frustration. The author hopes that the information, concepts and practical suggestions concerning democracy contained in this book will stimulate people to adjust their thinking in ways that will make possible the fulfillment of the splendid potentialities everyone possesses.

****

INDEX

Abortion, 78

Academic
freedom, 14

Acculturation
defined, 223-224

Adams, John, 206

Advertising and capitalism, 35

Africa, xi, 77, 361-362
countries' elections, x

African National Congress and
communism, 233-234
in South Africa, 233-234

Americanization
of immigrants to the United States, 185-188

Anderson, John B., 164, 392, 306

Aristotle, 88

Armed Forces - see military

Arms Trade
international agreements, 52

Articles of Confederation
of United States, 87, 217

Asia, 77

Australia
civilian control of military, 43-46

Balance of Power
military role, 51

Balance of Trade - see trade

Bancroft, George, 60

Banking System, 325, 346
and need to provide credit, 204

Beliefs - see values

Berardo, Felix M., 60

Bible, 74

Bi-lingualism
individuals, advantage of for, 189
nations, danger of for, 189

Bill of Rights, 212

Black Market, 171, 314

Boek, Dr. Heather D., i, 384

Boek, Millard E.
town Councilperson, 261

Bolivia, 334

Bork, Robert H., 140

Bosnia, xii

Boy Scouts, 183

Boys Clubs, 183

Brainwashing
defined, 21, 22, 173-174

Brandeis, Louis D., 196, 392

Bribery
and political campaigns, 114-115
a market of buyers and sellers, 249
method of attaining influence in
government, 112-115

Brunner, Edmund de S., 200

Buddhists, 67

Bundy, McGeorge, 196

Bureaucracies
advertising, 154
almost immune from examination, 156
controlling them, 288-290
danger to capitalism, 314
dangers to democracy, 127, 141-163
definitions, 141-144
expansion, 133
hinder science, 386
interpretation of legislation, 156
legislators, 144-145
organization, 141-144
orientation of new members, 148-149
prevents assessment of responsibility
and performance of personnel, 156

prevention of citizens' rights, 156
prevention of some democratic processes, 152-156
in private enterprises, 151
for regulations, 138
threat to new democracies, 289-290
used to control people, 102-103
why they grow, 144-147, 162

Bush, George Walker
and collapse of Soviet Union, 397
hero of United Nations war with Iraq, 323
reduction of federal regulations, 129
transfer of office, from, 107

Businesses
training for small, 327-331
how to be successful, 327-331
credit for, 331-336

Bylaws, 172

Byrnes, James F., 88

Campfire Girls, 181

Camp David Accords, ix

Canada, 222-223
civilian control of military, 43-46
Western Arctic and Subarctic, 223-226

Capitalism
and access to information, 36
and advertisement, 35
capitalistic objectives, 40
competition essential, 100
defined, 28-29
dependent on science, 383
and economic growth, 33-35
as an economic system, 28
effects of, 38-39
free market/ free enterprise, 314-327, 399
and free trade, 35-38
funding of science, 39
humanistic, 41
and individual independence, 42
individuals strive to improve, 274
Judeo-Christian Origin, 355
a method of distributing wealth, 40-41
and Protestantism, 72, 86
and scientists, 34
triumph over Marxism, 202

Carter, James Earl, Jr.
biography, ix-x
the Center, x
the Library, x
the Museum, x
Foreword by, v-viii
observer of elections, 242

Caste System - see Social Stratification

Castro, Fidel 109

Catholicism, 86
role in developing Poland's democracy, 74-75
missionaries, 224-225

Central American elections, x

Character
defined, 180-182
development in children, 183
foundation in the family, 177-183

Charters, 278

Checks and balances, 212

Children - also see parents
economic value, 358-359
why people have them, 357-361

Chile, 395

China, Peoples Republic of, ix
division into independent provinces, 219
control of industry, 340

Chinese Communists, 21, 344-345
citizens killed by government, 394

Chinese Nationalists
citizens killed by government, 394

Christianity, 70, 72
Bible, 74
in formation of United States democracy, 73-75
morality, 74
and Native Americans, 224-226
policies backed by police power, 224
promote enterprise, 316

Churchill, Winston S., 94

Citizens
ameliorating critical differences in a nation, 216-221

Citizens rights 13, 210-212
to appeal government decisions, 14, 23
bureaucratic prevention of right to object, 156

lack of restrictions, 9, 10
to meet and form organizations, 13
middle class, 80-81
to own arms, 14
to petition about grievances, 156
to trial by jury, 14
of the unorganized, 113

City Jurisdictions, 266-267

Civilian Conservation Corp
(CCC), 264

Civilized behaviour, xiii, xv

Clinton, President William J.
transfer of office, to, 107

Cold war, xiii

College of Democracry
Board of Advisors, iv
objective, iv
source of information, 205

Common Law
based on Constitution, 208-210, 278
defined, 7

Communication - see infrastructure

Communists and communisim, xii
Chinese, North Korea, North Vietnam
relearning centers, 21
party, 396

Community
government, 4
organization, 254-259

Competition
among animals, 90-91
in enculturalism, 95-98
essential in capitalistic societies, 100
and free trade, 38
for political office, 114
Soviet Union, v, xiii, 94
universality, 91

Conflicts
ameliorated by change in human
behavior, 232
how to resolve, 232
negotiation and concessions, 395
reason controls emotions, 395
resolution, 221-237
stopped by United Nations action, 235

Conspicuous Consumption
as a method of control, 98-100

Constitution
all men are created equal, 364
Bill of Rights, 212
for childrens' organization, 172
civilian control of military, 58
and common law, 278
defined, 6-7, 25, 211
development of, 207-216
first step in developing democracies, 207, 397
and free speech, 114
full rights for everyone, 397
and the judicial, 278, 282
laws derived from, 208
legalize talk, 397-398
cannot justify majority control at
expense of minorites, 214-215
may not be followed, 207
protect freedom of and freedom from
religion, 353-355
right to associate, 277
role of lawyers in preserving, 282-283
safeguard rights of people, 366
should require local governments, 270
how to write, 211-215
of United States, 74, 217

Contracts - see laws

Cooperatives
limitations of, 336-340

Corruption
bribery of government employees, 156-160
use of bribery, 112-115
controls, 248-252
of elected leaders, 108-109, 112-115
embezzlement, 251
payoffs for election help, 250-251
role of PAC's, 114-115
ways to prevent, 160-162
widespread malady, 248

Costa Rica
no national military force, 50, 58

Council of Freely Elected
Heads of Government, x

Councils
first step toward democracy, 395

Councilperson - see townships

Credit
needed in democracies, 204

supervised for businesses, 331-336

Crum, Bartley C., 2

Cub Scouts, 183

Cuba
and the United States, 109-110

Culture,
defined, 166-169
diversity, 219

Currency
free from government control, 316-317
sound currency needed, 346

Custom duties - see taxes

The Czech Republic
communist government treatment of heroes, 110-111
free from Soviet domination, 396
and political parties, 246

Debt
loans for production, 325-327

Decision-making
consensus method, 176-177
participative, 103-106, 117
process, 175-177

Declaration of Independence
of United States, 87

Democracy
advice, sources of 201-205
basic values, 399
and capitalism, 42
how children learn principles of, 171-173
danger from military industrial complex, 44
evidence of effectiveness, 394
and free enterprise, 27-42
and free enterprise study groups, 387-391
and free trade, 35-38
and freedom of thought and action, 68
Greecian, 69
ideal, 197-199
importance of immigrants to learn about, 184-189
and individual independence, 42
individualism, 193
issues in establishment and maintainence, 207-305
issues settled by concessions, 221
Judeo-Christian origin, 355
learned 165-194
learned by children, 382
lobbyists threat to, 112-116
modern participative, 69
number increasing, 393
organization from small local jurisdiction to national, 253-270
power is shared, 218
practical experience, necessity of, 203-204
principles defeated by forms, 158
principles learned by children, 171-174
and religion, 68
role of women, 77-78
structure compared to military, 54-57
successful, 393-400
superior type of government, 393
and value of human life, 55-56

Democratic
neglect, xiii

Dictators
dismissing legislators in parliaments, 49
fear political parties, 246
reasons they give for taking control of governments, 46-47
unmet promises after elections, 47
wealth transfer to other countries, 57

District of Columbia
in the United States, 254, 268

East Germany - see Germany

Economic freedom
and political freedom, 28

Economic growth
and capitalism, 33-35

Education, Formal, 376-382
available to everyone, 377
basic requirements, 377-379
compulsory, 12
curriculum, 190
and democractic values, 183-184
importance of instructional methods, 380-381
professional educators changed goals from performance to sensitivity, 190-191
public, 264
reason instead of emotions for judging issues, 376
relearning centers, 21
role of parents, 381

Ego, 65
extension with guns and knives, 96
and membership in organizations, 273

and political party membership, 243

Egocentrism, 243
cause of conflicts, 230-231
defined, 65, 193
and political parties, 243-244

Egoism, 231

Egypt
Camp David Accords, ix

Elected Officials
bond with voters, 120-121
rewards for people supporting them, 251

Elections
election process, 237-242
fraud, 237-242
may be method of manipulating people, 207
may not be democratic, 16
practical step toward democracy, 207
secret ballet, 237-239

Emory University, ix-x

Employees
labor unions, 71, 275
labor union leaders, 232-233
prevention of monopolies, 41
right to organize, 41

Enculturation
attention to in democracies, 193-194
competition for minds of children, 95-98
defined, 166-169
and leadership, 118
effect of population growth, 80
importance of normal, 177-180

Engineers
produce inventions and innovations, 385

England
Air Force, 111
and custom taxes, 287
immigrants, 188
media coverage of crimes, 97
and "shop girls", 362

English Language
and immigrants to the United States, 184-189
as a second language, 378-379

Eisenhower, Dwight D., 44-45

Ethnocentrism, 65, 193, 218-219
cause of conflicts, 230
defined, 170
diversity dangerous to a country, 189
maintained in democracies, 218-219
and membership in organizations, 273
and political parties, 243-244
religious, 76, 354

Evolution
human, 91-92

Evolution of a Democracy, The, iii, 216, 390

Executive
branch of government, 6
bureaucracy, 142-144
sessions not secret, 15

Family
farms, 333
foundation of all human societies, 82-84
gangs take place of, 180
importance of two
parent, 180-183, 193-194
limiting size, 80
natural limit of size, 81-82
and number of children, 355-363
provide security-giving
relationships, 182
single parent, 85-86
size and participation in democracies, 81-82
values and professional educators, 83

Family Planning
and capitalism, 39
and health care, 359-360

Farms
family, 338
transfer of government land to private
owners, 337

Formal education, 237

Fosdick, Harry Emerson, 2

Fountaine, Jean de La, 88

Four H Clubs, 183

Fox, Charles James, 392

France
gift of Statute of Liberty, 186

Free Enterprise/Free Market, 185, 194
capitalism, 314-327, 399
and corruption, 249
and democracy, 27-42

demand and supply in determing prices, 33
democracy study groups, 387-391
dependent on science, 383
and economic development, 36
learned by children, 382
and families, 82-83
and population size, 61

Free States, 386-387

Free press and free speech, 270-271, 385-386
and dictators, 270
life blood of democracies, 270
reporting of murders, 97

Freedom
of expression, 69
importance of sharing, 192-193
individual, xiii
to prosper, 80
of speech, 114
from want, 80
work of, xi

Freedom House, 393

Gangs,
of children, 172-173
take place of families, 180

Georgia Institute of Technology
and President Carter, x

Georgia Southeastern College
and President Carter, x

Germany, 20, 110
border with Poland, 293-296
Communist East Germany, 179, 308
free from Soviet domination, 396
punishment of youth, 179-180
Nazi, 394
population expansion, 356-357

Girl Guides, 183

Girl Scouts, 183

Glasnost, 396

God/Supreme Being
and Christianity, 69
communist attempts to eradicate belief, 63
God chosen leader, 66
widespread beliefs, 63

Goethe, Johann Wolfgang von, 164

Gorbachev, Mikhail Sergeyevich, 395-397

Government
communist, 23, 26
defined, 3-5
democracy rating, 16-17
democratic republic, 4
dictatorial, 23, 26
duties and limits controlled by citizens, 192
expenditures audited, 251
ideal characteristics of, 5-17
insurance for retired years, 368-370
learned, 4
maternalistic, 399
paternalistic, 399
regulations, 40, 78, 119-140
repressive, 27
role of women, 77-78
and social welfare, 367-376
theistic, 23, 26
totalitarian, 390
type of is learned, 165-166
utopian, 4, 5, 17

Governmentocracy, 130-136, 163
condition of dictators, 133-134
control by citizens difficult, 133-136
defined, 130, 132-133
disease of democracies, 133
inhibited freedom of citizens, 163
negative effect on individual rights
and freedom, 130-133
statesmen and stateswomen must
control it, 134, 139
effect on technological progress, 130-132

Government Employees
bribery of, 156-160
dedicated workers, 149
difficulty of citizens to petition, 156
number is a significant proportion of the
population, 162
objectives, 148-149
and private ownership, 149
procurement issues, 160-162
socialistic tendency, 147-150, 203

Government Forms
negative effect on democratic
principles, 158-159

Government Programs
negative effect on families, 85-86
should strengthen families, 85

Government Regulations
bureaucracy, 125-128
Cat Law, 122-128

citizen pressure for,123-124
control of supply and demand, 315-316
controlling, 295, 296-301
of currency, 316-317
danger to capitalism, 314
and decline of democratic
principles, 119-142
emotional bases of, 128
evaluating, 298-299
expansion of regulatory staff, 295, 298
further special interests, 297
hinder science, 386-387
imposing value on citizens, 78
incentives, 138-139
limiting number of children, 78
necessity for essential ones, 136-139
necessity to evaluate objectivity, 135
negative effect of, 120
origin of, 121-124
prevents scientific and technical
advances, 300-301
and profits, 297
reduced by President Bush, 129
restricting private enterprise, 128-130, 319
restrictions on freedom, 128-133, 139
should be limited, 301

Granada, 106

Grand Jury, 280

Grant, Ulysses S., 200

Great Britain, 24
civilian control of military, 43

Greed, 230-231

Gross National Product, 27

Hale, Nathan, 184

Haiti, 106

Hawaii
University of, 394

Headstart program
who benefits, 154

Hinduists, 67

Hirohito, 231

Hitler, Adolf, 110-111, 231
and population expansion, 356-357
youth organization, 20

Homelessness - see welfare

Hoover, Herbert C., 306

House of Representatives, 254

Hughes, Charles Evans, 206

Humans
equal brain capacity, 18-19
superior organisms, 3
unique personalities, 19

Human dignity, xiii

Human Evolution, 91-92
brain capacity, 62

Human Rights, ix

Humanitarian
standards of international conduct, xii

Hungary
free from Soviet domination, 396

Hussein, Saddam, xii

Immigrants
and free enterprise, 32
importance of learning democratic
principles, 184-189, 192
Korean, 32
problems due to, 188
to the United States, 185-187

India
1951 Planning Commission, 196

Individual
security-giving relationship needed, 272

Individualism
democracy, 193, 272

Infrastructure
improving the economic, 346-352
privately owned communication
services, 350-352
rapid transportation and communication
necessary, 346-349

Inkatha
in South Africa, 233-234

Interaction, human
defined, 167-169

equilibrium, 228-230
significance of, 169-170

International trade - see trade

Iraq, 226, 323

Islamic, 67

Israel
Camp David Accords, ix

Japan
citizens killed by government, 394

Jefferson, Thomas, 2, 164, 199, 306

Jews, 67, 109

Judaism, 86

Judeo-Christian
moral value, 87
origins of capitalism and
democracy, 355

Judges, 278-283

Judicial
branch of government, 6, 282
derive decisions from constitutions, 209
function, 142
independent, 8, 211
courageous and dedicated judges needed, 252
reasons for justice, 281
sessions not secret, 15
system, 278-283
varies among democracies, 24

Jury
trial by, 14, 278

Kay, P.E., 200

Keeping Faith: Memoirs of a President, x

Kiffer, Albert
town Councilperson, 261

Kinship, 3
government, 4

Kiwanis Key Clubs, 183

Komsomol Organization, 20

Korean War, 45
immigrants, 32

Kuwait, 226

Labor Unions - see employees

Language, 169, 377

Laws
authority over human behavior, 278
contract, 12, 319
patent, 385
private ownership guarantees, 318-319

Law enforcement
maintaining law and order, 283-285
well trained and paid police force
necessary to prevent bribery, 252

Language
one official, 12
human evolution, 91-92

Leadership, 17-18
attributes, 117-118
dictatorial, 390
risk of, 116-117
skills, 395

Lee, Robert E.
on characteristics of a gentlemen, 93

Legislative
branch of government, 6, 254
sessions not secret, 15

Legislators
dilemma faced by, 120-121
may seem unpredictable, 398
pressure from citizens, 121-123
selected, elected and rejected by voters, 7
staff growth, 126

Legislature
bureaucracy, 144

Lenin, 231

Level of Living
and advertiseing, 35
defined, 132
effect of government regulations, 132
improvement by immigrants, 188
effect of beliefs, 399-400
and quality of life, 204

Lincoln, Abraham, 88

Loans - see credit

Los Angeles, California USA, 32

Lobbyists, 113-115
extra branch of government, 113
power, 113
threat to democratic government, 114

Luther, Martin 69

Lux, Villiam
town Councilperson, 261

MacArthur, General Douglas
removal from command, 45-46

MacKenzie River, 224

MacKenzie, Sir Alexander, 224

Mafia, 280

Management
negotiating with labor, 232-233

Marshall, John, 196, 206

Marxism
and education, 201-202

Masloff, Sophie
mayor, 124, 148

Massachusetts
University of, 201

Maternalistic, 399

McCarthy, Eugene J., 140

Media
coverage of crimes, 97-98
influence on youth, 97
and legislators, 121
private ownership, 13

Men
importance to of fathering children, 358
normal and abnormal sex roles, 177-178, 191
roles in society, 222

Middle ages
Christian Inquisition, 22

Mierck, Lawrence
town Councilperson, 261

Military
and balance of power, 51
civilian career goals on retirement, 44
civilian Commander-in-Chief, 45
civilian control of, 11, 43-59
controlling, 301-305
dictators, 46-47
expansion of forces, 51-53
function, 11, 283
limitation of years of service, 44
is national military force
necessary, 49-51, 302
negative aspect of reviewing troops, 53-54
preparedness, 53
retrain for civilian employment, 304-305
standing army can be threat to peace, 49-50
structure compared to democratic, 54-57
techniques to enhance growth and power, 57
value of human life, 55-56

Minorities
and constitutions, 214-216

Mistick, Joseph Sabino, 124, 148

Molotov, Vyaches Lav, 111

Monarchs
and parliaments, 47-48
and elected councils, 395

Monopoly
by employee organizations, 41
prevention of, 41
slavery, 29

Morals - see values

Moscow City Council, xi

Moscow State University, 223-226

Mussolini, Benito, 231

Native Americans, 177
Inuit (Eskimo) and Arctic
Indian people, 223

National Graduate University
Board of Governers, iv

Natural law, 209-210

Natural resources
should be considered scarce, 343

Neighborhoods
organization, 255-259

<u>Negotiation: The Alternative to Hostility</u>, x

Nigeria
division into states, 218-219

North Korea, 21
communism, 274

North Vietnam, 21
retraining in communism, 179

Not free states, 393-394

Nuclear arms reduction, xiii, 397

Nuclear Submarines
and President Carter, x

Nye, F. Ivan, 60

Onorato, Don
Councilperson, 124-125

Panama, 106
canal treaty, ix

Parents
character and values, 178-179
conflicts in teaching children, 100-102
control of schools, 191
democracy, 178
failure in socializing children, 98
normal male and female sex
roles, 177-178, 191
necessity to teach normal values, 94
and number of children, 357-363
provide security-giving relationship, 178
respect for law and order, 178
role in children's formal education, 381

Pericles, 2

Parliamentary governments, 24
collapsing 48
dismissed by dictators, 49
inherent weakness for democracies, 49
operated by bureaucrats, 48-49
and military takeovers, 47-49, 58
and monarchs, 47-48

Participative management, 104-106, 117-118

Partly free states, 393-394

Patent laws, 385

Paternalistic government, 399

Peace, ix
threat by standing army, 50

Peacemaker, xi

Pennsylvania
highways, 348

Peoples democratic government
may not be democratic, 16

Peoples Republic of China, ix

Perestroika, 396-397

Pericles, 2

Permits, government
role of bribery in obtaining, 157-160
tool of government regulators, 132-133

Perot, Ross, 104

Personality
characteristics, 170
defined, 19
each is unique, 19, 26
how formed, 19, 20

Peru, 221

Petitions
for referendum, 267
to place candidates on ballots, 239

Phoenix
of fredoms, xi
of fear, xi

Philippines, 221

Plautus, Titus Maccius, 205

Poland, 74-75, 342
borders, 293-295
free from Soviet control, 395
and international trade, 342

Police
controlled and supervised by civilian
government, 284-285
locally controlled, 11
specialization to match specialization
of criminals, 284

Political Action Committees
can produce a monopoly by a minority, 145
lobbying pressure,115
provided with private funds, 114
support of campaign, 114-115

Political freedom
and economic freedom, 28

Political Parties, 13, 202, 398
defined and functions, 242-248
democratic, 107, 398
favor candidates trained in law, 247
major party may prevent other parties from organizing, 245
major and minor, 245
one party may be too powerful, 243
origin, 243
Republican, 107, 398
volunteer workers, 277

Pollution
air, water, soil, 137-139
nature's pollution of water, 138

Population Size
and democracy, 79-81
and enculturalism, 80
freedom from want and to prosper, 80
natural limitations, 81-82
over population a critical issue, 357
planning, 355-363
and resources, 80

Prime Minister, 24, 47, 375, 397

Prince, Dr. Julius, 360

President, 94, 129, 320, 321, 322, 323, 379

Private Colleges
costs lower than public, 151

Private Enterprise
auditing, 250
democracies must maximize, 203
restricted by government regulations, 128-130

Privatization
advantage of, 350-352

Procurement, government
problems with, 160-162

Productivity
and treatment of workers, 41

Property
advantage of government transfering to people, 310-314, 323-325, 337-339
ownership, 12, 307
sold to people by governments, 310-327

Protestants, 67, 224

Protestantism
and capitalism, 70-72, 86
freedom from control by Church leaders, 72, 86
and private enterprise, 320

Public Colleges
costs higher than private, 151

Public Education
importance of local control, 189-191

Public Hearings, 263, 267

Quality of Life, 29, 41, 204, 255, 399
as level of living, 132
improved by government regulations, 137-139

Reagan, Ronald W.
and the collapse of the Soviet Union, 323, 397
statements by, xi-xiii, 60

Referendum
petition for, 267

Regulations - see government regulations

Religion
characteristics inhibiting democracy, 75-77
Christianity, 69
defined, 353
and democracy, 67, 72
and ethnocentrism, 354
in the formation of the United States, 73-75
freedom, 72, 354-355, 399
freedom from, 10
freedom of, 10
freedom of and freedom from protected by constitutions, 355
function of officials, 64
hierarchy, 77
and number of children, 360-361
protected by Constitution, 355
and role of women, 362
subversion, 64-66
system of ethics and rules of behavior, 65
techniques of zealots, 68
terrorism, 68
tyranny when religion and government are united, 67-68

Respect
children must learn, 194, 382

Reston, James, 196

Revolutionary War, American, 184

Roberts Rules of Order, 382

Romania
free from Soviet domination, 396

Roosevelt, Franklin D., 94

Rummel, Rudolph J., 394

SALT II Treaty, ix

Science
defined, 382
dependent on capitalism and free enterprise, 383
directed, 383
free press and speech and freedom to form organizations, 385-386
hindered by bureaucracy, 386
inventions and innovations, 385
labs, xiii
major contributor to prosperity, 382-387
necessary to evaluate need for regulations, 135-136
and technology, 382-387, 399

Scientists
and capitalism, 34
funded by capitalists, 39, 383
at work in their laboratories, 384

Seaborg, Glen T., 200

Senate of the United States, 254

Seneca, Lucius Annaeus, 140

Socialism
children indoctrinated, 308-309
and consumer needs, 344
economic system failure, 166
superiority of state over religion, 64

Social security - see welfare

Social status, 399
and life cycle, 370-373

Social Stratification, 364-366

Social welfare - see welfare

Somolia, xii, 226

South Africa, 233-234

South America elections, x

South Korea
system of justice, 210-211

South Vietnam
retraining school scholarships, 179

Soviet Union, xii, 111, 219, 308, 323
citizens killed by government, 394
division into separate countries, 219-220
failure of socialistic government, xiii, 150
fall of, xiii
five year plans, 343-344
and Gorbachev, Mikhail, 395-397
marxist economy, 202
military, 396
President Reagan's policies caused its collapse, 323 397
reversion to independent countries, 219
SALT II Treaty, ix
youth organization, 20

Special interests
and legislation, 113

Spinning, James M., 164

Stalin, Joseph V., 111, 231, 343
killed non-believers in socialism, 307-308
five year plans, 343

Star Wars - see Strategic Defence Initiative

State jurisdiction, 267-268

Statespersons, 399
difficult role, 121
must control governmentocracy, 134, 139-140

Statue of Liberty
symbol of freedom, 186-187
tribute to, ii

Steelman, Dr. John R.,
and private enterprise, 320-322

Stewart, Edward C., 190

Stratification - see Social Stratification

Strategic Defense Initiative
and collapse of Soviet Union, 323

Study groups, 387-391

Successful Democracies, 393-400
may seem chaotic, 397

Supply and Demand, 34
balance is a problem in new democracies, 315-316
error of restricting, 36
matching after wars, 320

Supreme Court
of the United States, 254
of the states, 268

Tariffs - see taxes

Tasmania
native people killed by Europeans, 231

Taxes
customs at Polish borders, 292-295
on gasoline and diesel fuels, 347
greatest source of government funds, 286
limitation, 10
on property, 313
restrict economic development, 287
system, 285-288

Term Limits
of elected officials, 7-8

Terrorism, 68

Thatcher, Prime Minister Margret, 397

Tocqueville, Alexis de, 392

Totalitarian Leaders, 395
control of judicial system, 278
controlling individuals, 296
religious, 66, 67-68
rule, 395
theocracy, 67
treatment of resisters, 109-112

Totalitarism, xii, xiii
dictatorial domination of people, 117

Townships
Board membership and responsibilities, 260-263
school districts, 258-259

Trade, free
arms, 51
balance, 341
barriers, 95
and competition, 38
importance in democracies, 35-39
importance of international, 340-341
and infrastructure improvement, 36-37

Training
for succeesful businesses, 327-331

Transfer of Power
after elections and appointments, 107
children learn this, 106-107
from leaders of one party to another, 107
to new officials, 9-10, 106-108

Trial by jury
citizen's right, 14

Truman, Harry S., 320, 322

Turning Point: A Candidate, a State, and a Nation Come of Age, x

Tyrants, xii, xiii

Uhl, Francis,
town Councilperson, 261

United Nations, xiii, 19, 226
actions to stop conflicts, 235-236
armed forces, 210
and Iraq, 226, 323
and joint military action, 226
human rights, 227
peacekeeping, xii

United States, 201
Agency for International Development, 334
and Christianity, 73-75
civilian control of military, 43
campaign spending laws, 114-115
many thousands of democracies, 253
constitution, 217
and Cuba, 110
democracy, 86-87
early years as confederacy, 218
and government regulations, 129
great depression programs, 263-264
and immigrants, 185-189
meeting consumer needs, 320-321
Naval Academy
and President Carter, x
network of highways, 347-348
and People Republic of China, ix
privately owned roads, railways, canals, and ferrys, 349-350
and public roads, 263
Representatives, 46
and retirement social security, 368-370
Senators, 46
and social status, 370-372

support of anti-communists, 323

Universities
and faculty, 202

Values
behavior controlled by, 354
belief in Supreme Being, 63
change may be necessary, 400
changed by brainwashing, 21-22
capitalistic, 34
Christian, 73
conflict in values taught children
and the adults', 100-102
democratic, 178
family, 84
importance of formal education in
democracies, 183-184
Judeo-Christian, 87
limit or make possible satisfactory
level of living, 400
moral issues, 78
moral values of two-parent families, 85
morals, good and bad, 251-252
and number of children, 61
politeness, 92-94
regarding the past, present and future, 62-63
relayed by parents, 22
religious beliefs, 65
normal sex roles, 177-178
transfer to children by single parent, 85

Village Jurisdictions, 266

Voluntary Organizations
importance and function in
democracy, 271-278
integrating forces in nation, 273

Voltaire, 60

Voters
bond with elected officials, 120-121
undemocratic restrictions, 238

Voting
fraud, 238-242
observers to prevent fraud, 241-242
private and secret, 9

Washington, George, 88, 184, 200

Wagner, Jack
Council President, 124

Wealth
accumulation of, 29, 39-40
use of, 30-31

Weapons of mass destruction, xiii

Welfare
agencies need to change mission, 265
assistance in exchange for work, 375
change values of receivers, 375-376
entitlement tendency, 265
and homelessness, 374
and professional employees, 265
professionalization, 374
provided by township,, counties
and cities, 263
and retirement, 368-369
social welfare, 367-376
weakens work ethic, 263

Western World, 389

White, William Allen, 392

Why Not the Best?, x

Wilson, Woodrow, xii, 164, 199, 306, 392

Women
normal and abnormal sex roles, 177-178, 191
role in societies, 362

Work ethic, 82

Works Progress Administration (WPA), 264

Workers - see employees

World War II, 18, 94, 110, 323

Yeltsin, Boris, 396-397

Yoder, Dr. Hatten S., i, iv, 384

Young Pioneers, 20

Youngdahl, Luther, 206

Yugoslavia
free from Soviet domination, 396

Zaslaluskaya, Tatyana, 396